I0837358

RELIGIOUS TRUTH,

ILLUSTRATED FROM SCIENCE,

IN

ADDRESSES AND SERMONS

ON SPECIAL OCCASIONS.

BY

EDWARD HITCHCOCK, D. D., LL. D.,

LATE PRESIDENT OF AMHERST COLLEGE, AND NOW PROFESSOR OF NATURAL THEOLOGY AND GEOLOGY.

BOSTON:

PHILLIPS, SAMPSON AND COMPANY.

1857.

STEREOTYPED AT THE
BOSTON STEREOTYPE FOUNDRY.

PREFACE.

THE quarryman, who has made excavations in the rocks for architectural materials, sometimes looks over the fragments which have been thrown aside, and finds blocks that seem to him worth preserving. Thus have I been doing with the literary debris, which has been quarried and wrought on special occasions, and afterwards thrown aside. With some new dressing, I have ventured to hope that a part of them are worth preserving, and this volume is the result. A brief history of the several articles is subjoined.

The first article, entitled *The highest Use of Learning*, was my Inaugural Address when assuming the presidency of Amherst College, April, 1845.

The second, on *The Relations and Mutual Duties between the Philosopher and the Theologian*, was delivered as an Anniversary Address before the Porter Rhetorical Society, at the Andover Theological Seminary, in 1852. It was subsequently published in the Bibliotheca Sacra, from which it has been copied, by permission.

The third, on *Special Divine Interpositions in Nature*, was given before the Theological Seminaries of Bangor and Newton, in 1853. This, also, was published in the Bibliotheca Sacra for 1854.

The Wonders of Science compared with the Wonders of Romance, is a Lecture which has been delivered before literary associations in the cities of New York, Brooklyn, New London, Norwich, Lowell, Charlestown, Salem, Newburyport, and Springfield; also at Amherst College, and in some other places. It has never before been published.

The Religious Bearings of Man's Creation was preached as a Sermon before the Convention of Congregational Ministers, in Brattle Street Church, Boston, May, 1854. It was also delivered as an Address before the Theological Society of Dartmouth College, in August, 1854. It has likewise been preached in Amherst College, in Springfield and Conway, Massachusetts, Brooklyn and Buffalo, New York, and Milwaukie, Wisconsin. In August, 1856, it was preached in Rev. Dr. Sprague's Church, in Albany, on Lord's Day morning, at the time of the meeting of the American Association for the Advancement of Science. By the local committee of that association it has been published in connection with a Sermon by President Hopkins, of Williams College, delivered in the afternoon of the same day.

The Sermon entitled *The Catalytic Power of the Gospel* was preached before the Massachusetts Home Missionary Society, at its anniversary in Boston, in May, 1852. It was published by the Society in pamphlet form.

The Attractions of Heaven and Earth has been preached as a Sermon in Amherst College, in Amherst, West, East, and North Parishes; in Hatfield, Whately, Enfield, South Deerfield, Conway, and Richmond, Massachusetts. Its chief peculiarity is the employment of diagrams. It has never before been published.

The Sermon entitled *Mineralogical Illustrations of Character*, has been preached only in Amherst College, at an evening lecture. Its chief peculiarity is the employment of a few mineral specimens for illustration. This is the first time it appears in print.

The Inseparable Trio was an Election Sermon, preached January 2, 1850, in Old South Church, Boston, before His Excellency George N. Briggs, His Honor John Reed, the Honorable Council, and the Senate and House of Representatives of Massachusetts, by whom it was published in the pamphlet form. It is added to this volume from a growing conviction of the importance of the leading principle advanced in it.

A Chapter in the Book of Providence was delivered as an Anniversary Address before the Mount Holyoke Female Seminary, at South Hadley, in 1849, and published in a pamphlet form. I give it a place in this volume chiefly to exhibit the outlines of the character of one of the most energetic and benevolent females of modern times.

The Waste of Mind is also an Address at the anniversary of the same institution, in 1842. It was published by the trustees in a pamphlet form.

Excepting the two or three last of the preceding articles, it will be seen that scientific facts and principles are employed to prove or illustrate religious truths. This fact embraces so large a part of the volume, that I have felt justified in placing it upon the title page.

I might have added many more articles of analogous character, but fear that I have already presumed too much upon the interest of the public in such productions.

Amherst College, November 20, 1856.

CONTENTS.

THE HIGHEST USE OF LEARNING.

The cause of education, in this country at least, is almost universally popular. Yet were we to pass around the inquiry among the different classes of society, why they regard it so important, we should probably receive very different answers. One man, himself uneducated, places its chief value in the means it affords of defence against the impositions of the designing and unprincipled. Another values it chiefly because it enables him to take advantage of the ignorance of the world in promoting his schemes of self-aggrandizement. A third looks upon the means which education affords for acquiring property, as its highest use. A fourth regards the personal reputation, respect, and influence, which learning bestows, as its chief advantage. A fifth thinks of it mainly as an instrument of advancing civilization, and multiplying the comforts and luxuries of life. A sixth estimates most highly its influence in elevating the lower classes of the community above the condition of mere animals and drudges, and in making them understand that the body is not the only part of man to be cared for. A seventh places the highest use of learning in its power of disciplining and liberalizing the mind, and delivering it from vulgar fears, superstitions, and prejudices; and in giving to men just views of their rights, relations, and destinies. An eighth thinks most of the boundless fields of enjoyment which knowledge opens to the human mind, of a far more noble and refined kind than any dependent upon animal nature. A ninth makes its most important use to consist in its bearings upon religion, both natural and revealed.

Now, in my opinion, this ninth man has the right of the matter most decidedly; and yet I fear that his opinion is not the most common, or the most popular. But to my conviction, the religious applications of learning are by far its most important use; and the occasion seems to be a fit one to defend and illustrate this opinion. It needs, I believe, both defence and illustration. For though the belief is general that religion may derive some benefit from particular branches of learning, there is still an impression lingering on many minds, that some sciences are unfriendly in their bearings upon religion, and that others have no relations to religion. Much less is it generally believed that the strongest reason why we should sustain common schools, academies, and colleges, is, that we are thus promoting the cause of true religion. But if this be indeed true, then, when we give our property, our influence, or ourselves, to the cause of learning, we shall do it with a heartier good will and a more entire consecration; and we shall the more cheerfully bear up under the trials, fatigues, disappointments, and perplexities that lie in our path.

I would not, indeed, undervalue the secular advantages of learning. They are so obvious and so important, that I could not do it if I would. Those whose experience reaches back fifty, or forty, or even thirty years, have evidence in their own consciousness of the economical value of learning, too strong to be overcome by any speculative argument depreciating its importance. When we compare the present condition of the world, and our own condition, with what they were in our early days, we cannot but be deeply impressed with the rapid progress of society, and the multiplication of secular advantages, and the means of comfort and happiness, growing out of the advancement of learning. Branches of science and literature, which, at the beginning of this century, were *tabooed* to all who were not residents within the walls of universities and colleges, and even some branches that scarcely had an existence then, are now the theme of familiar conversation in the workshop, on the farm, in the stage coach, the rail car, the steamboat, and the packet. And so simplified are the elementary principles of many of these branches, as to be brought within the comprehension of the child at the primary school. Instead of the stinted sources of information then possessed in a few small newspapers and periodicals in some of the larger cities, and a few republications of small European works, the country is now flooded with newspapers of all sizes below one that will swallow up an octavo, and with periodicals and books to suit all tastes, all purses, and all fancies, from the penny pamphlet up to the seven hundred dollar volumes of Audubon.

Still more striking has been the progress of the useful arts from the application of scientific principles. In Great Britain, at this moment, steam performs a work that would require the unaided labor of more than four hundred millions of men; and a work as great probably, in proportion to the population, in our own country. Improvements in machinery and in chemical processes have doubtless within this century made a still greater deduction from the amount of labor necessary; and these improvements reach every class of the community; pointing out to them an easier path to competence, and affording them leisure to cultivate their intellectual and moral powers. Then, too, how striking the change in respect to intercommunication, both on land and water! We now hardly give a serious parting to our friend who starts upon a trip of only some five hundred or a thousand miles, so soon shall we see him again. And even when we have bid him adieu, as he starts on foreign travel, we hardly begin to reckon his absence by months, certainly not as formerly by years, ere he greets us again; having made the tour of Europe, or perhaps stood within the Holy City, or coasted the shores of the Black Sea and the Caspian, or gone down the Red Sea to India and the Celestial Empire, and returning by the Isthmus of Panama, he has completed the circuit of the globe. And besides the problem has just been solved, of carrying on a conversation and transacting business with our friend when absent, even though hundreds, and it may be thousands, of miles intervene between us.

Now, these are advantages derived from the progress of learning so obvious as to be known and read of all men; and, therefore, we are apt to suppose them the chief advantages. Whereas the applications of literary and scientific truths to religion lie more out of sight, and can be appreciated fully only by him who is well acquainted both with learning and religion, and who looks at their relations with the eye of a philosopher. We must dwell a little, therefore, upon these relations in order to sustain the position that has been taken.

I need not argue before such an audience as this the superior importance of religious principles to all others. This will be admitted; for all other truths have reference to time, these to eternity: all others regard man's mortal, these his immortal interests: all others are limited by created natures; these centre in the uncreated God. Religious principles, therefore, are in their very nature of infinite moment. Other truths have gradations of value; but these are invaluable, because necessarily immortal and infinite. Every thing, therefore, in literature or science, that discovers, illustrates, or confirms the eternal principles of religion, swells into an importance proportionably great. It remains, then, only to show that the wide fields of learning afford us such illustrations over their entire surface, and the position will be made out, that the religious applications of literature and science are the most important of all their relations; and that, consequently, when we consecrate our property, our influence, or our lives, to the cause of education, we consecrate them to one of the noblest of all human enterprises.

Accompany me now, my friends, as we rapidly pass around the circle of literature and science, in order that we may see what are the relations between religion and the different branches of human learning.

We meet, first, with the ancient classics, whose study forms so important a part of a liberal education in modern times. The religious principles which they contain are, indeed, fatally false; and not much more consonant with modern views is their philosophy. Nevertheless, they afford most important aid in elucidating revelation. The very absurdity of the mythology and philosophy of the classics brings out, by contrast, in bolder relief the beauties and glories of Christian doctrines and Christian philosophy; and instead of leading the student to embrace polytheism, they prepare his mind for the reception of the gospel. Besides, many passages of Scripture would be unintelligible, and others unimpressive, without that knowledge of ancient opinions and manners which the classics disclose. And then, too, how unfit to give a correct interpretation of Scripture is he who is unacquainted with the languages in which it was originally written! It does not prove this position false to state, what is certainly true, that many men have faithfully preached the gospel, and been instrumental of the conversion of great numbers, who were ignorant of classical literature. So there have been surgeons and physicians unacquainted with anatomy, physiology, and chemistry; and they may have performed many skilful operations and effected many cures, and thus done much good. But other things being equal, no one would feel as safe in the hands of such practitioners as in those familiar with the structure of the human system, and with the laws that govern it, and with the chemical nature and action of medicines. In difficult cases such practitioners would shrink from prescriptions and operations; or if they rashly attempted them, would be very likely to tie the omo-hyoid muscle instead of the carotid artery; or to administer nitric acid in connection with mercury; or by some analogous blunder, to put the patient's life in jeopardy. And mistakes alike dangerous, sometimes infinitely more so, because they involve the loss of the soul, must he be liable to make, who engages in the ministerial office ignorant of the original languages in which the Scriptures were written. And if one such fatal mistake should result from his ignorance, what a terrible drawback would it be upon a whole life of devoted usefulness!

In modern times human learning has become so prodigiously expanded, and so many new branches have been established, that it is difficult to discourse intelligibly concerning it without defining the terms which we employ. In France and Germany, the word *literature* embraces the whole circle of written knowledge; and with many English writers it has the same wide signification. But often the meaning is restricted to those branches which treat of the social, moral, and intellectual relations of man. Polite literature, or belles-lettres, is still more limited in its meaning; embracing poetry, oratory, and perhaps history, biography, and some other miscellaneous subjects. The term *science* is applied to those branches whose principles are considered as well settled; and with the exception of some parts of mathematics, the term is chiefly confined to the material world; although moral science, and intellectual science, are phrases frequently used.

Adopting these definitions, we might arrange all human knowledge under the three heads of Literature, Science, and Art. Let us first inquire into the influence of modern literature upon religion.

And here it must be acknowledged in the outset, that not a little of the influence of modern polite literature has been very disastrous to religion. For much of it has been prepared by men who were intemperate, or licentious, and secretly or openly hostile to Christianity; at least to its peculiar doctrines. And their writings have been deeply imbued with immorality, or infidelity, or atheism. Yet the poison has been often so interwoven with those fascinations of style, or thought, characteristic of genius, as to be unnoticed by the youthful mind, delighted with smartness and brilliancy. And even when the plague spots have been pointed out, it has tended, like the prohibition of the fruit of the tree of knowledge in Eden, to excite an irresistible desire to open the proscribed volumes, even though they should prove a second box of Pandora.

Perhaps no branch of literature has been oftener and more successfully employed as a vehicle for the propagation of infidel opinions than history. Rightly understood, and faithfully interpreted, it gives strong light and confirmation to revelation and to morality. But sceptical ingenuity has often been able to make its voice as ambiguous as a Delphic oracle, and as fallacious as ventriloquism. In pagan Greece and Rome, their historians, except perhaps Tacitus, were even over credulous on the subject of polytheistic religion. And so in modern times, previous to the last century, the historian was usually the supporter of revealed truth. But the talented yet anomalous Bayle, in that manual of irreligion, his Critical Dictionary, led the way in converting facts into an engine against Christianity. Voltaire and others learned the lesson, which was perfected by Gibbon and Hume. So often, however, have their sophistries and cavils been exposed, that it is only the unwary who are now entrapped. The great mass of historical literature also, your Rollin and Ramsay, Müller, Schlegel, Heeren, Goldsmith, Smollet, Russell, Turner, Robertson, and a multitude of others, are favorable to religion; although a Von Rotteck, in the costume of a baptized infidel, rejects biblical history as fabulous. Religion, therefore, need have no fears from her alliance with History; and, indeed, she may hope for many a rich harvest of illustration and confirmation from future researches; for there are other papyri to be unrolled, other hieroglyphics to be deciphered, and other Sir William Joneses and Champollions to be raised up.

Another most sacrilegious perversion of polite literature consists in clothing immorality and irreligion in the vestal robe of poetry. I say sacrilegious; for poetry is the natural handmaid of pure religion. Hence it was chosen by the Holy Ghost as the appropriate language of prophets and other inspired men. But it is the appropriate language of all strong emotions, and may, therefore, be employed for giving an attractive dress to immoral and irreligious sentiments, as well as to those which are virtuous and holy. Accordingly, so wide has been this misapplication of the poetic talent, that in almost every age its highest efforts have been consecrated to polytheism, or war, or amorous intrigues, or intemperance, or to secure favor from the great, by flattering their vanity. Indeed, though the Old Testament is full of poetry, and though it has ever been employed in the religious worship of Jews and Christians, yet it seems not to have been imagined till lately, that this delightful art had been perverted and degraded by being employed to sustain heathenism, and to pander to intemperance, licentiousness, and war; nor that it could ever be made thoroughly Christian, and thus exalted in character and effect. The great poets of antiquity were so fully heathen, and some of them, as Anacreon and Horace, had woven so many garlands for the intoxicating cup, that it seems to have been taken for granted that the muse could never be made to pour forth numbers as sweet and enticing on loftier and purer themes. Even the splendid efforts of Milton and Dante did not open the eyes of Christians to the true use of poetry. Indeed, the polytheistic and warlike numbers of Homer and Virgil, and the bacchanalian songs of the ancient lesser poets, were piety and purity, compared to the philosophic blasphemy of Shelley, the atheism and profligacy of Byron and Moore, and — must I add? — the bacchanalian songs of Robert Burns. Furthermore, if it be true, as Milton affirmed, that a poet's life is itself a true poem, we shall be obliged sadly to swell the list of modern poems devoted to vice and irreligion. For when biography informs us that Addison, Prior, and Steele were intemperate, that Thomson was a voluptuary, Goldsmith dissipated, Sterne a decided sensualist, and that even Johnson could practise abstinence but not temperance, and when we know, that though Pope's constitution was too delicate to allow him to indulge in luxurious excesses, yet his writings show a bad preëminence of wantonness and indecency, we are led to exclaim with Milton, —

"God of our fathers, what is man!
Nor do I name of men the common route,
That, wandering loose abroad,
Grow up and perish as the summer fly, —
Heads without name, no more remembered, —
But such as thou hast solemnly elected,
With gifts and graces eminently adorned,
For some great work — thy glory."

And then, too, consider the moral character of modern dramatic poetry, so decidedly worse than the noble tragic poetry of antiquity. From the days of Dryden to the present, — for even Shakspeare, with all his splendid moral sentiments, was undoubtedly a libertine in principle and practice, — scarcely a dramatic poet has appeared whose "entire unweeded volumes," as Hannah More calls them, can be conscientiously recommended, save the Comus and Samson Agonistes of Milton, and a few other plays of kindred character. We have seen, too, that lyric poetry — more influential than any other upon public morals — has been prostituted to the cause of intemperance and revelry, from the time when Anacreon indited his Ἡ γῆ μέλαινα πίνει, and Horace his *Nunc est bibendum*, down to the period when Burns exclaimed,

"We'll tak' a cup o' kindness yet,
For auld lang syne;"

or, still later, when the echo came from Moore, —

"Friend of my life, this wine cup sip."

But thanks be to God, that in these latter days he has created some greater and some lesser Christian lights, and placed them in the poetic firmament, where they already begin to rule the day and the night. First came Milton; a permanent sun, not immaculate indeed, but full of glory, and destined for a long time to rule the day. Then appeared a milder luminary; foremost in the train of evening, and delightful to look upon, as reflected from the volumes of Cowper. And a noble train of kindred lights, most of them indeed lesser stars, have since shone in the literary heavens, bearing the names of Watts, Heber, Montgomery, Young, and others; to which I might add several lights that have dotted the darkness of our western hemisphere. We were also startled, not long since, by the flash of a meteor shooting athwart the eastern heavens, and having marked out the Course of Time, vanishing from sight, —

"As sets the morning star, which goes not down
Behind the darkened west, nor hides obscured
Among the tempest of the sky, but melts away
Into the light of heaven."

Nor ought I to omit to point to that noble luminary, which, for so long a period, has been burning with a mild and steady light above the lakes and mountains of Northern England, and which gives us some foretaste of what the literary hemisphere will be when poetic inspiration shall consent to receive a higher inspiration from the fountain of Scripture — far purer than Castalia. To bring about that golden age of poetry, should be the grand object of its cultivators; especially of those who can claim the *nascitur, non fit.* Then, and not till then, will it be seen how noble an auxiliary to virtue and religion is the poetic element in man.

There is another department of polite literature that has been, still more than poetry, monopolized by vice and irreligion, and which, I fear, will be still harder to reclaim. To minds averse to close thinking, to those whose tastes and habits are all artificial, and who have never acquired a relish for the beauties and wonders of nature, as well as to those who are the slaves of appetite and passion, the novel and the romance have ever possessed irresistible attractions. And since these three classes form, to a greater or less extent, the principal part of society, this is the literature that is most widely and abundantly diffused. And while the demand has created a supply, so, according to a principle of political economy, a surplus supply has increased the demand. The pen and the press have been prolific beyond all precedent; and the quality of the article has varied according to the demands of fashion. At one time the gross and disgusting descriptions of Fielding and Smollet met the popular taste. Anon, what Hannah More calls the "non-morality" of the Great Unknown, was in excellent *goût*. And since that prolific fountain has been dried up, others, who, alas for the cause of virtue and religion are too well known, have not failed to disgorge tales of all sorts, suited to every variety of appetite, from the most delicate and refined to the most gross and grovelling. For, like the frogs of Egypt, these productions have not been confined to the *boudoirs* of the literati, nor to the centre tables and withdrawing rooms of wealth and fashion, but have found their way to the kneading troughs of the kitchen; coming there, it may be, in one of those enormous products of the modern press that might be mistaken for a winding sheet, and which, I fear, has proved the winding sheet of many a noble intellect.

I am aware that not a few authors, disgusted with these perversions of fictitious literature, have made many praiseworthy efforts to turn its current into the channels of virtue and religion. Nor have they failed to obtain many interested readers. But I fear that in most cases it is the well-arranged story, and not its moral, which has awakened interest;—

"First raising a combustion of desire,
With some cold moral they would quench the fire."

But Leviathan is not so tamed. Yet the fact that the love of novelty is so strong naturally in the heart, shows us that in some way or other it was meant to be gratified. And when we learn that the wonders of nature far transcend the wonders of romance, is it not evident, that if men can be brought to love nature, and those branches of knowledge which unlock her Elysian fields, this desire can be fully satisfied with realities, without the aid of fiction? I have little hope that any successful headway can be made against that morbid love of fiction which has become the almost universal passion, until you can implant in man's heart a love of unsophisticated nature. This once done, and the fascinations of romance would become powerless under the overmastering influence of the new affection. To restore nature, therefore, to the throne of the heart, and expel the meretricious usurper, is the noble work that lies before the scholar of the nineteenth century. And when it shall be accomplished, as I doubt not it will be, and the deluge of fictitious literature that now almost buries the civilized world, shall have passed into the limbo of forgetfulness, it will be found that a mighty barrier to the progress of true knowledge and true religion has been taken out of the way, and that the heart which is alive to nature's beauties is well prepared to love the God of nature, as well as the God of revelation.

It is not necessary to spend time in showing that rhetoric and oratory, two other important branches of polite literature, are capable of the same perversion to unworthy purposes as the subjects already noticed. In every human heart there are chords, which, when struck by the silver bow of the rhetorician, or the magic wand of the orator, cannot but vibrate and give back a response. But when stormy passion, or reckless irreligion, sweeps over those chords, they return only discordant sounds, that grate harshly upon the ear of virtue and piety. But when they are touched by the delicate and skilful hands of true benevolence, the tones which they return resemble the music of heaven, and they excite the spirit of heaven all around. To promote that spirit is doubtless the grand object to which the Creator intended the flowers of rhetoric and the strains of eloquence should be devoted. How immensely important, then, that Christian scholars should rescue these branches from the hands of the unprincipled and the wicked, and convert them to their legitimate use, as auxiliaries of virtue and religion!

Some worthy men, I know, look with a jealous eye upon the use of rhetorical and oratorical skill in aid of religion. They feel as if no attempt should be made to set off and recommend the naked truth. But, as remarked by Dr. Campbell, how much better for the minister of the gospel to write so as to make the critic turn Christian, than to write so as to make the Christian turn critic!

It is not in human nature to avoid receiving a powerful impression from a skilful choice and collocation of words; and why should not religion avail itself of this means of giving truth a keener edge? It may, indeed, be carried to excess, as Dante seems to have done in his descriptions of the physical torments of perdition. But Milton, while he has given an awful distinctness and force to those same torments, has not exaggerated them; and why may not religion use this power, as any other proper means, to impress divine truth? In this respect, thus far, the children of this world have been wiser than the children of light.

In passing from literature to science, on the great circle of human knowledge, we meet with intellectual and moral philosophy. But so obvious is the connection between the latter and the principles of religion, that we need not delay upon its elucidation. For every theory of morals, that is not radically defective, makes the origin of moral obligation identical with that of religious obligation. So that, in fact, moral philosophy is only one branch of natural theology. I regard politics, also, or the principles by which nations should be governed and regulated, as only a branch of ethics; or, rather, as a special application of the principles of morality and religion; though I greatly fear that expediency and self-interest have thus far been the basis of political action more frequently than moral or religious principle. By some writers, intellectual philosophy, or psychology, or metaphysics, as they would rather choose to denominate the science, has been supposed, upon the whole, quite disastrous to religion. For when they consult ecclesiastical history, they find that the most fatal errors in religion have usually been based upon some false system of metaphysics, and that behind its hypothetical and unintelligible dogmas, the ablest sceptics have intrenched themselves. They regard "the modern philosophy of the human mind, for the most part, as a mere system of abstractions," "having almost nothing to offer of practical instruction;" and although "the philosophy of the agency of sentient and voluntary beings is a matter of rational curiosity, it is nothing more."

I quote here, for the most part, the language of an able recent author. But admitting the truth of these statements, they show one thing at least; that unless theologians are familiar with the systems of mental philosophy, so ably defended by eminent men, how can they hope to expose and refute such men when they employ metaphysical subtleties to pervert religious truth? If the theologist does not display equal acuteness with the ontologist, the latter will triumph in his assaults upon religion. And if it be a false metaphysical philosophy that has led a man to adopt a false religious creed, how important that the advocate of religion should be able to meet the errorist on his own ground, and not only to show him that he started wrong, but to put him upon the right track! "If it be a murky or misty region," says a late writer, "carry the blazing torch of demonstrated truth into every cloudy cave and den, encompass every fastness where error lurks, and pour in the fire of a burning logic. The surest way to get protection from the open, and especially the secret ravages of a mischievous beast, is to hunt him down in his own lair." *

But it is said, that all experience shows that there is no safety save in keeping religion entirely aloof from metaphysics. What centuries of disaster followed the attempt of the ancient fathers to incorporate the metaphysics of Platonism with Christianity! And how much longer in the dark ages did the pall of ignorance and a perverted Christianity rest upon the world, because it was held down by the Peripatetic Philosophy, resting on it like an incubus! In our own day, too, we have seen a glacial period commence in a portion of the church, from the freezing influence of German metaphysics, which threatens to be as long and as rigid as the analogous geological period.

Now, were the question whether it were better for men to receive with childlike confidence the declarations of the Bible, without reference to ontological systems, all, probably, would reply in the affirmative. But the difficulty is, that in-

* Professor Fiske's Address at East Windsor, p. 8.

genious and speculative men will construct their philosophical strait jackets, into which they will force the doctrines of revelation. And when the friends of piety see that Religion is panting and almost strangled by this cramping Procrustean process, how shall they liberate her? They must have help to do it; and denunciation and mere zeal will not bring help. They must show by a careful examination and measurement of the entire warp, and woof, and cut of this philosophical dress, that however agreeable it may be to the latest fashion, it cramps the heart and the vitals, stops the circulation of the blood, and is shrivelling up the extremities; and then will all the friends of religion join in stripping off the murderous vestment. Do you suppose that the errors of Platonism, and the peripatetic philosophy would ever have been weeded out from Christian doctrines, except by men who had so thoroughly examined them as to be in no danger of plucking up the truth also? Who but metaphysicians could have exorcised that famous Plastic Nature, conjured from the "vasty deep," by so powerful a necromancer as Cudworth? Who but men versed in the subtleties of dreamy abstractions could have coped successfully with the Scottish prince of sceptics, when he had gathered a dense fog around him, and under cover of it had assailed the first principles of all religion? Had Kant been unskilled in the abstruse speculations of mental philosophy, he could not so effectually have demolished the pantheism of Spinoza; and still more essential is such knowledge to show the fallacy of those more recent forms of the same doctrine, the natural pantheism of Schelling, and the idealism of Fichte.

Another effort of the German mind is to show that the argument from design, to prove the divine existence, as advanced by Derham, Ray, Paley, and the Bridgewater Treatises, is false, and that the idea of God is derived from a sort of intuition of the pure reason; nor could the external world possibly excite the idea of God. These opinions have gained not a little credence in this country, falling in, as they do, with what is called a spiritual philosophy, or transcendentalism. Now that there is a moral order in the world, and in the mind itself, and that the understanding, perceiving this, naturally infers that a Being of infinite moral perfections must be the author of both, — because we instinctively refer every effect to a cause, — cannot be doubted. But on this view, this moral argument, as it is called, becomes only a single example of the argument from design; and by no means invalidates or supersedes other forms of the argument derived from the external world. Dr. Paley's argument was indeed defective, because he did not refer to mental philosophy to prove the spirituality of the Deity. But that defect is abundantly supplied by Chalmers, Crombie, and Brougham, so that now the argument which Paley labored to establish is impregnable; but it will require the vigorous efforts of men versed in abstruse metaphysics to bring it out of the fog and dust with which it has been enveloped.

I have alluded to transcendentalism, dignified as it has been by the name of "spiritual philosophy," in distinction from the Baconian or inductive, which is called "sensuous." This is also a product of German metaphysics; and when one sees what an absolutely unintelligible jargon is used in its enunciation, by its ablest originators, such as Fichte, Schelling, and Hegel, he finds it difficult to conceive how it has exerted such an influence upon religion. But the fact is, there is always to some minds, especially in youth, a wonderful charm in a philosophy that is esoteric. They love to believe themselves capable of discovering a hidden meaning in facts and principles, which the uninitiated cannot discover. Hence, let some man of real talents and learning, as Swedenborg, for instance, solemnly and pertinaciously declare that he does "see what is not to be seen," and he will not want followers, who soon come to have a clear vision for double senses and spiritual meanings. Indeed, a man of talents has only to be obscure in his style and meaning, in order to be regarded by a large proportion of the world, and among them not a few recently fledged literati, as very profound. On the contrary, that beautiful simplicity and clearness of style and thought, which are the result of long and patient investigation, and which characterize the highest order of talent, are regarded by the same class as evidence of a superficial mind and destitution of genius. Accordingly, the temptation is very strong with writers and public speakers, who would be popular, to wrap themselves in the mantle of mystery and obscurity; so that the remark of Dr. Griffin is too true, that the last attainment of the orator is simplicity; and we may say the same, also, in respect to the philosopher. But if men of talents will mount in the air balloon of metaphysical speculation, into transcendental regions of clouds and nebulæ, and through their speaking trumpets announce the discovery of new worlds, unknown to the Bible or to science, Christian men must ascend after them in a similar vehicle, bearing with them the torch of truth, to ascertain whether a fog bank has not been mistaken for a planet.

I have thus far spoken of the value of mental science as a necessary means of detecting religious errors originating in the same science. But it has also many direct and important bearings upon religious truth. Did the time permit me to point them out, however, it would be little more than a repetition of what has been recently said better and more fully than I can do, by one of my colleagues.* I pass, therefore, to another important sign in the great zodiac of human knowledge. On that circle mathematics follows naturally after metaphysics, because it furnishes us with the noblest examples of abstract truth in the universe.

But I fancy that I hear one and another whispering, "What possible connection can there be between mathematics and religion?" The pure abstractions of this science do not, indeed, lead the mind directly to a Deity, since they may be conceived to be necessary and eternal truths. They are not the result of an induction from facts, but of a comparison of ideas. And it is the facts of the natural world that most strikingly discover to us the wonders of adaptation and design, and lead the mind irresistibly to infer a Supreme Being. But what is the basis on which most of this adaptation and design rests? Chiefly, I answer, the laws of mathematics. Look up to the heavens, and you will find those laws controlling all the movements of suns and planets with infallible precision. Every movement on earth, also, which is either mechanical or chemical, is equally dependent upon mathematical laws. Vital operations, too, so far as they result from chemical and mechanical forces, must be referred to the same principles. I do not assert that life and intellect are governed by mathematical laws; but their operations have all the precision of mathematics, and, I doubt not, could be predicted by angelic minds, certainly by the Deity, with as much certainty as the astronomer foretells an eclipse or transit; and really I do not see but the same principles would guide the calculation in the one case as in the other. In short, so entirely dependent are the movements of the universe upon mathematical laws, that

* Professor Fiske's Address at East Windsor.

to alter or annul these laws would be to restore the reign of Chaos and old Night. Let but a single axiom or corollary of mathematics be changed, and I doubt not that wild disorder and ruin would soon take the place of the adaptation and beautiful design that now meet us at every step. Mathematics then forms the very framework of nature's harmonies, and is essential to the argument for a God. Instead of having no connection with religion, it lies at the foundation of all theism.

It seems to me, also, that mathematics aids us in the conception of some religious truths, difficult from their nature to be conceived of by finite minds. All the attributes of the Deity, being infinite, are of this description. But the contemplation of an endless series in mathematics gives us the nearest approach to an idea of the infinite which we can attain. Follow the series, indeed, as far as our powers will carry us, and we are still no nearer the end than when we started. But we have got hold of the thread that would conduct us, if our Dædalian wings did not fail us, across that interminable abyss which separates the finite from the infinite; and when we transfer our mathematical conceptions to the Deity, we can hardly fail to meditate upon his glories with deeper amazement.

To many minds all explanations of the biblical doctrine of the Trinity appear so absurd and contradictory as not to admit of belief. Let it, however, be stated to such a man, for the first time, that two lines may approach each other forever without meeting, and it will appear to him as absurd as the doctrine of the Trinity. But after you have demonstrated to him the properties of the hyperbola and its asymptote, the apparent absurdity vanishes. And so after the theologian has stated, that by divine unity he means only a numerical unity, — in other words, that there is but one Supreme Being, and that the three persons of the Godhead are one in this sense, and three only in those respects not inconsistent with this unity, every philosophical mind, whether it admit or not that the Scriptures teach the doctrine of the Trinity, must see that there is no absurdity or contradiction in this view of it. Hence it may happen, and indeed it has happened, that the solution of a man's difficulties on this subject may originate in a proposition of conic sections.

Other peculiar truths of revelation receive striking support from the application of mathematical principles. Among these is the doctrine of special or miraculous providence. Professor Babbage, in that singular yet ingenious work, called the Ninth Bridgewater Treatise, has shown mathematically, that miracles may have formed a part of the original and foreordained plan of the universe, and that their occurrence may be as really the result of natural laws as ordinary events—a doctrine which, indeed, had been previously advanced by Butler. And in this way is the famous objection of David Hume to miracles proved by mathematics to be groundless.

Other religious applications of mathematics might be pointed out. But we must hasten forward to that wide space on the circle of human knowledge, occupied by the inductive sciences. These comprehend, in fact, all those branches that relate to the material universe; and when we have glanced at them, we shall have completed the circuit of literature and science.

And here, at the outset, we remark, that from these sciences have been gathered that great mass of facts which constitute the essence of natural theology, by such men as Newintyt, Ray, Derham, Wollaston, Paley, Brown, and the authors of the Bridgewater Treatises. The *a posteriori* argument for the divine existence rests upon them, and, indeed, almost all the truths pertaining to the character of the Deity and his government that nature discloses. They are arguments which all men can readily understand and appreciate; for although a few metaphysical minds have endeavored to throw doubt over the validity of the argument from design, as I have already stated, yet this is in fact the only evidence that does interest and satisfy the great mass of men. When they see such wonderful effects as physical science discloses, they are led irresistibly, by a universal law of the human mind, to refer them to some adequate cause; and no cause can be adequate save an infinite Deity. Natural theology has selected only the most striking of these effects. But in truth every fact of inductive science furnishes an argument for theism. So that to a man in a morally healthy state, every scientific truth becomes a religious truth, and nature is converted into one great temple, where sacred fire is always burning upon the altars, where hovers the glorious Shekinah, and where, from a full orchestra, the anthem of praise is ever ascending.

In accordance with this view, we find that the most gifted minds, and indeed a large majority of all minds that have devoted themselves to inductive science, have been the friends of religion. And here we reckon the princes of the intellectual world, such as Newton, Kepler, Galileo, Pascal, Boyle, Copernicus, Linnæus, Black, Boerhaave, and Dalton; and among the living such men as Herschel, Brewster, Whewell, Sedgwick, Owen, and a multitude of others. The very same argumentation that leads such original discoverers to derive the principles of science from facts in nature, carries them irresistibly backward to a First Cause; and, indeed, the inductive principle, as developed by Bacon, forms the true basis on which to build the whole fabric of natural religion; and he who fully admits the truth of natural religion, is in a state of preparation for receiving revealed truth to supply its deficiencies. So that, upon the whole, the inductive sciences are of all others most favorable to religion, and the most intimately connected with it.

I shall doubtless be met here by the objection, that not a few distinguished men, found in the ranks of inductive science, have been thorough sceptics. And here the names of some of the most able mathematicians of modern times, such as La Place and D'Alembert, will be adduced. We shall be referred to the Nebular Hypothesis of the former, and to the Encyclopædia of the latter; both of them intended to lay the axe at the root of all religion, and to cover nature with the pall of atheism. But such anomalies as these are explicable in consistency with the general position that inductive science is eminently favorable to religion. For in the first place, these men were atheists in spite of science, rather than through its influence. The spirit of the times, and of the country in which they lived, was dissolute and atheistic; and the moral feelings of D'Alembert, at least, were so corrupt that nothing but atheism could keep conscience quiet. In the second place, they were distinguished in abstruse mathematics, rather than in inductive science; and it cannot be denied, that when men devote themselves almost exclusively to abstractions of this nature, they are apt to look with suspicion upon the less certain, but far higher and more important evidence of moral reasoning; or rather, they attempt to apply the subtleties of the higher mathematics to religion, and of course fail of arriving at correct results, because the subjects are totally diverse, and must be understood by entirely different modes of analysis. Bonaparte, who was quick to discover character, made La Place one of his ministers, but soon saw that he did not discharge his duties with much ability, because, as the emperor said, "he sought subtleties in every subject, and carried into his official employments the spirit of the method of infinitely small quantities," employed by mathematicians. But the grand difficulty with such men is, that by confining their attention so exclusively to one department of knowledge, and to the cultivation of one set of faculties, by a well-known law of physiology they dwarf all the other powers, and really become less capable of judging of other subjects than ordinary men, who cultivate all their faculties in due proportion. This is strikingly exhibited in the Nebular Hypothesis of La Place. He really thought that it rendered a Deity unnecessary in the formation of the universe. But the merest tyro in moral reasoning sees, that, even admitting the hypothesis, a designing, infinitely wise, and powerful Deity is just as necessary as without it. It only throws farther back the period when this designing and creative interposition was exerted; and even the Christian philosopher feels no difficulty in adopting this hypothesis, through fear of its irreligious tendency. The fact is, that La Place, though a giant in mathematics, was only a liliput on other subjects. It ought not to be forgotten, also, that neither of the eminent infidel mathematicians whom I have named were original discoverers, like Newton, Copernicus, and Boyle. In making their discoveries, these latter men were led to take broad views of science, and to examine the original as well as final causes of events; whereas such men as La Place and D'Alembert only carried out and illustrated the principles discovered by others. In tracing out these illustrations, they did, indeed, discover amazing acuteness; but their views were so much confined, that they were but poor judges of the relations of science to religion. They were excellent mathematicians, but poor philosophers. For in the noble language of Sir John Herschel, one of the brightest living ornaments of inductive science in Europe, "the character of the true philosopher is, to hope all things not impossible, and to believe all things not unreasonable." But the character of these men would be better described by saying, that they doubted and denied every thing that could not be proved by mathematics. They are examples of malformation and distortion in the philosophical world, instead of fair proportion and full development.

There is another circumstance which has deepened the impression that the inductive sciences are, to some extent, unfavorable to religion. Scarcely any important discovery has been made in these branches, that has not been regarded for a time, either by the timid and jealous friends of religion, or by its superficial enemies, to be opposed at least to revelation, if not to theism. When Copernicus demonstrated the diurnal and annual revolutions of the earth, the infidel saw clearly that the facts were in opposition to the Bible ; and the theologian was of the same opinion, and arrayed Scripture authority, as well as compact syllogisms, against the new astronomy. But the Christian soon learned that he had misunderstood the language of the Bible, because he had read it through the medium of a false astronomy. So too, when the Brahminical astronomy was first brought to light, and the epoch of the Tirvalore tables was thought to be nearly as early as the Mosaic date of man's creation, scepticism began to exult. But the tone changed when it was ascertained that this epoch was supposititious. More recently, French infidelity saw in the Zodiac of Denderah a refutation of the biblical chronology. But when it was ascertained that the position of the signs on that Zodiac, in respect to the colures, had reference to the commencement of the Egyptian civil year, and not to the precession of the equinoxes, this fancied discrepancy also vanished: and now, when both biblical interpretation and astronomy are better understood, every one confesses, not only that the science is in harmony with revelation, but that it affords some of the most splendid illustrations of religion to be found in the whole circle of learning.

When, at the beginning of the present century, the great discovery was announced, that the principal part of the solid materials of the earth had been oxidized, or in popular language had been burned, both the baptized and the unbaptized infidel at once declared, that the final destruction of the earth, as described by Peter, was impossible, since it is no longer combustible; and since the apostle had thus erred, because not acquainted with modern chemistry, the idea of his inspiration must be given up. It was ere long found, however, that the apostle's language had been misunderstood, through the influence of the false opinion, still widely entertained, that to burn a substance is to destroy or annihilate it. But when chemistry showed that combustion only changes the form of substances, and cannot annihilate a particle, the apostle's meaning was found perfectly to correspond to such an idea: and it is now obvious, that he meant to teach simply, that whatever upon or within the earth is combustible, will be burned, and the whole mass of the globe be melted. So that now the tables are completely turned; and we find, not only no contradiction between his language and chemistry, but a striking proof of its inspired origin, in the fact, that though written when chemistry was not known, it should be found in perfect harmony with the researches of that science. And the same remark may be applied to the whole Scriptures in their relation to all science. The most eagle-eyed sagacity of the nineteenth century has been unable to detect a single discrepancy between the two records. The same cannot be said of any false religion. The Shasters of Hindostan contain a false astronomy, as well as a false anatomy and physiology, and the Koran distinctly avows the Ptolemaic system of the heavenly bodies; and so interwoven are these scientific errors with the religion of these sacred books, that when you have proved the former you have disproved the latter. But the Bible, stating only facts, and adopting no system of human philosophy, has ever stood, and ever shall stand, in sublime simplicity and undecaying strength; while the winds and the waves of conflicting human opinions roar and dash harmlessly around, and the wrecks of a thousand false systems of philosophy and religion are strewed along its base.

But the religious applications of chemistry do not consist simply in illustrating a passage of Scripture. It abounds with the most beautiful exhibitions of the divine wisdom and benevolence; and notwithstanding the ingenious developments by Prout, in his Bridgewater Treatise, and by Fownes in his Prize Essay, I must believe that this field is only just entered, and that most precious gems will be found in almost every part of its wide extent. What admirable skill and benevolence does the doctrine of definite proportions and atomic constitution in chemical compounds present! Here we see nature incessantly performing processes, on which organic life and comfort depend, with a practical mathematics as perfect as the theory. And then, how wonderful is the isomeric constitution, recently discovered, of those proximate principles that form the food of animals and plants! How beautiful, too, the mode — only recently ascertained — by which this nourishment is brought within their reach, and introduced into their systems! See, too, what wonderful benevolence, as well as wisdom, is displayed in the laws and operations of heat, by which its very excess in tropical regions produces, by evaporation, the paradoxical result of cooling and rendering habitable that burning zone ; and on the other hand, the congelation and condensation, produced by its absence in frigid regions, renders the atmosphere warmer and the climate habitable. Think, also, how, in the case of water, by an apparent exception to a law of nature, just as it enters into a state of congelation, the great bodies of that liquid in our rivers and lakes are prevented from freezing up in the winter, so that the longest summer would not thaw them out. And finally, what substance in nature is so wonderfully adapted to its manifold and seemingly opposite uses as water!

> " Simple though it seem,
> Emblem of imbecility itself,
> As most regard it, yet in fact, the food
> Of all organic life; the fruitful source
> Of power in human arts ; and in the clouds,
> The storm, the mountain stream, the placid lake,
> The ocean's roaring and the glacier's sheen,
> The landscape's frostwork, or its icy gems,
> Hence springs the beautiful and the sublime.
> A power, indeed, pervading nature through;
> Now moving noiseless through organic tubes,
> To keep stagnation from the vital frame;
> And now the Atlantic dashing to the skies,
> Or rushing down Niagara's rocky steep,
> Earth trembling, staggering, underneath the shock :
> Effects so diverse, opposite, to gain
> By one mild element, a problem this,
> No wisdom, short of infinite, could solve."

No sciences have furnished so many and so appropriate facts, illustrative of natural theology, as anatomy and physiology. They have been the great magazine whence writers on that subject have drawn their most effective weapons in their war with atheism: but being so fully described in so many treatises, I need not enter into particulars. Comparative anatomy and physiology, however, of more recent date, have not yet been so extensively employed for religious illustration as they will be; although Bell's Bridgewater Treatise upon the hand affords us a foretaste of what may be done. The developments of these sciences are truly marvellous. Who would have believed, for instance, fifty years ago, that such is the mathematical correlation, not only of different parts of an animal, but of parts of different animals, that from a single fragment of the bone of an unknown creature, the skilful anatomist can construct his whole skeleton, and then clothe it with muscles, blood vessels, and nerves, and point out its food, its habits, and its haunts? Yet this has been done in many instances; and the subsequent discovery of the whole skeleton has confirmed the accuracy of the principle employed, and the results obtained. What a striking proof of the existence and agency of a Being infinitely wise and powerful, to contrive and create the universe! For, in fact, we find that the correlation of animal structures, so beautifully developed by Cuvier, Owen, and others, is but a specific example of the great law of harmony, that links together, by a golden chain, the great and the small, the past, the present, and the future, throughout the universe.

The science of physiology, however, has often been looked upon with jealousy by the friends of religion, as leading its votaries to materialism. It would not be strange, indeed, if men, who see such astonishing effects result from exquisite material organization, and who give but little attention to the functions and laws of intellect, should come to think it possible that even thought may be only a result of that organization. But the difficulty lies, not in the science, but in these partial views — in that common failing of literary men, to attempt to group every thing under a favorite science, and explain every thing by it. And further, when I find even professedly Christian men defending materialism, and some of its ablest advocates admitting that the soul may be something "immortal, subtle, immaterial, diffused through the brain,"* (I use their very words,) I cannot believe that the views of such men, as to the nature of the soul, differ much in reality from those of the strict immaterialist, although they use different terms. Nor will the practical influence of their opinions, false as they undoubtedly are, when understood in their strict sense, be likely to be very disastrous; although there is a grosser form of materialism, that is made the basis of a hateful system of atheism.

There are two recent offsets from physiology, which have been supposed fraught with influences unfavorable to religion. I refer to phrenology and mesmerism. The first has been thought to favor materialism, and to lessen human responsibility; and the latter, to bring miracles into disrepute, and to direct us, for the cure of the body and the soul, to a class of dreaming pretenders, whose responses are about as much to be relied on as those of the oracle of Delphos, the god of Ekron, or the witch of Endor, and whom it is about as impious to consult. The merits of these new branches of science, this is not the proper occasion to discuss; nor is it easy as yet to ascertain definitely what principles in them are settled. But admitting their pretensions, the first seems to leave the question of materialism just where it found it; since it is as easy to see how an immaterial soul should act through a hundred organs as through one. Nor does it seem to me more difficult, on natural principles, to see how the mind may

* Elliotson's Physiology, p. 39.

act at a distance, through the undulations of a mesmeric medium, than to see how light and heat are transmitted by the waves of a luminiferous ether. On the other hand, if physiology and phrenology tend to materialism, certainly mesmerism tends even more decidedly to immaterialism; as the conversion of several distinguished materialists will testify. It does, also, open to the Christian (admitting its statements to be true) most interesting glimpses of the mode in which the mind may act when freed from flesh and blood, and clothed with a spiritual body. Indeed, I doubt not that, in regard both to phrenology and mesmerism, the general principle will prove true, that the more ominous of evil any branch of knowledge seems to be in its incipient state, the more prolific it will ultimately become in illustrations favorable both to morality and religion.

The wide dominions of natural history, embracing zoölogy, botany, and mineralogy, the theologist has ever found crowded with demonstrations of the divine existence, and of God's providential care and government; and every new province that has been explored by the naturalist only serves to enlarge our conceptions of the Creator's works, and to impress us more deeply with their unity and perfection. These new conquests in unknown regions have been astonishingly numerous within the last half century; but in the direction pointed out by the microscope they have been most marvellous. The existence of animals too minute to be seen by the naked eye has, indeed, long been known; but it was not till the researches of Ehrenberg that any just conceptions of their infinite number and indefinite minuteness were entertained. We now know that nine millions of some of these animalcula may live in a space not larger than a mustard seed, and that their numbers are many million times greater than that of all other animals on the globe. Indeed, the microscope has laid open a field into the infinitesimal forms of organic and inorganic nature quite as boundless, both in number and extent, as the telescope discloses in infinite space. Nor can we find any limits in the one direction more than the other; and thus does the microscope, in the same manner as the telescope, prodigiously enlarge our conceptions of the perfections of the infinite Author of the universe.

These researches have cast not a little light upon a certain hypothesis, that has been, in one form or another, often thrown before the world since the days of Democritus and Epicurus, usually for the purpose of sustaining a system of atheism. It supposes an inherent power in nature, capable of producing plants and animals without parentage, by an imagined vital force, essential to some forms of matter. The ancient philosophers imputed these effects to a "fortuitous concourse of atoms." In modern times this general statement has been made more definite by Lamarck, Geoffroy St. Hilaire, Bory St. Vincent, and others, who suppose that Nature — in their vocabulary sometimes dignified by the title of Deity, but still unintelligent, and merely instrumental — gives origin only to "monads," or "rough draughts" of organic beings; and that these, by "an inherent tendency to improvement," and "the force of external circumstances," become animals of higher and higher organization; until at last the orang-outang abandoned his quadrupedal condition, and stood erect as man, with all his lofty powers of intellect. Before the invention of the microscope, a multitude of insects and worms were thought to have this equivocal origin, and to pass through these transmutations — an example of which every Latin scholar will recollect in the directions of Virgil for the production of a swarm of bees out of the carcass of an animal. But as optical instruments have been improved, and observations have become more acute, the origin of nearly every animal visible to the naked eye has been found to be by ordinary generation. The advocates of the spontaneous production of organic beings, however, still clung to the animalcula and the entozoa. But it is now clearly demonstrated that all the former class have been derived from parents; and that more abundant means are provided for their reproduction than for any of the higher tribes of animals. The same is true of the entozoa — a single individual of which is capable of producing more than sixty millions of progeny; and it would be very strange for nature to take such extraordinary pains for their propagation if it might have been accomplished spontaneously. Not a single certain example, indeed, of the spontaneous production of living beings can be adduced; and if there are a few cases where parentage has not been yet discovered, the past history of the subject makes it almost certain that it needs only more perfect instruments, or more extended observations, to prove that the same great law of reproduction embraces all animated nature. And as to the transmutation of species, geology has shown that it has never taken place; while physiology demonstrates that species are permanent, and can never be transmuted. The individual does, indeed, pass through different stages of development, some of which resemble the perfect forms of species inferior to it in the organic scale. But the limits of these developments are fixed for each species; nor is there a single known instance in which an individual has been able to stop at any particular stage, and thus become another species.

In view of these facts, it is not strange that most of the men best qualified to judge on such a subject — as for instance, Owen, the ablest of comparative anatomists; Ehrenberg, the first of microscopists; and Müller, most eminent in physiology — should reject these hypotheses of spontaneous generation and transmutation. Nevertheless, the unusual interest which has been manifested by the recent work entitled Vestiges of the Natural History of the Creation — wherein these hypotheses, as well as the nebular hypothesis, are ingeniously defended, and that, too, without denying the original intervention of a divine Power in nature — show us that a long-drawn contest is yet before naturalists on these subjects, ere these fancies shall be forced into that extramundane receptacle of things abortive and unaccomplished, described by Milton as "a limbo large and wide," on the back side of the moon. And yet, my conviction is that this contest will not have so important a bearing on the cause of religion as some theologists imagine. For, even though these hypotheses should be established, an intelligent, spiritual, infinite Deity is quite as necessary to account for existing nature as on the more common theory, which supposes the universe commanded from nothing at once in a perfect state. Indeed, to endow the particles of matter with the power to form exquisite organic compounds, just at the moment when circumstances are best adapted to their existence, and then to become animated, nay, endowed with instincts, and with lofty intellects, — all which results the advocates of these hypotheses must impute to the laws impressed upon originally brute matter, — such effects, I say, demand infinite wisdom, power, and benevolence even more imperatively than the common theories of creation. I doubt not that in general these hypotheses have been adopted to sustain atheistic opinions, or to remove the Deity away from his works. But unbiased philosophy sees that they utterly fail to accomplish either of these objects. And I confess that I reject them more because they have no solid evidence in their favor than because I fear that they will ultimately be of much injury to religion; especially so long as such works as Whewell's Indications of the Creator are within the reach of the scholar.

The religious bearings of geology alone remain to be noticed. And no science, except perhaps astronomy, has excited so much alarm as this for its supposed irreligious tendencies. But so soon as theologians discovered that while the Mosaic chronology fixes the date of man's creation, it leaves the antiquity of the globe unsettled, and, therefore, a fit subject for philosophical examination, they began to see that this science might be made to shed much light upon religion. Indeed, it already excels every other science in the importance of its religious applications; and notwithstanding the noble beginnings by Dr. Buckland, Dr. J. Pye Smith, Dr. Chalmers, and others, the work of development is but just begun. Would that my time and the reader's patience might permit us to take a leisurely survey of this interesting field. But a glance must suffice.

To say nothing of the illustrations of the meaning of revealed truth derived from this science, — of collision between them there is certainly none, — it furnishes us, in the first place, with a new argument for the existence of a Deity. This argument rests upon three leading facts of the science independent of one another; so that we may doubt or deny one or two of them, and yet not reject the argument. The first is, that there was a period when no animals or plants existed on the globe, and, therefore, an epoch when they were created; which must have required a Being of infinite perfections. The second is, that there have been on the globe several nearly entire extinctions and renewals of organic life, each of which demands the agency of such a

Being. The third is, that man was only recently created — almost the last of the animals; and since he is at the head of creation, nothing in nature has demanded a higher exercise of wisdom and power than his production; and, therefore, it must have required a Deity.

It is obvious that these same facts prove clearly the non-eternity of the present condition of the globe; and even though we admit the ancient doctrine of matter's eternity, yet its most important modifications, requiring a Deity no less than its creation, must have been produced in time, and this conclusion is all that is essential to theism. And thus geology, which has been supposed to favor the idea of the world's eternity, is the only science, as Dr. Chalmers has splendidly shown, that can prove its non-eternity.

These same facts, and others that might be named, demonstrate the occasional interference of the Deity with the settled order of nature: in other words, they show us splendid miracles of creation. And thus is all presumption against the miracles of revelation done away; and also all objections against special providence and special answers to prayer.

This science, too, opens to us views into the arcana of past duration, as deep and illimitable as astronomy does into the arcana of space; and there is made to pass before us a splendid panorama of the vast and varied plans of Jehovah; while chemical change is disclosed to us as the great conservative and controlling principle of the universe, superior even to the laws of gravitation. The unity of the divine plans is also exhibited to us by the records of this science, on a far wider scale than the existing economy of nature can show. And, finally, it brings before us a great number of new and peculiar proofs of divine benevolence, that throw new glory over this attribute of the Deity; derived, as they are, from facts heretofore supposed to prove divine malevolence, or at least vindictive justice.

We have now taken a glance at the entire and vast circle of human learning. And is not every mind forced irresistibly to the conclusion, that every branch was originally linked by a golden chain to the throne of God, and that the noblest use to which they can be consecrated, and for which they were destined, is to illustrate his perfections and to display his glory? If so, let me conclude my too protracted remarks by a few inferences.

In the first place, what a monstrous perversion and misapprehension of learning it is, to consider it as hostile to religion.

It is not difficult to explain how a Christian, who is very ignorant, and who learns that literary men are often sceptical, should distrust the influence of learning upon religion; nor how a mere smatterer in science, himself sceptical, should flatter himself that his great learning made him so. But how strange that any talented and well-informed man, be he Christian or infidel, should not see that all science and a large part of literature are

"But elder Scripture writ by God's own hand!"

It must be the strongest prejudice, or the most decided hatred to religion, which can suppose that one work of the same infinitely perfect God should oppose another; for, in fact, learning and religion are only different shoots from the same parent stock; and if their fruit be of opposite qualities, it must be because man has grafted upon one or the other the apples of Sodom. To set learning against religion is as unnatural as to array brother against brother on the field of combat.

We see, secondly, that those engaged in directly promoting

religion, and those devoted to learning, ought to look upon each other as laboring in a common cause.

If their labors are such as they should be, they will help each other; and, therefore, they ought to rejoice in each other's success. For though a new branch of learning but half understood may sometimes put on an aspect threatening to religion, we need never fear but the final result will be a new support to religion; and, therefore, the religious man should dismiss all fears and jealousies in respect to sound learning; while, on the other hand, every increase of true religion has an auspicious bearing upon the cause of learning.

We see, thirdly, that the preacher of the gospel may consistently devote himself to the work of instructing the young in literature and science. For, in the first place, he need not by such a change necessarily abandon the direct preaching of the gospel occasionally. In the second place, by faithful instruction in learning, he may greatly promote the cause of religion, and train up many, perhaps, to exert a still wider influence in its favor. Finally, how much better that such a man should use science and literature legitimately for the support of religion, than that they should be perverted by a sceptical teacher to undermine it! In spite of these reasons, however, we are frequently told that for a minister of the gospel to become a teacher of human learning, is to abandon his high calling, and forfeit his solemn vows; as indeed he may do, by engaging in such pursuits from merely secular motives.

In the fourth place, we see that the more eminent a man is for learning, the more eminent he should be for personal piety. Why, indeed, should not the latter increase in his heart, as the former does in his intellect? For every new accession of knowledge is but a development of some attribute or plan of the Deity. The entire field of human learning all rightfully belongs to religion, and should be regarded by the Christian scholar as consecrated ground. The farther he advances in it, the more does he see of the Deity; and as he returns from communion with Nature in the very holy of holies of her temple, he ought, like Moses from the holy mount, to show a radiant glory on his countenance.

In the fifth place, what importance does the subject give to the pursuits of learning, and the institutions of learning!

If knowledge is power in secular matters, it is no less so in religion. I know that a higher power is essential to the success of the latter. But I know, too, that religion without learning almost infallibly degenerates into fanaticism or dead formalism; and indeed, at this day, true religion will not flourish except in connection with learning; and, therefore, almost every denomination is now striving to found and sustain literary seminaries. Nor is their importance yet duly estimated, because but few realize how indispensable is their agency in promoting the noblest of all objects, the salvation of men; and, therefore, in our land at least, with a few exceptions, their foundations are too narrow, and the superstructure too frail.

In the sixth place, how justly are those honored, and how wide an influence do they exert, who found and endow literary institutions from religious motives!

They may be charged with unhallowed ambition, by men who think only of the secular influence of these institutions. But he who considers what is the highest use of learning, and how immense will be the influence of a well-endowed seminary upon the cause of religion, cannot but look upon such bequests as the noblest of charities; especially when he remembers how much more enduring is that influence than when money is given to most other benevolent objects. What names stand higher on the Christian's roll of fame than those of Harvard, and Yale, and Dartmouth, and Williams, and Brown? And through how many coming centuries of our country's history will their example stimulate others to go and do likewise! By liberal bequests to literary institutions while yet feeble and struggling for existence, their names have become inseparably fixed upon them, where they will remain long after the pyramids of Egypt shall be crumbled into dust. In what other way could they have exerted so desirable, extensive, and enduring an influence upon the world?

In the seventh place, what a noble yet immense work lies before Christian scholars, viz., to make all learning subservient to its highest purpose!

Sadly have many branches been perverted, and strong is still the disposition to divert all learning from its noblest use. To arrest this downward tendency, and to bring back all literature and all science to the service of religion, is an object of the highest ambition, adapted to call forth the strongest efforts of every Christian scholar. And let all such take courage. For religion is the natural home of all branches of learning; and though some of the sisterhood have been seduced into the service of sin and the world, and have forgotten their paternity, yet when reminded of their sacred origin, gladly will they return to the paternal hearth, and pile richer gifts upon the altar, where they presented their earliest offerings.

In the eighth place, we learn how important it is that every literary institution should make the promotion of religion the leading object of its system of instruction.

Other objects of subordinate importance it may and ought to endeavor to accomplish; but to make these the chief things

5

aimed at, while religion is thrust into the background, is as if a man should build an elegant mansion for the sake of improving the landscape, and with no intention of living in it; or as if a community should erect a church for the sake of holding town meetings and political caucuses in it, and hearing lyceum lectures, with no intention of using it as a place of worship, except perhaps occasionally.

There is, indeed, a great cry about excluding sectarianism from our literary institutions, and throwing them open to persons of all religious opinions. Now, in this country, where we have no established church, it is difficult to define a sectarian, unless it be a man who differs from us in religious sentiments. So that in fact, with the exception of a few, who have no opinions or care on this subject, we are all sectarians; and to exclude sectarianism from a literary institution is to exclude all religion from it. And such is usually the result, when it attempts so to trim its course as to suit all parties. But really, of all kinds of intolerance, that is the worst which is furious for toleration, and that the worst kind of sectarianism which is fierce for irreligion. The only true liberal and manly course for an institution to adopt, is, openly to avow its creed, and not to disguise its desire to have all the youth adopt it who resort thither; while at the same time it uses no other means but argument and example to convert them, nor permits their religious opinions, whatever they may be, to have any influence in awarding literary honors. In this respect the motto of the ancient Tyrian queen should be adopted by every teacher: —

> "Tros Tyriusve nullo discrimine mihi agetur."

Such a course does, indeed, make the institution sectarian, that is, it shows a preference for some particular system of religion. But it is an honest course, and the only honest one that can be taken. For if an institution professes to regard all religious opinions with equal favor, who can avoid the suspicion that it is either a stratagem for introducing some unpopular system, or that it indicates an almost universal scepticism on the subject? Indeed, how can a man, who has any just sense of religious obligation, consent to be placed in circumstances where he cannot recommend openly those religious views which he deems essential to salvation?

In the ninth place, we see that a professorship of natural theology is an appropriate one in a college.

The main business of such a professor is to go over the same ground as we have now glanced at, and to trace out the bearing of all literature and all science upon religion. And if this be, indeed, the most important use of learning, why should it be left unprovided for? or depend upon the voluntary efforts of the different instructors, whose hands are already quite full? I make these remarks, because such a professorship is unusual in our colleges; and I have feared that the one with which I have been recently honored may seem to have been got up for the occasion, to eke out a deficiency of titles. But it is not so; and it is proper to say, that I have in fact, for the last ten years, attempted to perform the duties of such a professorship.

Finally, to the principle which I have endeavored to prove, we owe the establishment of many modern literary and scientific institutions, and eminently of that within whose walls we are assembled.

By recurring to the history of the origin of some of the most distinguished scientific societies and literary institutions of Europe, it will appear that one of the leading objects which their illustrious founders had in view, was to extend a knowledge of the Christian religion, along with the arts and sciences, to remote and barbarous nations, particularly those of the south-eastern Asia. Among the institutions thus originating were the Royal Society of London, the French Academy, the Berlin Academy, the Academia Naturæ Curiosorum, the University of Halle, and the Institutions of Franke at Halle; and among the distinguished men who have labored in this work we find the names of Boyle, Montucla, Leibnitz, Wolf, and Humboldt.* I fear, indeed, that this object has been often lost sight of by these institutions; but their origin furnishes us at least with the testimony of most able and competent witnesses to the truth of the position which I have now vindicated and illustrated, as to the highest use of learning.

But to come nearer home: we shall see that this institution originated in a deep conviction of this same truth in the minds of those noble-hearted men, who, in faith and prayer, laid the foundations on which we are called upon to build. The very first paragraph of the constitution of what they then called a charity institution contains it; and in the first article it is said, "In contemplating the felicitous state of society which is predicted in the Scriptures of truth, and the rapid approach of such a state, which the auspices of the present day clearly indicate, and desiring to add our feeble efforts to the various exertions of the Christian community for effecting so glorious an event, — we have associated together for the express purpose of founding an institution on the genuine principles of charity and benevolence, for the instruction of youth in all the branches of literature and science usually taught in colleges." Here we see no other reason assigned for founding the institution but a wish to promote the cause of religion; as if no other benefits to result from it were

* Oratio in Academia Fridericiana Halensi, &c. habita ab. D. J. S. C. Schweigger, p. 4, Halle, 1834.

worth naming. Let this fact never be forgotten by those who manage and instruct in this college. God forbid that the time should ever come when any instructor here shall be ashamed, or backward, to acknowledge that the advancement of pure religion — even the Christian religion — is the grand object for which he labors and makes sacrifices.*

Let us never forget, that *promotion cometh neither from the east nor the west, nor from the south. But God is Judge. He setteth up one, and putteth down another.* How easy for him to blast the fairest schemes, and to prosper the weak and the trembling! Nor let our confidence in him, or in the prosperity of this institution, be shaken, because it has been called to pass through straits, and other conflicts may still await it. We believe that these storms in its youth are intended, by a wise Providence, only to make its roots strike deeper, and to give its trunk greater strength, and its branches wider extension in its maturity. Only let faith hold on firmly to the principle, that God will assuredly crown with success every sincere effort to bind the wreath of learning around the brow of Religion, and cheerfully and resolutely shall we consecrate ourselves to the great work of sustaining and advancing this institution; and though we shall not be allowed to labor long here, or elsewhere, yet while we live, and when we die, we may confidently utter in behalf of its pupils, its guardians, and all its future interests, the prayer of a heathen, with a Christian meaning and a Christian spirit: —

> "Dii probos mores docilii juventæ,
> Dii senectuti placidæ quietem
> Romulæ genti date remque prolemque
> Et decus omne!"

* Several pages relating to the college, its discouragements and encouragements, are here omitted.

THE RELATIONS AND MUTUAL DUTIES BETWEEN THE PHILOSOPHER AND THE THEOLOGIAN.

The history of the manner in which philosophy has been treated by theologians, and theology by philosophers, is very instructive and suggestive. Some of the former have taken philosophy into a close and most cordial embrace, and allowed it to modify, and even form a part of the foundation of their whole system of doctrines; and, as you looked at the stately pile, you could not be certain whether the human or the divine had most to do in its erection.

Another class have been as jealous of philosophy as if its touch were infectious, and its infection death; and it would seem as if they took special pains to make their professedly biblical system of truth look as distorted and angular as possible, lest they should be suspected of having used the moulding and the dressing tool of reason to give it form and symmetry.

On the other hand, the tendency among philosophers has been to rank theology below the other sciences. Some of them have maintained that the two departments are quite independent of each other, and that the question of agreement between them is one with which they are not concerned. Their business is to discover the truths of science, and to leave theology to take care of itself. Others admit the desirableness of a reconciliation, but are quite jealous of any claims, on the part of revelation, to superior authority.

But though thus diverse and conflicting have been the views of theologians and philosophers respecting their mutual relations and duties, yet the history of the connection or opposition between theological and philosophical systems has constituted no small part of the annals of the church. And from that history we learn two things: first, that there is an important connection, and consequently there are important duties, between the theologian and the philosopher; and secondly, that these relations and duties have been, and still are, sadly misunderstood or neglected. No code of principles, defining those relations and duties, has yet been elaborated; and hence these classes have often treated each other like the partisans in a border warfare; and prejudice and illiberality have been the impelling forces, rather than Christianity or philosophy.

These remarks will probably lead you, gentlemen of the society at whose request I stand here to-day, and other respected auditors, to anticipate a discussion on the Relations between the Theologian and Philosopher. Such is my intention; or, to state the subject more specifically, *I propose to enucleate and examine the principles which should regulate the intercourse and feelings of these two classes of society.*

I employ the term philosophy in its broadest signification, embracing all science, physical, intellectual, and moral. Yet, for special reasons, I shall rest my eye chiefly upon, and derive my illustration from, inductive or physical science. For, in the first place, circumstances beyond my control, and connected chiefly with health, have turned my attention mainly to this department of philosophy; secondly, the claims and bearings of moral and intellectual philosophy, oftener, and with a power which it would be in vain for me to aspire after, have been brought before you. And finally and especially, a deepening interest seems to be gathering around physical science, both as a rich repository of arguments for, and illustrations of, religion, and a magazine of missiles to hurl against it.

In attempting to discuss such a subject, it is gratifying to find one's self addressing the members of an institution where the freest and the fullest investigation of all truth is encouraged, and where evidence, not authority, is the test by which every principle is tried; an institution, which, while it boldly and honestly maintains its own views of religious truth, exercises the charity of the gospel towards those who reject them, and expects to convince them only by manly argument. It is not flattery, but justice only, to say that it is eminently by the labors of the distinguished men who have presided here, following in the steps of Edwards, Hopkins, Bellamy, and Emmons, that evangelical Christianity has assumed such a shape as to render its reconciliation with philosophy possible. Monuments evincing the truth of this position rise all around me. The Nestor of biblical philology is not, indeed, here to-day; but his works are, and they evince how much he has done to unfold the true meaning of the Word of God, and how fearlessly, yet impartially, he sought for the truth; never inquiring, while engaged in his investigations, whether the results would favor this or that theological system, but whether they brought out the true mind of the Spirit. And he well knew that if that could once be surely ascertained, it would be found in entire harmony with all other. The Nestor of theology is still here; and so are his works; especially the last and greatest one, which gives us results of nearly half a century's careful examination of systematic theology. Those results, presented in language of such simplicity as only true greatness and conscious strength know how to use, and with a calmness and fairness of reasoning which only a perfect knowledge of the subject, and a thorough conviction of its truth, could employ, stand up before my eye, as one of the noblest monuments which human skill and piety can raise to God's glory and man's good. I mean not that the work is perfect, nor that keen criticism, nor that the large-pupiled eye of prejudice and envy cannot find weak spots in it; nor that I should not myself dissent from some minor points defended in it. But as an American, and a Christian, I rejoice, and bless God that the venerable author has been spared to place the top stone on this column of eternal truth, which I predict shall abide fresh and strong, when the Washington Monument and the Bunker Hill column shall become only crumbling mounds.

As an American, and a Christian too, when lately on a foreign shore, it was gratifying, and I hope to some better feelings than mere national pride, to be able to point to a certain Bibliotheca, whose pages, each trimester, open, to the scholar and the Christian, productions which combine philosophy more profound with biblical analysis more accurate than any other evangelical periodical in the English language with which I am acquainted. Let this testimony, too, be regarded only as an act of justice, and not of flattery.

This allusion to the Bibliotheca reminds us — as indeed almost every thing else does to-day — of another strong pillar of this institution, whom Providence has recently smitten down.* Nor is it this Seminary alone that feels the stroke. When such a man falls, it brings a cloud over the whole republic of letters, and creates a wide blank, especially among the cultivators of sacred literature. It will be deeply felt even on the other side of the Atlantic, where his able works

* Professor B. B. Edwards.

have been long known and appreciated. This is not the place to give his life, or his eulogy, which has already been done in a most satisfactory manner. But there is one trait of his writings and his character which it is proper I should notice. Though devoting himself chiefly to classical and biblical literature, yet his active and scrutinizing mind was not satisfied till he had mastered the leading principles of almost all branches of learning; and he kept his eye open to the progress of secular as well as sacred literature and philosophy. His accurate judgment appreciated full well the importance of bringing all branches of human learning into harmony; for he well knew that there can be no real discrepancy between one kind of truth and another. Hence, when philosophy and revelation were in apparent collision, he knew that the one, or the other, or both, were not fully understood; and therefore he welcomed every new ray of light which literature and science, history and observation, might cast upon the Bible, and the Bible might cast upon philosophy. In a word, he had those enlarged and liberal views, in regard to the relations and mutual duties of the theologian and the philosopher, which made him, in this respect, a model man. From those narrow views and prejudices — the *odium theologicum* — which too often result from exclusive attention to one department of knowledge, he was remarkably free. He never substituted denunciation for argument; not because he was indifferent to the truth, but because he had so much confidence in its naked power and ultimate triumph. It is such men who are wanted in the ranks of theology, to command the respect of philosophers and the confidence of Christians. O Andover! how deep the wound inflicted upon thee in his removal!

"Hei mihi! quantum
Præsidium, Ausonia, et quantum tu perdis, Iule!"

But thanks be to God, that he was spared so long as to be able to make an abiding impress here. Nay, the cause of learning, of education, of religion throughout the land, shall long feel the influence of his labors; and other lands shall share in the rich legacy which he has left.

And now, before an audienee trained by such men, and under the influence of such principles, I feel confident that I shall be heard with candor, and, I hope, with sympathy, while I attempt to ascertain and enucleate the principles that should form the mutual creed of the theologian and the philosopher.

The first means which I shall employ for determining this platform of principles consists in an appeal to reason and Scripture.

We need, however, as a basis for our inquiries, to define the limits and the functions of philosophy and of theology. The first searches out and classifies the laws of nature; the second presents the principles of religion, natural and revealed, in a scientific or systematic form. Theology, therefore, has a right to employ whatever facts and reasonings it can find in philosophy, illustrative of religion. The principles of reasoning, too, are the same as in philosophy. But it possesses, in addition, an infallible standard of appeal for all subjects that are above reason. The object of philosophy is to explain the phenomena of nature, mental, moral, and material; that of theology is exclusively to defend and enforce the moral relations of the universe. Hence the two subjects are almost entirely distinct in their aim. The only point where they pursue the same track is in the department of moral philosophy, which has derived from revealed theology the only true foundation on which to build, and that is, the character of man as a fallen being. Incidentally, however, the two branches treat of the same subject; as, for instance, the creation, the deluge, and the destruction of the world and its organic races. But since revelation does not pretend to teach science, nor even to use language in its strictly scientific sense, we ought to expect, in such cases, only that there shall be no real, although there may be an apparent, discrepancy between the two records.

Thus distinct, in nature and in function, are these two great departments of human knowledge. Both do, indeed, connect with the same Infinite Source of all knowledge ; but they occupy separate and clearly defined provinces, and those at work in one field need not encroach upon, or despise and overlook, those in the other. Providence intended that they should be mutual helps, and mutually deferential. That theology has a vast preëminence, does not justify an undervaluation of philosophy, as if it were of no consequence.

This course of remark leads naturally to the attempt to lay down as the first article of the mutual creed of the philosopher and the theologian, this principle : That on the question of authority, while science should receive all the credit which its various degrees of evidence deserve, theology has a higher claim to any branch of knowledge not strictly demonstrative. A mathematical demonstration no sane mind can resist ; and little less certain are the physico-mathematical sciences. But where scientific conclusions depend only upon probable evidence, observation, and experiment, for example, there is some room for mistake and false inference. And is it not reasonable to maintain that theology has a higher claim to credence than the probabilities of any single science ? For the evidences of its truth, drawn from so many sources, and so diverse, must be considered as outweighing the evidence of any single science dependent upon experiment or observation. If, therefore, a direct collision could be made out between such a science and religion, and we were compelled to choose between the two, theology must carry the day.

I make this supposition, not because such an alternative ever has occurred, or ever will occur, but merely to show what are the relative claims to deference of theology and probable science. Not unfrequently, where only an apparent discrepancy has manifested itself between revelation and some yet imperfect science, the self-confident sceptic considers the fate of Christianity as decided. But that is only a flippant philosophy which will not rank revealed truth above any single science founded upon probable evidence. Not only does theology stand above all other sciences in the importance and dignity of its principles, but in the authority with which it speaks; for it rests mainly on inspired testimony.

On the other hand, however, not a few divines demand for theology, not only superior authority, but will allow none at all to science, in matters of religion.

"We have," say they, "an inspired record, and its declarations are not to be set aside, or modified in the least, by any pretended discoveries or theories of blind and perverted human reason. God has spoken, who cannot lie, and his Word is to be received implicitly, whatever may become of the supposed facts or conclusions of weak and ignorant man."

Such reasoning overlooks one important principle. All will agree that when we know certainly what God has revealed, we are to receive it without modification. But he has revealed himself through human language, and given us no inspired interpreters. We are to ascertain the meaning of Scripture essentially as we do that of any other writings. Accordingly we do not hesitate to resort to philosophy and history, as guides in our exegesis. Nor do we refuse the light that comes to us from the deciphered hieroglyphics of

Egypt, and the disinterred relics of Nineveh. Why, then, should not the testimony of science be employed to elucidate the meaning of Scripture, especially when it opens archives a thousand times more ancient, and no less distinct, than those of Egypt and Nineveh? No reasonable philosopher asks that science should be allowed to set aside or modify any thing which God hath spoken, but only that it should be employed to ascertain what he has spoken; for without the aid of science men have sometimes been unable to understand aright the language of Scripture — as in the rising and the setting of the sun, and the immobility of the earth, described in the Bible. Before astronomy had ascertained the earth's true diurnal and annual motions, the scriptural statements were not, and could not be, understood aright. And the same may be true in respect to phenomena dependent upon other sciences.

A second principle of this creed — if it be not too obvious, and too generally acknowledged, to require a formal statement — takes the ground, that as a means of moral reformation and regulation of human affairs philosophy has little power, and is not to be brought into comparison with theology. Both reason and experience have given so many striking illustrations of this truth that it seems strange any should wish to repeat the experiment. But it is done every few years; nay, at all times we find men zealous in advocating some new philosophic scheme for reforming and perfecting human society, whose essential element is something different from the method pointed out in the Bible. The new system may have some principle in common with Christianity; but the author of it relies rather on the differences which he has superadded than on the agreement. Yet what multitudes of such schemes, after an ephemeral excitement, become the byword of the world, and pass silently into that oblivious receptacle of things, "Abortive, monstrous, or unkindly mixed," described by Milton!

> "All these, upwhirled aloft,
> Flew o'er the back side of the world, far off,
> Into a limbo large and wide, since called
> The Paradise of Fools: — to few unknown
> Long after." —

A third important principle, which reason teaches as appropriate for this mutual creed, is, that entire harmony will be the final result of all researches in philosophy and religion. It is strange how any other view of the matter can be entertained by men who profess to believe that the God of nature is the God of revelation. For what are nature and revelation but different developments of one great system, emanating from the same infinite Mind? Yet not a few theologians look upon science as a dangerous ally of revelation, and maintain that we are not to seek for harmony between them. "The Bible," say they, "was given for our infallible guide, and it is of little consequence whether its teachings coincide with those of philosophy. The history of the church shows us that the two have always been in collision, and it is a dangerous enterprise for the religious man to labor for their reconciliation. Let him follow the teachings of revelation implicitly, nor suffer any of its statements to be modified by the pretended facts or theoretical deductions of science."

Does this seem to any to be a caricature? Take, then, the words of a distinguished American divine. "We are not a little alarmed," says he, "at the tendency of the age to reduce the great facts narrated in the Bible to the standard of natural science." "Human science is a changing and restless thing. It is well that it is so."

On the other hand, not a few scientific men, although professing respect for the Bible, and faith in it, yet feel as if its statements should have no weight, even upon any matter of fact which comes under the cognizance of philosophy. Science, it is thought, has its own appropriate evidences, which must be admitted, whatever else goes against it. The Bible was not given to teach science, and therefore it was never intended to be authoritative in such matters.

Now, if these two classes of men were to lay it down as a settled principle that all science and all religion are certain ultimately to harmonize throughout, it would remove this mutual jealousy and distrust; nor would the parties be disposed to stand aloof from each other, and to treat one another as enemies. If they are ultimately to be entirely one, then they are essentially so now, and all discrepancy is apparent only. Therefore should the philosopher and the theologian feel as if they were brothers, whose business it is, in mutual good will, to elucidate and bring into harmony different portions of the same eternal truth.

Another article of this mutual creed should be, that scientific men may have the freest and the fullest liberty of investigation. They have not always had it. "We remember," says Melville, "how, in darker days, ecclesiastics set themselves against philosophers, who were investigating the motions of the heavenly bodies, apprehensive that the new theories were at variance with the Bible, and therefore resolved to denounce them as heresies, and stop their spread by persecution." Open persecution is unpopular now; but I fear that a remnant of the same feelings still lingers in some minds. They will not say directly to the scientific man, "Abstain from your researches, for they seem to threaten injury to religion," but their fears of some disastrous influence make them jealous of the man, and fearful that his scientific conclusions may lead himself and others astray; and hence they withdraw their confidence from him, and thus take the most effectual way to alienate and make a sensitive mind sceptical. But how narrow are such views! and how idle the fear of collision between science and revelation! How much more noble and truly Christian are the sentiments of Dr. Pye Smith! "Only let the investigation be sufficient, and the induction honest; let observation take its farthest flight; let experiment penetrate into all the recesses of nature; let the veil of ages be lifted up from all that has hitherto been unknown, if such a course were possible — religion need not fear; Christianity is secure, and true science will always pay homage to the divine Creator and Sovereign, *of whom, and through whom, and to whom, are all things, and unto whom be glory forever.*"

The difference in the character of the language of science and that frequently employed in religion suggests a fifth article of the supposed platform. Different principles of interpretation, to some extent, are demanded in the two departments. True science employs terms that are precise, definite, literal, with scarcely more than one meaning, and adapted only to cultivated minds. Religion, especially the Bible, makes use of language that is indefinite, loose, and multiform in signification, often highly figurative, and adapted, not only to the popular mind, but to men in an early and rude state of society. Science, for instance, could not, as the Bible can and does, represent the work of creation in one chapter as occupying six days, and in the next chapter as completed in one day. It could not, like the Bible, speak of the sun's rising and setting, and of the earth's immobility. Meteorology could not describe the concave above our heads as a solid expanse, having windows or openings for the rain to pass from the clouds beyond. Nor could physiology represent the bones to be the seat of pain, or psychology refer intellectual operations to the region of the kidneys. Neither could systematic theology in one place represent God as having repented that he had made man, and in another exhibit him as without variableness or shadow of turning. But all this can the Bible do in perfect consistency with its infallible inspiration, because it was the language of common life; and common sense can interpret it, so that every suspicion of self-contradiction shall vanish. Indeed, had its language been strictly scientific, it might have formed a good text book in philosophy, but it would have been a poor guide to salvation. Yet the attempt to force the language of the Bible into the strait jacket of science has been prolific of mistakes and errors.

Another principle, which maintains that the Bible has anticipated some scientific discoveries, should be settled and form a part of this mutual creed. In my view it should be settled in the negative. For if we admit that one modern discovery can be found in the Bible, how can we vindicate that book in those numerous cases where it speaks of natural phenomena in accordance with the monstrously absurd notions which prevailed among those to whom it was originally addressed? If it describes the science of the nineteenth century in one instance, why not in all? But admit that it was foreign to the object of revelation to teach science, and we can see why its descriptions of natural things accord with optical, but not physical, truth; and, then, there is no difficulty in enucleating the true meaning of the sacred writers. Interpreted by such a principle, we should not conclude that Job meant to reveal the Copernican system because he speaks of the earth as hanging upon nothing; especially as in another place he refers to the pillars on which the earth rests.

But both phrases are quite natural and proper for one of the most allegorical books of the Bible when regarded as vivid poetical images. The grand distinction between the Bible and all other professed revelations is, not that it has anticipated scientific discoveries, but that there is nothing in its statements which those discoveries contradict or invalidate. Often has the sceptic announced such discrepancies; but, in the end, the Bible has always been shown consistent with itself and with science. Now, this is true of no other professedly inspired books. The Koran and the Vêdas are often in direct collision with astronomy, geology, anatomy, and physiology; and when you have proved them false in science you have destroyed their authority in religion. Proudly above them all stands the Bible; and so long as it can maintain this position we may be sure of its divine original; for any mere human production, embracing so many authors, and reaching through so many thousands of years in its history, could not have avoided collision with scientific truth.

Once more: theologians and philosophers should mutually require that those who undertake to pronounce judgment upon points of connection between science and religion should be well acquainted with both sides of the question. I do not say equally well acquainted; for so limited are the human faculties that he who is eminent in one department of knowledge can hardly be expected to be equally familiar with another. But a respectable knowledge of any subject is essential to decide upon its relations to other subjects. And it ought to be a settled principle, that an opinion upon any point of science or religion is entitled to no respect if it can be shown that the man does not understand the subject upon which he writes. For eminence in one department of knowledge gives a man no claims to credence in another which he has never studied. A man, for instance, may be most distinguished in science, so that his word is law; and yet, never having given his attention to theology, he is utterly unfit to judge of the bearings of scientific facts or theories upon religion. We listen with great respect to the opinions of an eminent divine upon those theological principles to which he has devoted so much thought and study. But if he undertakes to dogmatize upon matters of science, when his very language shows him quite ignorant of its principles, and swayed by prejudice, what claim can his opinions have to our reception or respect?

The distinguished Scotch divine, who uses the following language respecting geology and geologists, no doubt supposed himself doing an important service to religion by his denunciations. "Geology," says he, "as sometimes conducted, is a monument of human presumption, which would be truly ridiculous were it not offensive by its impiety." "Thus puny mortals, [geologists,] with a spark of intellect and a moment for observation, during which they take a hasty glance of a few superficial appearances, dream themselves authorized to give the lie to Him who made and fashioned them, and every thing which they see." The same may be said of another eminent divine, who applies similar remarks to the whole of physical science. "The third fact," says he, "here revealed, [in Genesis,] is, that this world was created in six days. Here, again, the Scriptures are at issue with science. Modern geologists tell us that this is not possible; and all we need reply to the bold assertion is, *with men this is impossible, but with God all things are possible.*" "Natural science is confessedly progressive, and, therefore, comparatively crude. Geology is in its infancy." — *Spring.*

Now, whatever effect such language may have upon persons

who have given no attention to science, what but a bad influence can it have upon the naturalist, who sees, on the very pages from which I have quoted, the most decisive evidence that the writers do not understand the subject? not from want of ability, but because other studies have engaged their attention. Suppose that, in reading a commentary on Job, the writer had inadvertently disclosed the fact, that he knew nothing of the Hebrew grammar, nor even of the Hebrew alphabet. From that moment his criticisms, however much of talent they might discover, would be regarded with indifference, if not with pity or contempt, by the Christian and the scholar.

It would be easy to quote examples of an analogous character from the philosophers. I might refer to the extraordinary and even ridiculous exegetical principles adopted by the physico-theologists of the last century to prove their favorite dogma, that the principles of physical science are all to be found in the Bible, as given by Catcott in his work on the Deluge, and by Hutchinson in his twelve volumes entitled "Moses's Principia." But more appropriately may I refer to a writer of our own times, eminent enough in science to be selected to write one of the Bridgewater Treatises. In his interpretation of the phrase "windows of heaven," in Genesis, Mr. Kirby makes it mean "cracks and volcanic vents *in the earth*, through which water and air rushed inwardly and outwardly with such violence as to tear the crust to pieces."

I quote another example from a naturalist and philosopher still more eminent, not because it has the dreamy character of that just given, but because I know how the following passage has struck some of the most distinguished and liberal Hebrew and biblical scholars in our land. While they sat gladly at the feet of this author in all matters of physical science, they regretted that the same discrimination and long study had not been given to the science of biblical interpretation before an exegesis of Genesis had been thrown out so confidently, which is contrary to the obvious sense and to the almost universal opinion of biblical writers. I speak not here of the truth or falsehood of the theory of this distinguished man, whose writings exhibit so much of the true spirit of religion, and who takes so noble a stand against the flippant scepticism of sciolists, but refer simply to this particular exegesis of Genesis.

"The advocates of identity of origin for all the several races of men, as springing from only one primitive pair," says Professor Agassiz, "have no argument to urge in support of that position, but simply a vulgar prejudice, based on some few obscure passages of the Bible, which may after all be capable of a different interpretation." "To suppose that all men originated from Adam and Eve, is to give to the Mosaic record a meaning that it was never intended to have."

It is very probable that some may be ready to apply to me personally the exhortation, *Physician, heal thyself.* For some do regard me as having violated the rule which I am urging upon others, by advancing interpretations of Scripture which no sound biblical scholar can admit. On two points especially has this charge been made. I have advocated that exegesis of Genesis which permits the intercalation of a long and indefinite period between the beginning and the first demiurgic day; and, also, that exegesis of Peter, which makes him teach that this earth and its atmosphere, after being burned up and renovated, will become the new heavens and the new earth.

Now, were these interpretations original with myself, and now first proposed in opposition to the whole array of biblical critics, I might well confess myself guilty, and conclude that my zeal to sustain a favorite theory had blinded my judgment. But in fact, these views, both of Genesis and of Peter, have been advocated by the early fathers of the church, and by a large number of the ablest modern interpreters and divines. As to the meaning of Peter, Dr. Griffin says, that the view above referred to "has been the more common opinion of the Christian fathers, of the divines of the reformation, and of the critics and annotators who have since flourished." I must disclaim, therefore, both the honor and the odium of these views, and say, that if I am wrong in their advocacy, it is because I have been led astray by such men as Augustine, Theodoret, Justin Martyr, Origen, Luther, the elder Rosenmüller, Tholuck, Dathe, Pye Smith, Patrick, Chalmers, Knapp, and Griffin.

Finally, it ought to be a position admitted by the philosopher and the theologian, that the facts and principles of science, brought before an unsophisticated mind, are favorable to piety. A contrary impression prevails extensively; just because not a few scientific men, in spite of science, and not through its influence, have been sceptics. Their hearts were wrong when they began the study; and then, according to a general law of human nature, the purest truth became only a means of increasing their perversity. But had their hearts been right at first, that same truth would have nourished and strengthened their faith and love. Why should it not be so? For what is true science but an exhibition of God's plans and operations? And will any one maintain that a survey of what God has planned and is executing should have an unfavorable moral effect upon an unperverted and unprejudiced mind? If it does, it must be through the influence of extraneous causes, such as pride, prejudice, bad education, or bad habits, for which science is not accountable. O, no! the temple of Nature is a holy place for a holy heart. Pure fire is always burning upon its altar, and its harmonies are ever hymning the praises of its great Architect, inviting all who enter to join the chorus. It needs a perverse and hardened heart to resist the good influences that emanate from its shrines.

A consideration of the mutual interest of the theologian and the philosopher constitutes a second means for determining the principles by which their feelings and intercourse should be regulated.

It hardly needs a formal argument to show, that it is for the interest of both to bring revelation and science into entire harmony. The established and intelligent Christian will not, indeed, be greatly disturbed because an alleged scientific discovery is said to come into collision with the Bible. But there are others, predisposed to believe revelation, who will gladly seize upon such examples to fortify themselves in scepticism. Religion, therefore, suffers by merely apparent incongruity between science and revelation. Nor can it be a matter of indifference to philosophers, to be looked upon as throwing doubt upon man's highest hopes and interests, by those who defend these interests, and who have taken a most important part in time past in advancing science. Suspicion and alienated feeling between these classes operate most disastrously upon both; and, therefore, mutual interest demands their united efforts to remove apparent discrepancies.

A second consideration of importance, in this connection, is, that science is the great storehouse of facts on which is based the whole system of natural religion. And when we recollect that natural religion does not stop with the mere demonstration of the being and attributes of the Deity, but establishes his natural and moral government over the world, and man's correspondent obligations, — also his common, special and miraculous providence, and the doctrine of his purposes or decrees, — we see how important is this use of science. At this day, indeed, how can the theologian dispense with its facts in their religious applications? Let the works of Ray, Derham, Wollaston, Paley, Crombie, Brown, Chalmers, and the other authors of the Bridgewater Treatises, testify to their importance. For though the divine may stand firm upon the evidence of history, prophecy, and internal character to sustain the Bible, yet if he can show that its truths are in agreement with nature, and are even sustained and illustrated by it, his appeal, in this thinking and reasoning age, will come home with much more convincing power. He cannot dispense with the facts of science and yet be *a workman that needeth not to be ashamed.*

On the other hand, the philosopher should not forget that the religious applications of science are its most important use. When he thinks what knowledge has done in elevating and civilizing society, and in multiplying the comforts and luxuries of life, he is apt to forget its religious bearings. But these, in fact, transcend in importance its worldly influences, as much as eternity transcends time. And most sadly does he degrade science who overlooks its religious applications. These form the ground of its truest dignity, and they alone link it to the permanently grand and the eternal.

But philosophy may also be employed in defending and illustrating revealed truth. Of this we have a splendid example in the "Analogy" of Bishop Butler, whose grand principle has been applied successfully by Barnes to nearly all the peculiar doctrines of revelation. Of all efforts to meet sceptical objections to evangelical Christianity, this is the most thorough and complete; and were this work more carefully studied, along with such authors as Chalmers, Harris, Whewell, Sedgwick, Isaac Taylor, and McCosh, who extend and illustrate analogous principles, the flippant and superficial sciolism of the day, that would metamorphose the Deity into natural law, would find little favor.

Nor are these religious applications of philosophy confined to the older and more mathematical sciences. Nay, those more recent, and dependent mainly upon experiment and observation, when rightly understood, are remarkably prolific of religious illustrations. Chemistry and physiology, for example, throw much light upon the doctrine of the resurrection of the body, and vindicate it against objections otherwise unanswerable. The former science, also, points us to the true meaning of those scriptures that describe the destruction of the world by fire ; showing us that it is change of form in the matter of the globe, but not its annihilation. Meteorology teaches us how to understand the language of Scripture respecting the firmament above us. And geology, especially, lends confirmation to the biblical history of man's creation as a comparatively recent event; it shows us how we should understand the scriptural cosmogony, points out a new argument for the divine existence, and lends such decisive corroboration to the revealed doctrines of special and miraculous providence, and divine benevolence, that these truths could not consistently be excluded from the creed of philosophy, though the testimony of the Bible were lost.

Surely, then, the interests of theology demand that the religious applications of science should not be overlooked ; and, on the other hand, science should count it the highest honor to be able to throw even a ray of light upon God's written word.

I venture here to suggest another use to which science may

be applied by the theologian. It is well known that sharp discussions not unfrequently occur respecting the meaning of the language of the ablest divines after their decease; and they are charged with teaching contradictory principles. It is well known, also, how great complaint is often made, by controversial writers, of the misunderstanding of their views by their opponents. But how seldom do discussions of this sort occur respecting the meaning of eminent mathematicians, natural philosophers, and naturalists! Nor does this result from entire unity of views, and the certainty of every principle discussed in these sciences. But it springs mainly from the definiteness and precision of the language which is employed. Take botany or chemistry, for example: how can men be in doubt about the meaning of a sentence, when almost every word in it has a settled and usually a single sense? I do not suppose that equal precision could be introduced into theology, because it treats of natures more subtile than those of physical science. But I suggest whether divines, in the definition of their terms, might not advantageously consult the directness, singleness, and precision of physical science more, and the wariness, subtilty, and equivocal senses of metaphysics less. I fancy that in the style of Dr. Chalmers, which, although sometimes too stately, is always clear, we have an example of this improved phraseology. I doubt whether posterity will hesitate much as to the meaning of his writings; and perhaps the unsanctified ambition of the earlier periods of his ministry, which led him to devote so much time to mathematics, chemistry, and natural history, will be thus overruled to the benefit of theology.

Every true philosopher, no less than the religious man, should be desirous that his pursuits may accomplish the most possible for the good of society; for benevolence is a duty of natural as well as revealed religion. Now, the cultivation of science alone, in a community where atheism or infidelity predominates, is most likely to prove a great curse. Knowledge puffeth up; and hence mere scientific acquisitions tend to foster pride, selfishness, and inordinate ambition, and to exalt the brilliant few at the expense of the degraded many. The result will be, that the most furious passions of our nature will exhibit their deadliest malignity in a community where science is cultivated, but spurns the aid of religion.

What a terrible illustration of this truth has been exhibited during the last century in the centre of European civilization! Never did France show more of brilliant scientific skill than during the savage days of her first revolution; and her whole subsequent history teaches us how dangerous it is to commit the power which science bestows into irreligious hands. The meteoric explosion which was the result, not only rent that unhappy country to atoms, but sent its iron fragments into every European land; and the death groan that followed has hardly yet died upon our ears. It was a dear-bought yet impressive lesson of the danger of committing scientific power into the hands of irreligion; and it should lead the philosopher to feel the necessity of spiritual influence to control the energies of science. Truly, as Coleridge remarks, "all the products of the mere understanding partake of death;" and as Lord Bacon still more appropriately observes, "in knowledge, without love, there is ever something of malignity."

But there is another important fact on this subject. The general diffusion of scientific knowledge through a community can never take place without the aid of Christianity. There may be an aristocracy of learning, as in the case just quoted, but religion alone will provide for general education. Left to the influence of any other principle, the favored and enlightened few will keep down and oppress the ignorant masses. Popular education is found only in connection with revelation. So says the history of the world; and an analysis of human nature shows us that it must be so. Hence every philosopher who is a friend to his species will feel it his duty to promote the diffusion of Christianity as well as of science. Thus only can the greatest good be secured to the whole.

The third means of ascertaining and settling the principles that should regulate the intercourse and feelings of the theologian and philosopher is by an appeal to history and observation.

We thus learn the results of many well-tried experiments on this subject; and these should have all the force of law, and be incorporated into the code of mutually obligatory principles. They are more certain than the *a priori* deductions already considered, and I could wish that my space would allow a fuller enumeration of what has thus been taught.

One of the principles thus developed is the danger of exalting philosophy above revelation. Unhappily, we can hardly glance at a page of ecclesiastical history without finding instructive examples. Perhaps the Platonizing tendencies of the Christian fathers for many centuries are the most striking illustration in former times. It is hardly strange that those who came out of the schools of philosophy into the school of Christ should be gratified to find, and be ready to suppose they could find, a correspondence between the doctrines of their old and new masters. And how natural, in such a case, to accommodate the principles of the new leader to those of the old one; or rather to exalt the teachings of the first above those of the last. Thus did the fathers; and though Platonism was again and again driven out of the church, again and again was it brought back — demanding from time to time a new exorcism.

But though this incubus rested on the church for so many centuries, and often well nigh stopped its breath, modern divines seem to have gained little wisdom by the severe lesson. Plato and Aristotle, indeed, no longer vex the church by name. But their spirit, like the exorcised demon of old, walking through dry places, and seeking rest in vain, has commissioned seven other spirits to return into the sacred enclosure, not merely to modify Christianity, but to expel it. Hence, in modern theological literature, we have profound works on the gospel, whose object is to prove the gospel a fable; treatises on dogmatics, without any doctrines; and lives of Christ, from which Christ is excluded. Instead of one or two leaders, as of old, we now have scores. Having the shoulders of those old giants, Plato and Aristotle, to stand upon and start from, it is only necessary to be provided with a huge pair of transcendental wings to seem very large to a wondering world, as they soar away into the mysterious ether, into which those old giants found it difficult to rise, because the clogs of common sense hung so heavily upon them.

Justice requires me to add, in this connection, that the philosophy which has thus been exalted above revelation so often and so disastrously is not that of induction, but of abstraction; not that of Bacon, and Newton, and Whewell, but that of Hobbes, and Hume, and Diderot. I know that there always has been, and still is, a strong jealousy of physical science, as if it were hostile to religion; but where is the evidence of such hostility? What philosopher of the Baconian school has ever erected within the church a tower that overlooked and overawed Christianity itself, and made it a resort for those too proud to submit to revealed truth? But how often has the deductive philosophy done this! Divines seem prone to forget the distinction drawn with such a vigorous hand by Isaac Taylor. "The entire mass of intellectual and theological philosophy," says he, "divides itself into two classes—the one irreconcilably opposed to the other. The first is, in its spirit and in all its doctrines, consentaneous with human feelings and interests. The second is, both as a whole and in its several parts, paradoxical. The first is the philosophy of modesty, of inquiry, of induction, and of belief. The second is the philosophy of abstraction, as opposed to induction; and of impudence, as opposed to a respectful attention to nature and to evidence. The first takes natural and mathematical science by the hand; observes the same methods, labors to promote the same ends, and the systems are never at variance. The second stands, ruffian-like, upon the road of knowledge, and denies progress to the human mind. The first shows an interminable and practicable, though difficult, ascent. The second leads to the brink of an abyss, into which reason and hope must together plunge. The first is grave, laborious, and productive. The second ends in a jest, of which man and the world and its Maker are the subject."

A second instructive fact taught us by history and observation, is the strong tendency to substitute a dogmatic and denunciatory spirit for knowledge and argument. Men of superior intellect and extensive erudition are very apt to do this in respect to subjects to which they have never given special attention. Some new science or discovery has been brought forward in such an aspect as seems to the theologian to conflict with religion. He has never studied the science, it may be, and cannot therefore hold an argument on the subject. But he feels deeply the wound inflicted on revelation, and he cannot sit still and see that cause suffer which he loves so well. He denounces the new discovery, therefore, and gives no doubtful intimation that its advocates are sceptics, trusting to his reputation as a theologian to enforce his opinion upon the public. Some, whose organ of veneration is large, swallow the *ex-cathedra* judgment with no wry faces. Others, more discerning, see through the ruse, and sigh over human weakness. Scientific men look upon the whole with silent contempt, nor deign to attempt an answer to dogmatism and personal abuse.

Sometimes, however, a scene equally absurd is witnessed on the other side. A scientific man, desirous of extending his discoveries into the domain of religion, ventures upon interpretations of Scripture, or statements of doctrine, that show him quite ignorant of both. The practised theologian points out the fallacy of his reasoning so clearly as to wound his pride. But, instead of generously confessing his error, he resorts to charges of bigotry, narrow-mindedness, and ignorance of science, and dogmatically maintains that science is to be followed, whatever becomes of revelation. He shows towards it and its defenders the same bitter, bigoted spirit which he censures in his opponents. Their arguments he cannot answer, because he has never studied hermeneutics or theology. And so he wraps himself up in the cloak of self-conceited wisdom, and substitutes contempt for logic. Men talk much of the *odium theologicum*, as if it were the quintessence of gall. But really, the *odium scientificum* is often a much more concentrated mixture. The most illiberal of all bigots are those who fancy themselves the very pinks of liberality; and pride never assumes such lofty airs as when it curls the lip of the self-satisfied philosopher who is destitute of Christian humility.

The disastrous influence of mutual jealousy and hard speeches between theologians and philosophers is a third lesson most impressively taught by history and observation. Although many distinguished divines have been eminent philosophers, and science is largely indebted to the clerical profession, yet, in general, the two classes have kept very much apart from each other. This is particularly the case in respect to the cultivators of physical science. In general they have an impression that theologians feel no sympathy with their pursuits, and are not only ignorant of science, but prejudiced against it, as unfriendly to religion. And the fact that so few in the ministerial office do regard attention to natural science, by the ministry, as entirely appropriate, fosters this false notion. But it awakens deep prejudices in these scientific minds against clergymen, because they cannot see why the ministers of God should not take interest enough in his material works to study them. Prejudice prevents that intimate acquaintanceship which would be its cure. It engenders distrust, and produces severe judgments, and keeps those apart who should be cordial friends, because they are both engaged in the same great business of developing the works and ways of the Almighty.

This jealousy and want of acquaintance with each other produces a reaction on the part of theologians, who, also, become censorious and distrustful of men of science. They learn that some such are sceptics, and they presume that nearly all are. Hence, when some new scientific discovery is announced, which seems unfavorable in its bearings upon revelation, theologians are at once suspicious that the author of it is intentionally aiming a blow at Christianity — although the greater probability is that its bearings upon religion never entered his mind. But too often, in such cases, the zealous vindicator of the truth throws out such an insinuation in the public ear, and if the scientific man is not a meek Christian, the ungenerous suggestion may convert into an enemy of the faith one who before was only negligent of it, or indifferent towards it.

But this is not the worst of it. Such a course produces a conviction on the public mind, that men of science teach one thing, and theologians another. Nor can there be a doubt that there is a strong disposition among intelligent men, who are not pious, to take sides with science, even when it seems hostile to revelation; and thus may the severe and unfounded judgment of the theologian, in respect to science, confirm and multiply men of sceptical views.

This point may be illustrated by the history of geology. Ever since Cowper, in his oft-quoted lines, charged geologists with digging and boring the strata in order to disprove the history of Moses, almost all subsequent writers have repeated the accusation; and I doubt not that the almost universal belief now is, that the works of geologists abound with open or covert attacks upon revelation. But the impression is entirely erroneous. In perhaps four out of five of those works, you will find able attempts to reconcile the facts of geology with Scripture; but I have never met with a single attempt, in any language, by any respectable geologist, to adduce the facts of the science to the discredit of revelation. Many of them are, doubtless, sceptical; but they have not done this thing, as they are charged. If it has been done at all, it is by men of no reputation as geologists. Yet probably it will require another quarter of a century to rid the public mind of this false impression.*

* How easy would it be to substantiate these statements by quotations from the most eminent geological writers of the last fifty years; such as Jameson,

Now all these false notions would be avoided, if men of science and theologians would cultivate a closer acquaintance. If men of science were often to come into contact with divines, instead of finding them narrow-minded, bigoted, and unfriendly, as they now suppose, they would, in general, be gratified by their enlarged and liberal views, their ability and candor in looking at scientific truth, and their ardent love of all kinds of knowledge, and cordial efforts to promote it; and many they would find to be successful and eminent cultivators of science. In like manner would scientific men appear in a quite different light to theologians. Instead of subtle and designing enemies of Christianity, they would find many to be its firm friends; and nearly all entertaining for revelation the

Silliman, Buckland, Coneybeare, Mantell, Sedgwick, Lyell, MacCulloch, Miller, &c. But I will refer only to a recent work by two eminent French geologists, C. D'Orbigny, and A. Gente, published in Paris in 1851, entitled "Geologie appliquie aux Arts et à l'Agriculture." Coming from a city generally regarded as the centre of European scepticism, and whose learned men have been considered as unfriendly to the Bible, it is gratifying to find that these authors, after a laborious attempt to bring revelation and geology into harmony, pass the following noble eulogium upon the sacred volume: —

"In view of the chronological agreement between Genesis and the most authentic geological facts, we cannot but accord to this mysterious book something profound and supernatural. If the mind is not convinced, it at least bows reverently before such writings, brought out in an age when we cannot suppose the first elements of the natural sciences were known, and which embraces a development of the principal events of which our globe has been the theatre. We find in Genesis something so simple, so touching, and so superior in respect to morality and philosophy, that the sceptic, astonished moreover at the genius that could foretell facts which scientific researches should demonstrate so many ages afterwards, is forced to acknowledge that there is in this book the evidence of an inspiration secret and supernatural; an inspiration which he cannot comprehend, which he cannot explain, but which strongly affects him, presses upon him, and controls him." — p. 107.

highest respect. Their chief fault is, that in their ardent and exclusive devotion to science, they are apt to neglect that higher attention to religion which its claims demand—a charge, however, which I fear lies equally against most other classes of society. They would find, in fact, almost without exception, that these men were ready publicly to express their regard for religion; and while they would contend for the fullest liberty of investigation into every department of nature, they would resent the charge of intentionally aiming to injure the credit and authority of revelation.

If I mistake not, a reference to the British Association for the Advancement of Science will not only confirm these suggestions, but show that British divines are ahead of Americans on this subject. That association embraces all the most eminent scientific men in the kingdom, as well as many from the continent; and they meet yearly to spend a week together in scientific discussions. Here we might expect, if any where among the cultivators of physical science, an exhibition of religious scepticism. But the fact is, a decidedly religious tone has always been exhibited in that meeting. Whenever a fitting opportunity presented, the addresses of the presiding officer, and of the members, have exhibited a spirit not only religious in the general sense of the term, but in its Christian sense. Said Sir R. H. Ingliss, the president, in 1847, "I will only add my firm belief, that every advance in our knowledge of the natural world will, if rightly directed by the spirit of true humility, and with a prayer for God's blessing, advance us in a knowledge of himself, and will prepare us to receive his revelation of his will with profound reverence." In echoing similar sentiments from Dr. Abercrombie, at the meeting in Edinburgh, in 1834, Professor Sedgwick remarked, that "the pursuits of science, instead of leading to infidelity, have a contrary tendency; they tend rather to strengthen religious principle, and to confirm moral conduct."

One of the most gratifying features of the meeting of this body in Edinburgh, in 1850, which I had the pleasure of attending, was the strong religious influence which was manifested. This resulted, in part, perhaps, from the fact that the meeting was presided over by that truly Christian philosopher, Sir David Brewster. But his noble address was warmly seconded by others. Said Dr. Robinson, the eminent astronomer, in complimenting Dr. Mantell's lecture on the gigantic extinct birds of New Zealand, "This lecture speaks to us of God; yea, more, it speaks to us of Jesus Christ," — alluding to the fact that these birds were discovered by missionaries; and that sentiment was warmly cheered by the immense audience, of more than one thousand persons, embracing some twenty of the nobility, a hundred members of the Royal Societies of England and Scotland, sixty professors in the universities and colleges, a hundred physicians, and a hundred clergymen. Ay, a hundred clergymen; and in the fact I discover the main secret of the religious tone that has characterized these meetings. And here it is, as it seems to me, our British brethren are ahead of us in this country. For there is also an American Scientific Association, on essentially the same plan as the British. It has now been in existence twelve years, and I have attended all its annual meetings save two; nor have I ever seen any other feeling manifested than respect for religion. But I am sorry to say, that I have met there only a very few of my clerical brethren. If they desire to witness in this body as decided an influence in favor of religion as is exhibited on the other side of the Atlantic, they have only to attend its meetings and take an active part in its labors.

A fourth lesson taught by history and observation is, that neither philosophy nor biblical interpretation have yet arrived at a perfect and unchangeable state.

Mathematics is the only science that can lay claim to infallibility, and even this admits of progress; so that new religious applications may arise from new researches. The other sciences range widely along the scale of probability and certainty in their conclusions. Many points in them all, and in some nearly every point, admit of further elucidation, such as may considerably modify their religious bearings. Let the history of philosophy, even in the exact sciences, and eminently in the psychological and moral, teach us how vain is the pretence that they can assume no new phase in relation to religion. How cautious, therefore, should the philosopher be, to distinguish between the settled and the changeable principles of science, before he pronounces any of them in collision with inspired truth!

On the other hand, however, let the theologian remember, that, though the principles of the Bible be infallible and unchangeable, not so is its interpretation. Passing by the wild rationalistic theory of accommodation in biblical hermeneutics, it is still true, that on many principles of their science exegetical writers are not agreed. The result is diversity of signification, when they interpret the word of God. Yet to avoid misapprehension, let me avow my conviction, that, so far as the essentials of salvation are concerned, the Bible is so plain a book, that no theories of interpretation, advocated by honest Christian men, can conceal these great truths. In fact, so prominently do they stand out in the Scriptures, that it needs no rules to make them intelligible, save what common sense and common honesty supply; and hence no sophistries of the interpreter can long conceal them from the people. But very different is the case with some of those parts of Scripture *hard to be understood*, and of others, which cannot be understood till researches and discoveries in philology, history, and science have given us the clew. So long as these discoveries continue to be made will the meaning of some passages of Scripture be liable to modification; and at present these branches of learning are far enough from perfection. It is impossible, therefore, that the meaning of some portions of Scripture should not receive some modifications for a long time to come; and he does the most injury to the cause of religion, who rejects every new interpretation, and considers it dangerous to disturb the settled notions of men as to the meaning even of the less important portions of Scripture. He must have a weak faith in the Bible who fears to have every passage in it subjected to the most thorough scrutiny, under the concentrated light which all literature and all science can pour upon it. And he must have a very narrow view of literature and science who fancies that they have done all they can do to elucidate the sacred text. Yet how common the notion among divines, that, while "human science is a changing and a restless thing," theology — not merely its framework, but its entire covering, coloring, and appendages — has long since received its last finish!

The fifth lesson taught us by history and observation is the weakness and folly of predicting or apprehending injury to Christianity from scientific discoveries. Such fears and predictions are not uncommon. On the one hand, the infidel, by a hasty inference, feels confident that the new discoveries will give a deadly blow to what he regards a false system; and he exults in the anticipated discomfiture of the Christian church. Some intelligent Christians, also, become alarmed at the threatening aspect of the new views, and tremble for the result. But how vain are all such fears and predictions! It is the fiftieth time in which Christianity has seemed to the sanguine sceptic and the timorous believer to be in great peril; and yet not even an outpost has been lost in this guerilla warfare. Discoveries in astronomy, geology, chemistry, and physiology have often looked threatening for a while; but how entirely have they melted away before brighter light and more careful study! Moreover, every new assault upon Christianity seems to develop its inherent strength, and to weaken the power of its adversaries; because, once discomfited, they can never rise again. It will be time for the infidel to begin to hope, when he shall see, what he has not yet seen, a single stone struck from one of the bastions of this massive fortress by his artillery. And strange that any believer should be anxious for the future, when the history of the past shows him that every science, which for a time has been forced into the ranks of the enemy, and made to assume a hostile attitude, has, in the end, turned out to be an efficient ally.

History and observation sustain us in going further than this; they show us that, as a general rule, the more threatening have been the developments of any science in its earlier periods in respect to Christianity, the more strong and abundant have been its ultimate support and illustration of religion. The introduction of the Copernican system of astronomy seemed, to the divines of that day, utterly irreconcilable to revelation; and they contended against it as if the life of religion were at stake. Nevertheless, the demonstrations of physics triumphed over councils and decrees; but instead of proving the death of religion, what Christian does not rejoice in the rich illustrations and auxiliary support which revelation has derived from astronomy? especially in furnishing to the commentator the true principle of interpreting texts of Scripture that relate to natural phenomena. So, too, chemistry was employed for a time by the exulting sceptic, and to the alarm of the timid believer, in disproving the future conflagration of the earth. Yet not only has this envenomed arrow fallen harmless to the ground, but the science has furnished materials enough for at least one volume as a prize essay, entitled "Chemistry as exemplifying the Wisdom and Beneficence of God;" and other similar volumes might easily follow. During the early part of the present century, no science excited so much of this false alarm as geology. But already, if I do not mistake public opinion, the tables are well nigh turned, and, save here and there a disconsolate few, who have so long been chanting the death song of Christianity that they can never change their notes, the ministers of Christ now find among the religious applications of this science rich illustrations of divine truths; and from the disinterred relics of the deep-bedded strata there come forth a voice in defence of the peculiar doctrines of the reformation, and a new argument for the divine existence. So that, in fact, this new field of religious literature is already becoming attractive and prolific in publications. To geology, therefore, may be applied the riddle of Samson: *Out of the eater comes forth meat, and out of the strong comes forth sweetness.*

Now, in view of such results, we may confidently predict that some recent and yet imperfect sciences, lying on the outskirts of physiology and psychology, although at present greatly perverted by sciolism, and made to bear unfavorably both upon morals and religion, will in the end afford a support to both, proportionably strong. What they need now is careful investigation by clear-headed men of the Baconian school, who are familiar both with physical and intellectual science. But so long have these subjects been in the hands of charlatans, or of men with limited and partial views, that able and respectable philosophers, especially among the clergy, shrink from their investigation, lest the title of phrenologist, or mesmerist, or spiritualist should destroy their reputation and usefulness. It ought not so to be; and I am satisfied that not until this thorough investigation takes place will these branches of knowledge be placed upon the same sure footing on which other departments of experimental science rest. At present they seem to me like some large temple, or palace, mostly buried by rubbish, with only here and there some tower, or minaret, or column projecting above the surface. Around these detached parts groups are gathered, endeavoring to show that each tower or column is a complete temple. But not till the vast piles of rubbish are removed will the real temple exhibit its true proportions and character. When this is done, I fancy that the structure will be found a noble one, and worthy of the infinite Architect.

I have time to derive only one other lesson from history and observation on this subject. They show us how unwise it is to denounce any new discovery, or theory in science, when they are first broached, as hostile to religion; and especially to take the ground that if the new views are true, the Bible must be false. There is a strong temptation to do this. Men of ardent temperament, who love the Bible, when any thing is advanced which can be construed into hostility to its statements, feel as we all do when any thing is suggested derogatory to the character of a near friend. We rush to the defence without waiting for the dictates of prudence; and thus we may injure instead of assisting our friend. Much more liable are we to injure the Bible. There is no need of such haste. Christianity stands on too firm and broad a base to be overturned by one or a hundred such blows as have hitherto been aimed against it. The true policy is to wait for a time, to see whether we fully understand the new views, and whether they conflict with the letter or the spirit of revelation. Suppose the theologian should take ground which he is compelled afterwards to abandon, and to fall in with the new discovery. With how bad a grace will he come over to the new ground after severely denouncing as infidels those who adopted it! How likely to lose the public respect, and to make sceptics of those who were before only indifferent! How mortifying must it have been to the theologians who, one hundred and fifty years ago, denounced astronomy, to see its discoveries at length introduced into the almanac, and testifying of their bigotry to all classes! Who can doubt that many a man, in despising them, was led to despise the sacred cause which they were appointed to defend? Yet the theologians honestly believed that to admit the earth's annual and diurnal revolution would overthrow the Bible. But how much better to have waited a little before avowing their convictions!

How little heed, however, do men give to the mistakes of their predecessors! The same eagerness and hot haste have been manifested in our own day to rush into the conflict with scientific men, as they have brought out new discoveries apparently unfriendly in their bearing upon revelation. Divines, eager for the onset, have not waited till they could study the subject and understand it, but have rushed upon the foe, confident that by abstractions and denunciation, if by no other weapons, they could crush him. Often have they found themselves in conflict with a windmill, and all they have accomplished has been to make themselves ridiculous, as with fallen crest and trailing plumes they have left the field. A little delay would have taught them that sometimes, at least, the better part of valor is discretion.

Allow me to refer to a very recent example, where the caution which I recommend would have been wisely adopted. Some of our zoölogists have advanced views respecting the specific unity and unity of origin of the human race, that are in conflict with the common understanding of revelation; and at once able divines took the ground that such views are irreconcilably opposed to the whole scheme of the Bible. They may be so; but why declare it before the subject has been more thoroughly discussed, and we are sure that we understand it? It may turn out — and such is my own conviction — that the zoölogists have too hastily decided this question, because they judged of it chiefly from facts in the limited field of their own science. Suppose it should appear that eminent naturalists are divided in opinion on the subject. Suppose that, when they assert that there are several species of men, they are unable to tell us what constitutes a species, and cannot draw a line of distinction between species and varieties. Suppose that we should find zoölogists entirely disagreed on the subject of hybridity. Suppose it should appear that the laws of distribution in the species and varieties of the lower animals, which is the grand argument for proving a diversity of origin in the case of man, should be found greatly modified in respect to him, by his cosmopolite character and ability, through superior mental endowments, to adapt himself to different circumstances. Suppose we should find examples of varieties of men, who have passed from the highest to the lowest races, save in color, through the influence of deteriorating causes long acting. Suppose it should appear that ethnology and psychology are entitled to as much weight in their testimony on this subject as zoölogy, and that they should pronounce in favor of a unity of origin. Suppose it should be found that many other elements of this most difficult subject are yet not well enough understood to reason from, and demand long and patient investigation. Or make the most unfavorable supposition, viz., that the preponderance of evidence favors the idea of a diversity of origin. Is it quite certain that we must give up the Bible, or its more important doctrines? Would the discrepancy appear so great as it did when the Copernican system was first announced? Shame on us, that we feel so fearful in respect to God's Word, and those eternal truths that form the groundwork of the scheme of salvation! Right is it that we should address ourselves manfully to every argument that bears upon revelation; but how unwise, when it is wholly unnecessary, to take ground which we may be compelled with a bad grace to relinquish!

In conclusion, let me recapitulate the principles, which, as I have endeavored to show, should be the common creed, and regulate the intercourse and feelings of the theologian and philosopher.

They should start with the principle that theology is entitled to higher respect, as a standard of appeal, than any branch of knowledge not strictly demonstrative.

It should also be admitted that, as a means of moral reformation and a regulator of human affairs, philosophy has little comparative power.

They can agree, also, in the position, that entire harmony will be the final result of all researches in philosophy and religion.

To the scientific man should be granted the freest and the fullest liberty of investigation.

The language of science and of Scripture, as well as of popular religious literature, requires different, or at least modified, principles of interpretation.

Revelation has not anticipated scientific discovery.

It is required that those who pronounce judgment on points of connection between science and revelation, should be well acquainted with both subjects.

The facts and principles of science, to an unprejudiced, unsophisticated mind, are favorable to piety.

They form a vast storehouse for the use of natural theology.

They cast light upon and illustrate revelation.

The harmony of science and revelation is mutually beneficial.

The cultivation of science, without the restraints of religion, often proves very disastrous.

The general diffusion of science through a community is impossible without religion.

The precise language of science may be useful in stating the principles of theology.

History shows impressively the danger of exalting philosophy above revelation.

And the evils of substituting a denunciatory spirit for knowledge and argument.

It shows us also the evils of mutual jealousy and hard speeches between theologians and philosophers.

And the folly and weakness of predicting injury to revelation from scientific discoveries.

The more threatening to religion the developments of any science at first, the more abundant will be its defence and illustration of religion ultimately.

Finally, it is unwise hastily to denounce any new discovery as unfriendly to religion, and much safer to wait till its nature and bearing are well understood.

Now, in conclusion, is not a code of this description needed? I feel the imperfection of this first effort to draw it out; but I offer it as the beginning of a necessary work. Had the common ground on which divines and philosophers may stand, been cleared up and marked out centuries ago, how many violations of sacred charity and good manners, how many unreasonable jealousies and prejudices, how many angry controversies might have been prevented; and how much nearer to entire harmony might science and religion ere this have been brought! And how many more examples would the page of history have presented of genuine, humble-hearted, Christian philosophers, and of high-minded, liberal-hearted, philosophic divines!

It is such men that are wanted in the ranks of science and the ranks of theology; and the principles which I have pointed out at this time are well adapted to form them. Could I excite a desire in the hearts of our students in theology to take this high position, I should not have written in vain. For what is a Christian philosopher? He is a man who loves Nature, and with untiring industry endeavors to penetrate her mysteries. With a mind too large for narrow views, too generous and frank for distorting prejudice, and too pure to be the slave of appetite and passion, he calmly surveys the phenomena of nature, to learn from thence the great plan of the universe as it lay originally in the divine mind. Nor does he stop when he has found out the mechanical, chemical, and organic laws of nature, but rises to those higher principles by which the moral relations of man to his Maker are disclosed. Hence he receives with gratitude and joy those richer disclosures of truth which revelation brings. To its authority he bows reverently and rejoicingly, and counts it the best use he can make of science to render it tributary to revelation, and to the cultivation of his own piety. He exhibits a generous enthusiasm in the cultivation of science; but he has a stronger desire to have it associated with religion; and hence he cherishes a high respect for those whose business it is to teach it. Indeed, the noblest example of a true Christian philosopher is seen in the able and faithful minister of the gospel, who employs a thorough knowledge of science, not merely to enlighten the ignorant, but to illustrate and enforce the higher principles of religion.

On the other hand, if I were to give a definition of the highest style of a philosophic divine, it would be synonymous with that of the Christian philosopher. I should represent him as one whose grand object is to glorify God in the salvation of men, by means of the gospel of Christ, but who made the whole circle of knowledge, literary and scientific, subservient to his great object.

Thus may the philosopher and the theologian be combined in the same individual. And why should they not? To whom is it more fitting to be an interpreter of nature, than to him who interprets God's work of revelation? Were such an identity more often realized, there would no longer be need to draw out a code of principles for regulating the conduct and feelings of those no longer twain. It would be like laying down a set of rules for regulating the conduct of the different members of the same individual towards one another.

If, then, the theologian and philosopher may be thus identified, it must be because the principles of theology are in harmony with those of philosophy. Theology does, indeed, develop principles which the sounding line of philosophy cannot reach. But so far as the two systems can be compared, they coincide. And we may be sure that whatever goes by the name of science, which contradicts a fair and enlightened exhibition of revealed truth, is only false philosophy. To develop this harmony should be an object of the Christian ministry, second only in importance to its first aim — that of the personal salvation of men. Indeed, so enlightened at this day is the popular mind in matters of science, that a large class of intelligent men will not listen to the claims of Christianity till they are satisfied it does not conflict with science. It is gratifying to find our young brethren, as they issue yearly from our theological institutions, so well qualified, by their enlarged and accurate knowledge both of science and theology, to engage successfully in this noble work. We bid them God speed in it; and so does the voice of history. For it tells them that the issue of every assault upon religion, with weapons drawn from science, has been to bring revelation and philosophy into closer agreement; and hence may we confidently anticipate ultimate and entire harmony. It is gratifying, also, to remember, amid all the conflicts of opinion on earth, that all truth originally sprang from the same pure source — the infinite mind. But as it enters this world, its rays are separated, colored, and distorted, by the media through which they pass; by human ignorance, prejudice, pride, and passion. It is the noble work committed to divines and philosophers, so to prepare and adjust the rectifying glasses of reason and revelation, that they shall collect and rearrange these scattered rays into a pure and uncolored beam, that shall spread the light of heaven over the darkness of earth. O, as I look down the vista of years, the sweet vision rises before me. The storm of conflicting opinions has passed by, and I hear only the distant, dying thunder, while the spent lightning plays harmlessly around the horizon. The sun of truth looks forth in glory behind the retiring cloud, on whose face it has painted a bow of harmonious colors — a sign of peace to the world, as its evening comes on, and a pledge of the cloudless and immortal day that is to succeed.

SPECIAL DIVINE INTERPOSITIONS IN NATURE.*

No subject of theology has in it more true moral sublimity than the government of God over this world. Yet it is eminently a practical subject. Our views of it afford a test of our piety and a type of its character. Nay, there is one feature of this government that has been regarded as the chief distinction between revealed and natural religion. We refer to Special Divine Interpositions. These have been supposed to be peculiar to revelation; while nature moves on by uniform, unchanging and unchangeable laws; nor does the whole history of those laws, as given by natural science, show a single example of interference or modification on the part of the Deity.

We venture to call in question the correctness of these views. If we have read nature aright, it teaches a different lesson. That lesson may be worth learning. We choose for our subject, therefore, SPECIAL DIVINE INTERPOSITIONS IN NATURE, *as made known by science.*

Let us, in the first place, endeavor to affix a definite meaning to the phrase *Special Divine Interpositions.*

But here, perhaps, it may be necessary to interpose a re-

* This address, essentially as here given, was delivered at the anniversaries of the Newton and Bangor Theological Seminaries.

mark, to prevent misunderstanding. We assume, as the basis of much of our reasoning, those views, now almost universal among geologists, and very common among theologians, which teach that this world existed through a vast and indefinite period before man was placed upon it. Such an opinion we think perfectly reconcilable with a fair interpretation of Scripture, though this is not the place to go into the proof. But let no one imagine, when we take such views for granted, that we mean to cast the slightest doubt upon the inspiration and literal truth of revelation. Let us be believed rather, when we express the conviction that, if admitted, they afford a strong corroboration and illustration of some most important doctrines of revelation.

We proceed now to affix a definite meaning to the phrase *Special Divine Interpositions.*

It requires but a few years' experience in this world to satisfy any observing mind, that natural operations are carried on in a settled order; that the same causes, in the same circumstances, are invariably followed by the same effects. We call this uniformity of operation the course of nature; and the invariable connection between antecedent and consequent we call the laws of nature. If we should see a new force coming in to disturb this settled order, we should call it a miracle. It might do this by a direct counteraction of nature's laws; and this is the common idea of a miracle. But if an unwonted force were added to those laws, the result would be a miracle; and so would a diminution or suspension of their action; for in either case, the effect would be out of the ordinary course of nature, and this we take to be the essential idea in a miracle. Perhaps the best and briefest definition of a miracle is, an event that cannot be explained by the laws of nature. It may, and usually does, contravene those laws;

but it may show only that their force has been increased or diminished.

This, then, is one example of special divine interposition. Is there any other? Most writers, theologians as well as others, would probably answer in the negative. For they admit only two classes of events in the universe — the miraculous and the ordinary; the supernatural and the natural. And yet most of them maintain that God exercises over the world a special providence. It is, indeed, true, that very wide differences exist as to the meaning of this phrase. One theologian tells us that the providence of God "over the human family is termed special," and that "over those persons who are distinguished for virtue and piety is called most special." * Another calls that providence special "which relates to the church." † Another regards providence "special when it relates to moral beings, to men and human affairs." ‡

But whatever may be the views of this phrase among technical theologians, the leading idea attached to it among Christians generally is, that God provides and arranges the circumstances in which men are placed, so as to meet the exigencies of individuals, just as he would have them met, and so as will be best for them. In other words, he provides means exactly adapted to meet the specific wants of individuals.

Now, it is an interesting inquiry, whether this can be accomplished by the ordinary and unmodified operation of the laws of nature. We confess ourselves unable to conceive of but two modes in which it can be done.

It is not difficult to imagine how God, at the beginning, when

* Storr and Flatt's Biblical Theology, p. 240.

† Buck's Theological Dictionary.

‡ Knapp's Theology, Vol. I. p. 501.

he established the laws of nature, did so arrange their operation as to bring about such results as the exigencies of every individual would demand, and at the exact moment desired. Human intellect is, indeed, confounded, when it attempts to conceive of a foresight so vast as to embrace in a glance the history of every individual of the race, and then so to arrange the countless agencies of nature, that every item in the history of the numberless millions of our race should be as carefully and exactly provided for as if only one individual were concerned. But we are certain that all this is perfectly easy to infinite intelligence. To suppose the contrary, is to destroy the idea of omniscience; and therefore we are bound to believe what we cannot comprehend.

It will help us to conceive how God might thus arrange and adapt the laws of the universe to meet particular exigencies, if we consider how it is that most events are brought about in our experience. We are apt to regard them as dependent upon a single second cause, or, at most, upon a few causes, just because one or two are the immediate antecedents. But how few events are there that have not been essentially modified, at least as to the time and manner of their occurrence and in intensity, by what may be called lateral influences! We see a given cause operating, and we are apt to feel that we know what will be its ultimate effect. But we forget that every event in the universe has a connection with all other events; that, in fact, the whole series of causes in the universe constitutes a plexus, or network, in which if you remove one of the fibres, you remove the whole. Every occurrence is, indeed, dependent mainly upon a leading cause; but the result may, after all, be prevented, or greatly modified, by any other cause. So that, as Bishop Butler remarks, "any one thing whatever may, for aught we know to the contrary, be a necessary condition to any other." *

Conceive of a vast hollow sphere, in which balls of various sizes are moving in every direction, and with all degrees of velocity. Fixing your eye upon a single ball, you see it moving towards a given point, and, if it meet with no obstruction, you are sure that point will be reached. It may pass through its whole course untouched. But when your eyes are opened to discern the countless multitude of other balls flying through the same sphere, you feel almost sure that it will be deflected from its course, and its motion accelerated or retarded, by a multitude of collisions; nor can you predict, by any mathematics which the human mind can master, what will be the exact course of that single ball. But how easy for God to do it! and how easy for him so to place the other balls, and to give them such momentum, as will carry the single one to a given point at a given time!

Now, this supposition gives us a not unapt representation of the manner in which the events of the world of matter and of mind are brought about. They are almost never the result of a single secondary cause, acting directly and simply, but of a great multitude of causes, modifying one another, and conspiring to bring out the final development. All these agencies were originally ordained and arranged by the Deity, in the manner that seemed best to infinite wisdom, which had infinite power at command. Can it be that they were put into operation without any plan, or with only a general object in view? Who does not see that God might, at the beginning, have given to these countless forces such degrees of strength, and such adjustment and direction, that they would

* Analogy, Part I. Chap. VII.

bring about just such results in the history of every individual as would be desirable? Thus would every case of special providence be met as certainly as if he should interfere miraculously at the moment in each man's life when special interposition would be desirable.

But with such a complex system of second causes in operation, it is easy to see how the same object could be accomplished by such a modification of some of those causes by the Deity, at any given moment, as would produce the desired result. And this might be done out of human view, so that man would see only the ordinary operation of nature's laws, and, therefore, there would be no miracle; for any event that can be explained by the regular operation of nature's laws, as already remarked, is not a miracle.

To most men these two modes of providing for special providences — the one by a disposition of the laws of nature in the divine mind from eternity, the other by some change effected at the moment by divine interference in the complex causes of events — we say, these two modes will seem to most persons very unlike. Indeed, they cannot see how there should be any thing special in an event that was provided for in the counsels of eternity, and which transpires as the result of arrangements then made. In order to make it special, they feel as if it were necessary that the Deity should interpose, in some way or other, at the time of its occurrence, just as the mechanic finds it necessary to modify his machine, if he wishes to accomplish some specific object not provided for by its regular operation.

Now, we feel confident that such impressions result from our limited views; or rather, from the difficulty which finite creatures experience in understanding the mode in which an Infinite Being thinks and acts. It is hard to divest ourselves of the idea that, in his processes of thought and action, God is altogether such a one as ourselves. But there are certain principles, true of the divine mind and divine action, that cannot enter at all into human powers and human conduct. One is, that no new plan or motive of action can ever enter the divine mind; and, consequently, whatever plans we find developed in God's government must have been perfectly formed in the counsels of eternity. Another principle is, that God never acts except under the guidance of those fixed principles which we call law. Hence miracles are brought about by fixed laws as much as common events; that is, in the same circumstances we may expect the same miracle. The law of miracles does, indeed, differ from all others; and this constitutes a miracle. But to suppose that God ever acts without the guidance of a settled principle is to impute to him a want of wisdom and character which we should be slow to charge upon an eminent man. No less absurd is it to suppose the Deity ever to act by the impulse of after thoughts, as men do; or that he ever does any thing which he had not, eternal ages since, resolved to do in manner and time exactly as it takes place.

If these are correct positions, what possible difference can it make whether we suppose God to have arranged the agencies of nature at the beginning so as to meet every exigency, or to interpose whenever necessary to accomplish specific purposes by some new force or law? Why is not the one as special as the other? If he did in eternity arrange and balance the forces of nature in a particular manner, with the express design of meeting a particular exigency, what matter how many ages intervene between the arrangement and the event? If a miracle was needed at a particular moment of human history, and God originally so arranged the universe that the law of miracles should come in just at the right moment, would the event be any the less special than if we suppose he stood by at the moment, like a finite being, and by his power arrested or counteracted the laws of nature? And the same is true of the means by which a special providence is brought about. An eternal provision made for it shows merely the perfection of the divine plans and operations, but takes nothing from its speciality.

A question may arise in some minds whether such views do not make all events special, though such a statement be a solecism. For if God has arranged the agencies of his natural and moral government so that all events happen just as he intended, on what ground is it proper to say that one of them is more special than another? Do they not all meet some particular exigency? And what more can any of them do?

The fallacy of such an objection lies in the assumption that all events are equally the objects of God's intention. If it were proper to apply such a term to God, we might say that there is such a thing as an *incidental* providence — that is, an event which transpires as the necessary result of a certain arrangement, but which was not the specific object of such arrangement. Perhaps our meaning may be made obvious by reference to an illustration already employed.

We refer to the supposition of a vast hollow sphere, with balls flying through it in all directions, and of course often interfering with one another. Take a particular ball, and admit that God has so adjusted its direction and velocity that, in spite of collisions, it shall reach a given spot at a stated time. Suppose that thus to reach the point is the grand object God has in view in setting the ball in motion. Yet, on its way to that point, it might encounter a multitude of other balls; and each collision would constitute events as distinct and as certainly foreseen and determined upon as the final one. But they might not accomplish any specific object, and be merely incidental to such a system of moving bodies. God might, indeed, in infinite wisdom, make them subservient to other objects besides the ultimate one; but they might be mere incidental occurrences in such a system, which even Omnipotence could not prevent without altering the system.

Now, have we not here two classes of events, equally the result of divine power and wisdom? Yet one of them is special, and accomplishes a definite object; the other is merely incidental, and may or may not be used for a special purpose. Just so can we see how the special providence of God may be distinct from common providence, although both are equally the work of God. He has so arranged the agencies of his government, that certain specific objects shall be accomplished infallibly. But through the operation of those agencies a multitude of other events are brought about incidentally, which, although related to special providences, are not such in themselves.

Another inquiry may arise in reference to some of the preceding reasoning. We have endeavored to show that special providences may be the result of an original adjustment of the agencies of the natural and moral world, or of direct interposition by the Deity out of sight in modifying those agencies. Now, the question is, Which of these methods is actually employed in the divine government? Can we determine which? If by special interposition at the moment, is not the evidence of such interposition precluded by the very supposition we have made? For the statement is, that the interposition must be made out of our sight; while within view, the event seems to be brought about by the ordinary laws of nature, since, if made within sight, it would be miraculous. All we can prove, therefore, is, that God can thus interpose and modify events within sight, by altering their antecedents out of sight; and this is all that seems necessary for the purposes of religion. Hence it is that the Scriptures never raise any such questions as this, but simply and boldly assert the agency of God in the leading events in the history of nations, communities, and individuals.

From the preceding course of reasoning we think we may consider the following positions as established: —

First, that there are two modes in which divine interposition may take place — the one by miracles, and the other by special providences.

By a miraculous providence we mean such a superintendence over the world as interferes, when desirable, with the regular operations of nature within the sphere of human vision, and brings about events either in opposition to natural laws, or by giving them a greater or less power than in their normal state.

By a special providence we mean an event brought about apparently by natural laws, yet in fact the result of some special agency on the part of the Deity, either by an original arrangement of natural laws, or the subsequent modification of second causes which lie beyond man's sphere of vision.

Secondly, that both these modes of interposition take place in accordance with fixed laws or rules of action; so that there is a law of miracles and of special providence, as well as of common phenomena.

Thirdly, that the difference between miracles and special providence lies in this, that the former cannot, and the latter can, be explained by the laws of nature.

Fourthly, that special providences may be the result of an

original arrangement of the laws of the natural and moral world such as to produce special results, or of a direct modification of those laws at any time by divine power in some of the links of causation out of sight.

And, finally, that the events are equally special, whether the result of an original ordination in the divine mind, or of direct modification of natural agencies at the time of their occurrence; nor can we, from the nature of the case, prove in which mode, or whether by both modes, divine wisdom acts.

The main question now returns upon us — whether there is any evidence of special divine interposition in nature, save those which revelation has recorded. All such interpositions must, indeed, occur in natural operations, since it is their suspension or modification that constitutes the interposition; but the inquiry is, Does science, or common history, apart from revelation, contain any such records?

We waive the inquiry, at the present time, as to the evidence which uninspired civil history may contain of special interposition, both because the field is too wide for the limits of this article, and has already been to a considerable extent explored. But the records of physical science have not hitherto, to our knowledge, yielded much of this kind of fruit. Our object, at this time, is to attempt to gather at least one cluster from that field.

It must be confessed that, as a general fact, physical science seems barren of any evidence of special divine interference — presenting us, instead, with operations as uniform and unchanging as mathematical laws can make them. Nevertheless, if we do not greatly mistake, on some portions of the vast field we can discover the imprints of special and miraculous providence.

We shall speak first of special providence, but only in a brief manner.

From the nature of the case it might be presumed that we should need a revelation to show that God had originally arranged, or directly modified, natural agencies so as to meet exigencies in the case of individuals or communities. For, as man sees it, such providence seems to be brought about by unmodified natural operations. It is hardly sufficient to prove special providence to find that great wisdom is shown in contriving and adjusting the laws and agencies of nature so as to meet the necessities of the animate creation. We want the proof that those laws and agencies have been so arranged and modified as to meet particular exigencies, and with those exigencies specially present in the divine mind. For all the purposes of religious faith, it is sufficient to show that God can do this; and therefore we need not expect that nature will offer many examples which clearly show it to have been done. But believers in special providence suppose that they can find proof in their own experience, or that of others, that God has thus interposed either to bless or punish them. When they perceive that various causes have conspired — causes, it may be, both remote and undesirable — to bring about a certain result, they call it a special providence. We know that we need to be slow and cautious in drawing such inferences; but not unfrequently the evidence is so clear and decided, that not to do it would be hurtful scepticism. We will mention one or two analogous cases in nature.

It is no longer a conjecture, but a settled fact, that our globe has been the seat of several distinct economies of animal and vegetable life; that whole races, if not over the whole globe at once, yet over wide districts, have become extinct, and been succeeded by new families; and the new species have been quite different from the old, requiring new conditions as to location, climate, and food. Now, in every instance yet known to us, the new races have been met by conditions exactly adapted to their wants. And this has taken place although the state of the globe has been one of slow but constant flux, both from the escape of its internal heat, the vertical movements of continents, and the action of volcanoes and water. When we consider how delicate a balancing of these and a multitude of other agencies would be requisite to accomplish such an object, how many causes must have been adjusted and made to converge to a given point through a long series of ages, it does seem to us that this case should be regarded as something beyond a mere wise and benevolent ordination of nature's laws, and as a special adaptation foreseen and provided for by the Deity, either by an original adjustment of natural laws, or by their subsequent modification, so as to bring the case fairly within the definition of a special providence. If any think that, by thus regarding a case of this kind, we should include all examples of wise adaptation as special providences, we can only say that there certainly is a difference that should be recognized between cases of this sort, which seem to have been the special object of divine wisdom and intention, and those incidental events which result from the adjustments necessary to bring about the special events.

But the records of science furnish us with another class of examples in nature, still more indicative of a special providence. They are cases in which complicated causes have operated through vast periods of duration anterior to man's existence, or even anterior to that of scarcely any of the more perfect animals, in order to provide for the wants and happiness of those animals, especially of man. Laws, apparently conflicting and irregular in their action, have been so controlled, and directed, and made to conspire, as to provide for the wants of civilized life untold ages before man's existence. In those early times, vast forests, for instance, might have been seen growing along the shores of estuaries; and those, dying, were buried deep in the mud, there to accumulate thick beds of vegetable matter over large areas; and this, by a long series of changes, was at length converted into coal. This could be of no use whatever till man's existence, nor even then, till civilization had taught him how to employ this substance for his comfort, and for a great variety of useful arts. Look, for instance, at the small island of Great Britain. At this day 15,000 steam engines are driven by means of coal, with a power equal to that of 2,000,000 of men; and thus is put into operation machinery equalling the unaided power of 300,000,000 or 400,000,000 of men. The influence thence emanating reaches the remotest portions of the globe, and tends mightily to the civilization and happiness of the race. And is all this an accidental effect of nature's laws? Is it not rather a striking example of special prospective providence? What else but divine power, intent upon a specific purpose, could have so directed the countless agencies employed through so many ages as to bring about such marvellous results?

Or take an example on a still more gigantic scale. It is already ascertained that, by the same process of vegetable growth and decay in the hoary past, thick beds of coal have been accumulated in the rocks of the United States over an area of more than 200,000 square miles, and probably many more remain to be discovered. Yet, upon a moderate calculation, those already known contain more than 1100 cubic miles of coal; one mile of which, at the rate it is now used, would furnish the country with coal for a thousand years; so that a million of years will not exhaust our supply. What an incalculable increase of the use of steam, and a consequent increase of population and general prosperity, does such a treasure of fuel open before this country! If our numbers should become only as many to the square mile as in Great Britain, or 223, there is room enough this side of the Rocky Mountains for 500,000,000; and including the western slope of those mountains, for 700,000,000; equal almost to the present population of the globe. And yet all that has been thus far seen in this country, and all that is in prospect, is only an accidental, or incidental, event in his theology who admits no special providence in nature. We are not of that number, for we not only believe that God, through vast cycles of duration, directed and controlled the agencies of nature, so as to bury in the bosom of this continent the means of future civilization and prosperity, but that a strong obligation hence results for every one living here to throw all his energies into the work of making this land a glory and a blessing to the nations.

Let us go once more on the wings of imagination back to that remote period of our world's history, when most of its present continents were beneath the ocean. As we hover over the waters, we see them agitated by internal forces, and now and then smoke and ashes, and it may be flames, issue from their surface. Submarine volcanoes are pouring forth their contents; and could we look beneath the troubled waves we should probably see beds of various kinds thrown out by the volcano, spreading themselves along the bottom. Among these beds we should probably see gypsum and common salt. But what has this to do with special providence? Let the ages roll on and we shall see. By and by that ocean's bed is slowly lifted above the waves. Those waves, during its emergence, cover it with a soil adapted to vegetation. Man at length fixes his dwelling upon it. He discovers, among the exposed strata, the gypsum and salt which he so greatly needs, and which by ingenuity and industry he can extract. And thereby can he greatly multiply his comforts and his numbers.

In like manner might we go back and trace out the origin of the various ores, the marbles, the granites, the porphyries, and other mineral treasures so important to an advanced state of the arts, and of civilization and happiness. And we should find them originating in agencies equally remote, equally chaotic and irregular, and seemingly as much removed from all connection with man's long subsequent appearance. But it does seem to us that, during the long series of preparatory agencies, we can every where see the finger of God's special providence pointing to the final result.

But we turn now to inquire, in the second place, what evidence we have, in the records of science, of God's miraculous providence? And we take the position that, in the natural history of our globe, we meet with phenomena explicable only by miraculous intervention.

Not to speak of the earliest condition of the world, which hypothesis alone can describe, let us follow back its history only to the time when legitimate theory shows it to have been in a molten state. That its internal parts are still in that condition, and that its now solid crust was once so, seem to us to be proved by fair inference from facts; and such is the opinion of almost all scientific men. Think of it now in that condition — a shoreless ocean of fire. It is not difficult to conceive how, by the radiation of its heat, a solid crust should form, and at length the water condense upon its surface, while volcanic force should form such inequalities as would make beds for the oceans, and elevations for continents. Nay, by the action of the waves and the atmosphere, soils might be accumulated upon the surface. But, in spite of all that merely natural operations could do, what a scene of utter desolation and loneliness would it present! That wonderful power which we call life, and the still more mysterious principle of mind, would be absent. How, then, were the numberless forms of organism, animal and vegetable, possessed of life and instinct, and some of them with powers of intellect, — how were these introduced? If miraculous interposition be not necessary here, we know of no exigency in which it can be; and we may as well dismiss the idea from our philosophy and our theology. Just see what the problem is: nothing less than to take a world of rock, more or less comminuted by water, and to convert it into essentially such a world as the present; to take a world utterly dead and desolate, and spread through its atmosphere, its waters, and its solid surface, ten thousand forms of life and beauty. Has nature any hidden inherent power to do all this? Why, then, can we not lay our finger upon a single manifestation of creative power in nature in these latter times? O, that power is the prerogative of the Deity alone. Who shall have the boldness, and even the impiety, to transfer to blind, unintelligent law, what demands infinite intelligence and infinite power, miraculously exerted?

And yet there have always been men who have done this; not, indeed, in the bold language in which we have stated the principle. Yet some of them have confessed that their object was to sustain atheism. Others have said merely that they meant to show that every thing, even the creation of animals and plants, was accomplished through the inherent self-creating power of law; but they left the origin of the laws to each one's own convictions. Nay, some have attempted to reconcile this creation by law, not merely with theism, but with a belief in revelation. This is the form in which this hypothesis has clothed itself in our own day. In such a dress it has ventured forth from the philosopher's study, where it has so long been isolated, and become incorporated with the fashionable literature of the day. And it has enough of plausibility about it to make it popular with men who have only a general, but not a minute acquaintance with science, and who, afraid to live without some religious system, are yet unwilling to adopt one that brings God near. This is not the place to discuss such views. We will only say, that true philosophy must reject this hypothesis; first, because the facts adduced to sustain it, when scrutinized, are too few; and secondly, because for every fact seemingly in its favor, a thousand testify against it. Accordingly, all the great living and recently deceased masters of physical science reject it. Does it appeal to anatomy and physiology? Cuvier, Owen, and Carpenter cry out against it. Does it evoke the aid of chemistry? Berzelius, Turner and Liebig see its shallowness. Does it call on zoölogy for aid? Agassiz and Ehrenberg can refute its claims. Does it search the archives of geology for support? Sedgwick, Miller, Lyell, and D'Orbigny can show how certainly they will fail there. Or, finally, does it appeal to botany? Hooker and Lindley, Torrey, and Gray, know that it will certainly glean nothing to sustain it on that flowery field. The fact is, it is only here and there that a second-rate naturalist will sympathize at all with such dreamy views.

But there is another, and perhaps a more plausible mode of evading the general argument for the miraculous introduction of organic life upon our globe. When we descend into the rocks a certain distance, say six or eight miles, we reach those that contain no remains of animals or plants, and show the metamorphic action of heat, by which they have been partially or wholly melted. Now, most geologists consider this horizon as the starting place of life on our globe, and that the rocks below it were formed before the existence of animals or plants. But some — and they eminent geologists — maintain that these lower rocks did once contain organic remains, which have been obliterated by the influence of the intense heat, and that, therefore, we cannot tell when life first appeared on the globe. For aught we know, these metamorphisms may have been going on forever.

A few years ago it might have been difficult to prove directly that this hypothesis is false, though the history of the rocks afforded many presumptions against it. But the researches of the last few years among the oldest of the fossiliferous rocks have furnished its full refutation. For it has been ascertained, that both in Great Britain and in this country, stratified rocks, several miles in thickness, exist below those containing fossils, and yet retain so much of a mechanical character, and are so partially metamorphosed, that if ever animals and plants existed in them, they would not have been obliterated. The metamorphic action has not been sufficient to melt down the pebbles and fragments originally deposited, and therefore not great enough to destroy the harder parts of organic beings, had they been present. Here, then, we have an indisputable horizon of life, below which there is no reason to suppose it ever to have existed.

But even if we admit that the apparent is not the real horizon of life in the rocks, there is another scientific fact that proves it did once begin, however far back we may suppose the metamorphic cycles to have extended. In other words, we can prove that there was a time when life did not exist on this globe, and consequently a time when it was first introduced. And this is the argument: —

If any body, such as the earth, having a certain temperature, be surrounded by a medium, or by other bodies, with a lower temperature, it is certain, from the laws of heat, that the warmer body will continue to give off its heat to the colder ones, till at length they will be brought to the same temperature, unless the higher temperature of the central body is maintained by the perpetual generation of heat within itself. Now, we know that at present the earth is placed in exactly this condition; for it can be proved that the temperature of the space surrounding it is at least fifty-eight degrees below zero. Consequently heat must be continually given off into the planetary spaces; and unless there be some internal source of heat, the earth must be growing colder. When did this cooling process commence? Those who believe an indefinite series of organic beings to have existed on the globe, will not surely fix a beginning, because that would be yielding the main point in their hypothesis. Yet it is certain that, if the earth has been cooling for an indefinite period, the time must have been when its surface was too hot for animals and plants to live upon it; nay, when it was in a melted state. There must have been a time, therefore, when the first animals and plants were commanded into existence by the miraculous fiat of Jehovah. For the idea that the earth possesses within itself a power for the indefinite renewal of its heat as it escapes, finds no support in philosophy. We can conceive how heat might be produced while combustible substances were burning, but we know of no possible way by which an indefinite supply could be evolved.

We are unable to conceive how any philosophic mind can escape the force of such reasoning as this, which natural theology brings forward to prove a period in the history of this world when it was destitute of organic races. But this is not the only argument which science can offer to prove miraculous interposition in nature. A second proof, quite independent of the first, is found in the fact that the earth has been the seat of several nearly independent systems of life, since animals and plants were first introduced. A certain group, wisely adapted to one another, and to the state of the air, the waters, and the surface, as well as to the food and the temperature, have flourished for a long period; and, as some of these circumstances have changed, they have either gradually died out, or have been simultaneously destroyed by some catastrophe; so that few if any species have survived. Afterwards new races have been introduced, exactly fitted to the altered condition of things. These also, after flourishing long, have disappeared, and another and another system has succeeded, until we can distinctly trace five economies previous to the existing races. Many writers say that the number of systems has been much greater; and, were we to limit our views to portions of the earth, it is undoubtedly true. But we can show that all the races, animal and vegetable, have been changed at least five times, over the whole globe; and five such changes are as good for the argument as five hundred. For though we can see how, by natural operations, organic beings can be destroyed, yet what but infinite wisdom and power can repeople the lifeless waste? This question we have considered under our first argument, and hope we have shown that nothing but miraculous power could have done it.

But there are some peculiarities that attended the introduction of successive races, which deserve notice. From the nature of the case, the world must have been preparing, by the reduction of its temperature and increased productiveness of its soil, for a greater variety of organic beings, and for those of more delicate and perfect organization. And we find that, at the successive epochs of creation, there was a correspondent increase of the higher races, "a gradual ascent towards a higher type of being,"* in connection with "a gradual improvement in the style and character of the dwelling place of organized beings." † This is called the *doctrine of progression;* and it obviously points to a beginning, not only of organic races, but of the present system of inorganic nature, and requires miraculous divine interposition.

It is well known, however, that at least one distinguished geologist takes opposite views of this subject, and maintains "that the existing causes of change in the animate and inanimate world may be similar, not only in kind, but in degree, to those which have prevailed during many successive modifications of the earth's crust." This is called the doctrine of *uniformity*, or *non-progression.* It is not intended by its able advocate to teach the world's eternity, although it has that aspect; nor does it conflict with the idea of miraculous intervention in the creation of animals and plants; for it admits that "the succession of living beings has been continued, not by the transmutation of species, but by the introduction into the earth, from time to time, of new plants and animals; and that each assemblage of new species must have been admirably fitted for the new states of the globe as they arose, or they would not have increased, and multiplied, and endured for indefinite periods. ‡

Even the doctrine of non-progression, then, is consistent with miraculous interpositions in nature. Much more does

* Sedgwick. † Hugh Miller.
‡ Lyell's Manual of Elementary Geology, p. 501.

the doctrine of progression demand it. And we confess ourselves compelled to subscribe to the latter doctrine. So far as inorganic nature is concerned, we have already assigned a reason for this opinion. Perhaps the evidence from organic nature is not as strong, because we cannot say certainly how many of the more perfect animals will yet be discovered in the older rocks. But so far as we do know, the progression has been very decided. More than 24,000 species of animals have been dug out of the rocks, 700 of which are mammalia or quadrupeds. But 695 of these occur within 2000 or 3000 feet of the surface, while in all the 54,000 feet below, only five species have been found. Birds, the next less perfect class of animals, are scarcely more abundant in these lower rocks. Reptiles are more numerous, and extend to a greater depth, while the fishes, the least perfect of all, are still more abundant, and are found nearly at the bottom of the series. And the same increase of numbers would be found were we to descend still lower on the scale of animals. All this accords with the doctrine of progression, and so do the facts respecting plants. Now, making the largest allowance for future discoveries, it seems hardly possible that it will ever appear, that as large a proportion of the higher orders of animals and plants existed in the earlier periods of our globe as at present.

But we hasten to offer one more proof of God's miraculous interposition furnished by the records of science. It is the creation of man. All observation teaches us that he was one of the last of the animals that was placed upon the earth. In vain do we search through the six miles of solid rocks that lie piled upon one another, commencing with the lowest, for any trace of man. And it is not till we come into the uppermost formation, — we mean the alluvial, — nay, not till we get almost to the top of that, merely in the loose soil that is spread over the surface, that we find his bones. And yet these, formed of the same materials as the bones of other animals, would have been as certainly preserved as theirs in the lower rocks had he existed there. The conclusion is irresistible, and it is acquiesced in by all experienced geologists, that man did not exist as a contemporary of the animals found in the rocks. At least five vast periods of time, with their numerous yet distinct groups of organic beings, passed over this globe before the appearance of man. This is not a dreamy, hypothetical conclusion, but a simple matter of fact, which has been scrutinized with great care, and by some unfriendly to revelation, who would gladly have found it otherwise. But no fossil man or works of man have been discovered below alluvium, (in which we include drift;) nor would any really scientific man risk his reputation by maintaining the existence of the human species earlier than the alluvial period.

What an astonishing exhibition does this scientific fact bring before us! Suppose we could explain by chemical and organic laws how the inferior animals were gradually developed from one another in the successive periods of our world's history. Yet here we have the phenomenon of a being introduced at once, superior somewhat in organic structure to the other animals, but raised immeasurably above them all by his lofty intellectual and moral powers — a being destined to take the supreme control of all inferior natures, and, so far as need be, to subject them all to his will; and, in fact, to convert the elements into servants to do his pleasure. The anatomist can, indeed, describe his organization; the physiologist can point out the functions of his organs; and the zoölogist can assign him his rank at the head of animate creation; but how is the psychologist baffled when he attempts to unravel the wonders of his spiritual powers! and the theologian, when he looks into the depths of his moral and immortal nature! And did it demand no miracle to bring such a being upon the stage, and fit him exactly to his condition? What greater miracle does even revelation disclose? Admit, if you choose, that all other events on the globe — even the creation of all other organic beings — might have been accomplished by ordinary laws; yet, so long as the great fact of man's creation stands out so conspicuously on our world's history, we need nothing more to establish, beyond cavil, the reality of divine interposition in nature. God has impressed his own signet so deeply upon this last act of creation, that scepticism dare not directly attempt to deface it. And this grandest miracle of nature is also the greatest of revelation. It stands up a lofty and immovable rock, amid the ocean of existence, to arrest and beat back the waves of unbelief, and to reflect the glories of divine power and wisdom.

We might add other arguments corroborative of the same principle. But if the three which we have adduced, independent and cumulative as they are, do not satisfy, we despair of producing conviction. We may be laboring under some hallucination on this subject; but we cannot see why the evidence of special divine interpositions in nature is not as clear and decided as in revelation. The only difference seems to be, that in the one case we depend on the testimony of living witnesses; in the other, upon the conclusions of science. But if such interpositions have been made in nature, it is easy to see how important are the bearings of the fact both upon theology and upon piety.

See, for example, how the miracles of nature take away all presumption against the miracles of revelation. We all know that this has been a favorite point of attack both in ancient and especially in modern times. The grand argument has been, that miracles, being contrary to all experience and all analogy, cannot be proved by human testimony. We remember the metaphysical network woven by Hume on this subject, which he fancied too strong for any Christian champion to break through; and we know, too, how many professed Christians at this day assume in their theology that miracles are only ingenious myths. Little did these men imagine what a record on this subject lay concealed within the stony leaves of the earth's crust, or that the hammer of the miner and the geologist would bring facts to light that would sweep away at once all their ingenious quibbles. So long as Christians could meet them only with abstract reasoning they felt strong. But now we lay open the solid rocks, and show them there miracles of creation as wonderful as the miracles of revelation, and of them, the creation of man, perhaps the most remarkable of all, is the same in both records. We show them that interference with nature's usual course has been a rule of God's government from the remotest times; and the conclusion is irresistible, that what God has done during the earlier economies of our world he will be likely to repeat during the human era, should his purposes require it.

Not less effectually does this subject remove all improbability from the doctrine of special providence in the case of individuals and communities. Nay, the facts which we have presented form an *a fortiori* argument for the exercise of such a providence. For if we find proof registered on the rocks, that God has taken care to adapt the state of the world wisely and benevolently to the nature and wants of the lower animals that have peopled its changing surface, and prospectively and specially for the comfort and happiness of man as a race, we may with still stronger confidence presume that he will see to it that the exigencies of individuals of that superior race will be taken care of. Henceforth, then, when we witness the exhumation, from the quarries, of the strange beings that once occupied the earth, let us not regard them as mere objects of an idle curiosity, but as so many arguments to show us that God will take care of our individual interests; and when we wander through the deep-seated coal mine, or any other excavation where human industry is extracting mineral treasures to advance civilization and happiness, let our faith gather thence an argument for implicit trust in that providence which, in the depths of past ages, buried up these deposits for the special use of civilized man. How delightful for the Christian thus to find food to nourish his faith, where most men see only rugged rocks, and think only of accumulating wealth!

So, too, this subject takes away all presumption against the doctrine of special divine influence on the human mind; for if God would work miracles to accomplish his purposes in the natural world, much more ought we to expect that he would exert those influences upon the human mind which are not inconsistent with free agency, and are essential to prepare it for a higher state of existence. This he can do without a miracle; and it is an exigency which the whole history of his providence leads us to expect will be met in this manner.

See, too, what a new and interesting argument may be derived from this subject for the divine existence. The usual argument, that from design, requires us to prove, or assume, a beginning to the matter of the universe; and here the atheist, hiding himself in the fogs of the doctrine of chance, and an eternal series of things, can make a quite formidable show of argument. But admitting miracles in the modifications of matter, we need not carry our thoughts back beyond those modifications, and may leave the question of the origin of matter untouched, without any injury to theism. We thus get rid of a multitude of dreamy abstractions which have so long enveloped the argument for the divine existence with a mist. We force the atheist out of the obscurities of the deductive, into the clear light of the inductive, philosophy. We bring the subject down from the airy region of metaphysics, and place it on the firm ground of common sense.

This subject, also, may be made to subserve another purpose, no less important. It aims a deadly blow at all those subtle systems of religion founded on the supposed unending uniformity of nature's laws, and their inherent power to accomplish all the changes of the organic and inorganic worlds. Some of these systems, as we have remarked in another connection, admit that there might be a Deity to ordain these laws originally; but that is a question of no great importance, since it is the laws themselves, and not divine intervention, that have taken the world in the state of nebulous vapor, condensed it into a sphere, brought in at first a few species of animals and plants of the simplest organization, in the state of monads, and from them gradually developed all the higher forms of life by the force of external circumstances and an internal tendency to improvement, until, at length, as the last act of the drama, man, in the form of the negro race, was evolved from the semi-quadrupedal orang, and, still pressing onward, has assumed the loftier character of the Caucasian.

Now, either the entire history of our globe, which has been dug out of its stony archives, is false, or this hypothesis is untrue. The history is based on facts, gathered from a thousand fields, widely scattered, yet all teaching the same lesson; the hypothesis is speculation merely, springing from a few supposed facts, half buried in fog and twilight. Which shall we adopt? Philosophy cries out, responsive to the voice of nature, It is God, and not mere law; an infinitely wise and powerful God, the God who doeth wonders, whose miraculous interpositions are recorded in the volume of nature, as well as in the volume of revelation.

Finally, this subject identifies the God of nature with the God of revelation. We greatly mistake the general sentiments of mankind, if they do not feel that the Deity recognized by science, is a quite different being from the Jehovah of the Scriptures. The first is regarded, indeed, as infinitely perfect, but as distant and uninterested in human affairs, binding the iron chain of law around all created things. But the God of revelation is an infinite Father, who is ever near his children, watching their every step, with an ear ever open and quick to hear their cry for help, and with a heart of boundless love to sympathize with them in all their trials. It is these different aspects in which the Deity is presented, that makes the religious man jealous of those views of theology which science offers; and it is because he does not wish to feel that God is so near, and so observant of his actions and thoughts, that often the scientific man is disgusted with the God of revelation. But this subject shows us the same God in both dispensations. He who so often interposed miraculously for his ancient chosen people, and providentially, at least, for the followers of Christ in every age, — that same God, as modern science informs us, has shown the same watchful care over the material creation in all ages, and specially interposed, whenever necessary, for the welfare and happiness of all sentient beings. And herein does the pious heart recognize in the God whose glory is seen in the heavens, and who has filled this lower world with beauty, the same infinite Father, whose wisdom and mercy shine so gloriously in the plan of redemption.

If these views be correct, do they not give to the works of creation a double charm to the Christian heart? And do they not suggest the inquiry, whether those who preach the gospel might not make much more use than they do of natural religion? If we mistake not, there is a prevalent jealousy of facts and principles derived from nature; just because those facts have been sometimes perverted to throw discredit upon revelation. But we have long been satisfied that, from the fields of natural science, efficient support may be derived to some of the peculiar, and to the carnal mind the most offensive, doctrines of revelation. We have brought forward, in this article, only a single cluster of the fruit from that field. But other and richer clusters, we doubt not, would reward the search of abler minds. See what such men as Chalmers and Harris have done; and let all, who now preach or who mean to preach the gospel, follow in their steps, and we doubt not that Christians, instead of being fearful that science and revelation are in conflict, would find that they sustain and illustrate each other, and that the heart of piety might be warmed at the shrine of nature, as well as at the cross; for, in an important sense, the cross may be found in nature, and nature in the cross.

But, after all, the tendency of the age is to substitute that which is artificial for that which is natural. Hence it is, that the Christian passes with indifference the works of God, while his soul rouses and his eye brightens when it turns to the works of man. O, what a magnificent temple it is which Jehovah has made our dwelling place! It is a vast whispering gallery, echoing and reëchoing with his name and his praise. How much do they lose who always have its vast dome above them, and its lofty columns around them, and yet hear none of those whispers or echoes, nor feel any of the inspiration of the place, but whose supreme attention is devoted to "the gewgaws and trinkets, the puppet shows and histrionic feats, which fashion, and ambition, and sensuality have surreptitiously introduced there!" How insensible to every noble impulse has his heart become who has neither eye nor ear for the charms of Nature! For she is the kind mother of us all. In her arms were we cradled, on her bosom were we nursed, and her voice falls on every well-attuned ear like the music of heaven. It is indeed the music of heaven; for Nature's harmonies are but a transcript of the divine perfections, and her voice is, therefore, the voice of God.

We fear, however, that such sentiments do not accord with the experience of most Christians. They look upon the system of nature as a field well adapted to regale the fancy, gratify the taste, and delightfully exercise the understanding, but not to warm the heart and feed the spiritual taste of piety. Creation is, indeed, a splendid temple, but it is cold and lifeless. No sacred fire burns upon the altar; no crucified Redeemer is there to fix the attention and absorb the affections; no Spirit of grace speaks gently to the soul. The religion of sentimentalism may flourish by communion with nature; but the piety that saves the soul and blesses the world must seek for its nourishment at the foot of the cross.

True, it is at the cross we must learn how to be saved, and how to save others. But because we cleave with supreme affection to the God of redemption, must we abjure the God of nature? If it feed our devotion to muse on the character of that God who devised and executed the marvellous plan of redemption by a long series of miracles in human history, shall it afford no nourishment to our new-born nature to find that the Author of this vast universe has interposed, in a no less special and wonderful manner, to fit up this world that it might become a proper theatre for the display of redeeming love? Is there not something wrong in our hearts, if we do not recognize the same wonder-working, beneficent God in the natural as in the moral world? Creation and redemption are but parts of one great system, and we may not disjoin what God has united; neither may we depreciate one part of the scheme in order to exalt the other. We will try to unite them in our experience, as well as in our judgment. Then shall we see the same great truths imprinted upon nature which shine forth in redemption. Then shall all our communion with nature serve only to strengthen our love of the cross, while the more powerfully we are constrained by the love of Christ, the more delightfully and profitably shall we wander among the works of God. O, how meagre is his enjoyment of creation's beauties who looks at them with only the eye of the cold, calculating philosopher, or the mere enthusiasm of the poet, but not with a Christian's heart! It is only such a heart that can vivify the scenes of the natural world with the presence of God. Nature has charms, indeed, for the mere man of taste, and of philosophy. But it is not till we bring in the religious element, that the affection becomes such as God would have it, a pure and a sanctifying emotion.

It is no wonder that such a love as this should be a deep fountain of happiness in every condition of life. It does not, like almost all earthly affections, become weaker with advancing life, when the pressure of cares, disappointments, and the infirmities of old age come upon us. The man may become weary of the world, and be deserted by it. Feeble health may infuse wormwood into the common pleasures of life; treachery and ingratitude may convert professed friends into enemies, and pierce his heart with many a pang; and old age, with its failing senses and failing powers, may deaden his sensibilities to almost every thing else; but if in early life a religious love of nature has taken possession of his soul, he will ever find it a sweet solace in the hour of desertion and bereavement; and, even amid the frosts of old age, the sacred flame, less bright only than his immortal hopes, shall spread a sweet light along his dark passage to the grave.

Such a view of nature as this was taken by the writers of the Bible. The labored distinctions which we make between common and miraculous events were unknown to them. In every event they saw and joyfully recognized God's hand; and hence it so often happens that the sentence which begins with praise to the God of nature ends with ascriptions of glory to the Redeemer.

Nor is this all; for these same views of this subject are taken in heaven. For the redeemed from among men, as they stand upon the sea of glass, and sing the song of Moses and the Lamb, exclaim, "*Great and marvellous are thy works, Lord God Almighty.*" Yet these ransomed ones are ever ready to join in what seems the common chorus of heaven: "*Blessing, and honor, and glory, and power be unto Him that sitteth upon the throne, and unto the Lamb forever and ever.*" In heaven, therefore, at least, will the God whom science describes be identified with the God of redemption. Would that it were so on earth! It will be, when educated men, especially ministers of the gospel, shall have fully developed the harmonies between nature and revelation. Here, then, is an object, second only to that of the personal salvation of men, inviting the labors of those who go forth, after long years of preparation, from our theological seminaries, burning with the desire to do what they can for the good of man and the glory of God. The field is open and inviting, and the ripening grain abundant. May those who take the sickle have a large share in so noble a work, and late in life *return, bringing their sheaves with them.*

THE WONDERS OF SCIENCE COMPARED WITH THE WONDERS OF ROMANCE.

Ladies and Gentlemen: The whole number of works, original and reprinted, that were published in the United States during the year ending with June, 1834, was 623. Of these, 126, or about one fifth, were novels and tales. In Great Britain, 1112 works were published in the year 1833; of which 71, or about one fifteenth, were novels and tales. In France, during the same year, 7011 works were issued; of which 355, or about one twentieth, were novels and tales.

I have not been able to obtain a complete correspondent statement for any year subsequent to 1834. The following numbers, however, from the American Publishers' Circular for April, 1856, show a great increase of works of fiction. "In all departments, except that of fiction," says Mr. Norton, "there were published in this country, in the year 1855, about 800 different works; adding for the new and old novels that owed birth or resuscitation to this year, the new issues will reach, in round numbers, to *two thousand.*" This makes the works of fiction three fifths of the whole.

These numbers afford some criterion of the taste of the reading part of the community in the countries specified. And what I wish particularly to be noticed at this time is, the much greater demand in this country for works of fiction than in Great Britain or France. Were I to include poetry in the list, however, it would swell the works of imagination in France to one ninth of the whole, and in Great Britain to one seventh; while the poems published in this country during the same time were not numerous enough to alter the proportion above stated. But it is to novels and tales that I wish to confine my attention. For very few of the injurious effects supposed to result from romances can be charged upon poetry, especially if it be not read in connection with romances.

I think I may safely draw the inference, from the facts stated, that our countrymen show a very strong predilection for a light and fictitious literature. And I might add other evidence, were it needful. It would be shown in the register of every circulating library, as it is in almost every public original exhibition in the college and the academy. Young men, in such a case, will select those subjects in which they feel the most interest; and how much more common is it, on such occasions, to hear discussed the character and merits of writers who address chiefly the fancy, than those who develop the substantial principles of accurate science and philosophy! It is seen, also, in the character of a large part of our periodicals, which their editors scarcely dare send forth to the public, if not set off with one or two original tales. Excepting a few business newspapers in our larger towns, most of our hebdomadals also must be adapted in the same way to the public taste; and the amorous story often stands in singular juxtaposition with the solemn realities of practical religion in the adjoining column. But the taste of all classes must be suited.*

* Yet it would be but an act of justice to readers that the motto for such newspapers should be, in the words of Burns, —

"Perhaps it may turn out a song,
Perhaps turn out a sermon."

And last, though not least, our religious literature must be clothed in the drapery of fiction, or it will be passed by as old-fashioned and uninteresting; while the latest religious romance will be seen occupying a conspicuous place upon the centre table. Nor will the devoted Christian — devoted, at least, to this kind of reading — suffer sleep to close his eyes, till it has been read through, and the enchanting story, if not the religion of the book, is deeply lodged in his memory.

But it is not my object at this time to go into a detailed exposure of the evils of novel reading. Suffice it to say, that when the father learns that his son, who is in a course of public education, has become devoted to this kind of literature, he abandons the hope that he will ever rise higher as a scholar than to become a writer of tales for some newspaper or periodical, or possibly the author of a play, that shall at least once appear upon the boards of Thespis. Or if his son be destined for business, instead of learning, the father expects that remissness and effeminacy will take the place of manly enterprise and success. The mother, too, who finds her daughter, in spite of all her warnings and rebukes, given up to secret midnight communings with the latest romance, almost abandons the hope of ever interesting her in those domestic pursuits that have always been the glory of New England women, or even in the higher and purer branches of literature. Indeed, she will be thankful if her daughter, in the ebullition of some glowing fancy scene, does not evaporate into ether, and pass into that place described by Milton, —

> " ——— All these, upwhirled aloft,
> Flew o'er the back side of the world, far off,
> Into a limbo, large and wide, since called
> The Paradise of Fools : — to few unknown
> Long after." —

But I forbear: for I repeat that I have no intention of making a direct attack upon the passion for romance that has taken so deep a hold upon the community; and I beg pardon if any should be led, from my remarks, to fear a transmigration into the limbo of Milton. I wish to look at the fact, that so general a taste for romance exists, with the eye of a philosopher; and to inquire what that strong, deep-rooted principle of human nature is, that lies at the foundation of this taste. And although I doubt not that some are attached to romances because their baser passions there find fuel to inflame them, yet I prefer to believe, in general, that this taste has a nobler origin, and results from that strong love for whatever is new and wonderful, which is found in every human bosom, — especially in the morning of life. That desire was given us for wise purposes. Whenever it is suffered to waste itself upon fiction, it is perverted; and what was intended for our happiness becomes our bane. God has filled this beautiful world with enough of thrilling realities to feed and gratify this passion to the utmost, through the whole course of our pilgrimage. Passing by all other sources whence it may receive gratification, I request the attention of this audience — especially the youthful part of it — to some of the wonders developed by modern science. My object is to convince my hearers, that here is a far wider and nobler field, and a profusion of more delicious fruit, and sparkling gems, than fiction can offer. My hope is, that I may thus divert the attention of some who have begun to sip of the Circæan cup of romance, to the pure Castalian fountains of science, where the sparkling nectar of truth rises up to meet them.

But in exhibiting the wonders of science, where shall I begin? The field is immense: it is the universe; and it is all filled up with wonders; and the more critically these are examined, the more do they multiply and enlarge. It must be, therefore, only a glance that we can now take. I feel like the man who has undertaken to exhibit in one short hour the mazes and the beauties of an extensive series of gardens and parks, where the labor of centuries has been expended in collecting, arranging, and ornamenting the fruits and the flowers of every clime, and in forming every variety of alley, terrace, and arbor, of cascade, lake, and fountain. The conductor, as he hurries his visitors through one enchanting and mazy spot after another, can only pluck here and there a flower, or point to the clustering fruit, or to some charming landscape. This is all I can hope to do, as we move at railroad speed through the wide fields of science.

I begin with the science of mind, which, although abounding in unprofitable speculation, still presents us with many important and wonderful truths. There is reason to believe, for instance, that no idea which ever existed in the mind can be lost. It may seem to ourselves to be gone, since we have no power to recall it; as is the case with the vast majority of our thoughts. But numerous facts show that it needs only some change in our physical or intellectual condition to restore the long-lost impression. A servant girl, for instance, twenty-four years old, who could neither read nor write, in the paroxysms of a fever, commenced repeating fluently and pompously passages of Latin, Greek, and Hebrew; and it afterwards appeared, that in her early days a learned clergyman, with whom she lived, had been in the daily habit of walking through a passage in his house that opened into the kitchen, and repeating aloud the very passages which she uttered during her fever. How many interesting inferences crowd upon the mind in view of such facts! What an amazing power do they prove to exist in the soul! And what astonishing developments will be made in this world or another, when the vast magazine of thoughts within us shall be unsealed! And who can avoid the inquiry, what kind of thoughts he is daily pouring into this storehouse!

The capacity of the human mind for knowledge is another of its wonderful powers. By every accession of knowledge is that capacity enlarged; nor have the limits of that expansion ever been reached, or imagined. Indeed, the nature of the mind leads us to the conclusion that there are no limits. And it has already been shown that whatever knowledge the mind acquires it can never lose. What a magnificent conception, to attempt to follow the mind along the path of its immortal existence, and to see it forever drinking in the stream of knowledge, whereby it constantly accumulates strength, and has the sphere of its capacity enlarged, yet remaining eternally infinitely inferior to the Deity! Yet who can conceive of the vast amount of knowledge it will ultimately attain, or its more than angelic intellectual might?

No less wonderful is man's capacity for happiness. Here too we find no limits but infinity. The happy emotions of today only qualify the soul for stronger emotions to-morrow, provided all the strings of the delicate instrument are in tune. Nor is the increase in an arithmetical, but in a geometrical ratio. Who shall set limits to the expanding series? or who will doubt but God can fill to overflowing the most enlarged capacity through eternal ages?

Alike unlimited is man's capacity for misery. In this world his sufferings sometimes rise to a fearful height. Nor can we discover in the nature of mind any reason why an increase of knowledge should not add a proportionate intensity to suffering. Who can tell what fountains of misery may be broken up, or when, in the round of eternal ages, the angry billows shall cease to roll over the soul that has broken loose from the great law of rectitude and happiness? O, it is not strange that an inspired writer should declare, that man is not only *wonderfully* but *fearfully* made. His unlimited capacity for misery is surely a most fearful trait in his intellectual constitution.

Not less fearful is the supremacy that is given to Conscience in his moral nature, especially when we recollect with what unbending severity she applies her scorpion lash upon the soul that has fallen under her displeasure. Yet no less promptly does her approving voice cheer the soul that is struggling along the strait and narrow path of duty, and brings down into the heart the spirit of heaven. In short, to the mastery of conscience every one must sooner or later submit. Rightly has it been called God's vicegerent in the soul; and though it be a part of ourselves, we can as easily annihilate the soul as to escape from its dominion. And when we think how terrible are its inflictions sometimes upon the guilty, and recollect our unlimited capacity for misery, we cannot but inquire with solicitude whether its commission does not extend to another world; and though an affirmative answer may shock the ear of guilt, it will make the heart of virtue beat high with delightful anticipations.

Even this slight reference to some of the powers of the human soul show that it is a maze of wonders. What is there in the boldest flights of imagination to compare with it? Here then the ingenuous mind can find enough to feed its strongest love of the new and the wonderful, without the aid of romance.

Another department, no less interesting, is mathematics. And in the entire certainty of its conclusions it possesses an advantage over every other branch of knowledge. I know that it is not uncommon to speak of mathematics as a dry study; but it is dry only for the reason that the grapes were sour to the fox — because he could not reach them. The truth is, that to those who have the resolution and perseverance to master its noble truths, it becomes one of the most fascinating of all pursuits. This is particularly true of the higher and more difficult parts of the subject — those sublime heights where your own fellow-citizen, the prince of American mathematicians,* soared so high, and gathered so many laurels, which he wreathed around the very cycles of the heavens. It is said that he who has the strength of wing to carry him fairly into the ethereal regions of the differential calculus, often becomes more fascinated than men in any other pursuit. So many new and unthought-of truths flash upon his mind, as he follows the golden thread of demonstration, that he seems to breathe an atmosphere almost freed from the grossness of earth. In such pursuits we can easily believe the English mathematician sincere when he exclaimed, *Crede mihi, extingui dulce erit mathematicarum artium studio* — "Believe me, it will be sweet to die in the study of mathematics."

But though mathematics be full of curious and fascinating truths, yet such is the nature of the subject that I shall scarcely be able to clothe even one fair example in a popular dress. Let me attempt one or two founded upon the doctrine of infinitesimals. To one who has not thought on the subject this proposition seems not a little paradoxical, viz., that a man may approach nearer and nearer to a fixed object eternally, and yet not be able to reach it; yet by slackening his pace in a certain ratio, the result would be that he could never reach

* Dr. Nathaniel Bowditch, formerly a resident of Salem, where this lecture was first given.

the object, although he might make an infinitely near approach to it.

Another proposition may be new to some, and worthy of being named. It is this: two lines may approach nearer and nearer forever without meeting, — the asymptote to the hyperbole, for example. This, too, is very easily conceived, though likely to produce scepticism when first announced.

A third proposition asserts that one infinitesimal may be infinitely smaller than another. Here the mathematician starts with something infinitely small, — for that is the meaning of an infinitesimal, — and he asserts that another thing may be infinitely smaller. And this he demonstrates. How stupid must that intellect be which is not roused and interested by such paradoxes!

The science of moving forces, or mechanics, abounds with principles and demonstrations that are novel and striking to the beginner. But for the reasons mentioned in speaking of mathematics, they cannot be now exhibited. Perhaps the following proposition may at least be amusing, although it can hardly be regarded as true, except theoretically. Any force, however small, can put in motion a body however large, and by a sufficient number of repetitions, give it a velocity infinitely great. When, for instance, a man stamps with his foot, he moves the earth; and could he prevent the reaction of gravity, and were to continue to stamp long enough, he would not only put the earth in motion, but give it a velocity greater than it now has in its orbit. But the *που στω*, the place to stand on, which Archimedes demanded, can never be obtained; and therefore this experiment can never be tried.

The mechanical properties of fluids, and especially of the atmosphere, are some of them of a remarkable character. Light and yielding as we regard the air, what but experiment would satisfy us that a musket ball, that has a velocity sufficient to range seventeen miles in a vacuum, actually falls short of half a mile; and that so rapidly does the resistance increase with the velocity, that it would become at length so great that a ball would be stopped as if fired against a stone wall!

Another property of fluids that leads to some singular results is their power of pressing in all directions alike. Hence it becomes true that any quantity of a fluid, however small, will balance any quantity, however large. Hence the hydrostatic bellows; by standing on which and blowing forcibly into a tube, a man may raise himself from the floor — or still more certainly by pouring into that tube a single pint of water. Hence, too, by inserting a tube, not more than the tenth of an inch in diameter, in the strongest vessel filled with water, and then making the tube sufficiently strong and pouring water into it, the vessel may be burst; that is, the weight of a single quart of water is sufficient to burst asunder an iron-bound vessel. Or by fitting a strong piston to a large cylinder, the powerful machine called the hydrostatic press is formed, by which trees are torn up by the roots, porous bodies astonishingly compressed, and enormous weights elevated.

This same principle (of equal pressure in all directions) prevents us from being conscious of the great weight of the atmosphere. Indeed, we are not aware that any pressure is upon us; and unless we move very rapidly, or against a strong wind, we scarcely realize that the air offers any resistance. Hence a man unacquainted with pneumatics can hardly be made to believe that every square inch of surface upon his body does in fact sustain a weight of fifteen pounds, and that the whole weight of the atmosphere that lies upon him is not less than fourteen and a half tons; while the whole surface of the earth sustains a pressure of twelve trillions of pounds, or six thousand billions of tons.

The extent to which matter may be divided, both mechanically and chemically, may be regarded as one of the wonders of modern science. Little, indeed, is said at this day respecting the infinite divisibility of matter; which, if theoretically possible, is now generally regarded by philosophers as in reality untrue. With Sir Isaac Newton, they now mostly consider it "probable that God in the beginning formed matter in solid, massy, hard, impenetrable, movable particles, of such sizes and figures, and with such other properties, and in such proportion to space, as most conduced to the end for which he formed them."

These ultimate particles are called atoms; and although none of them have ever been rendered cognizable by the senses, yet it can be shown that they must be inconceivably small. Gold may be spread over silver wire so thin that fourteen million films of it would make a pile only one inch thick; while fourteen million films of common writing paper would form a pile three quarters of a mile thick. Gold may be beaten so thin that one twenty millionth part of a grain is visible to the naked eye, and one fourteen hundred millionth part through a microscope. Yet in each of these fragments there may be, for aught we know, millions of atoms. A certain species of fungus, (*bovista giganteum*,) has been known to attain the size of a gourd in one night; and it is calculated that the cellules, of which it is composed, must amount to 47,000,000,000. If it grew in twelve hours, this would give 4,000,000,000 per hour, or more than 66,000,000 each minute. Animalcules have been discovered so small that 1,000,000 would not exceed a grain of sand, and 500,000,000 could sport in a drop of water. Yet each of these must have blood-vessels, nerves, muscles, circulating fluids, &c., like larger animals. What, then, must be the almost infinite littleness of a particle of these fluids! Yet chemical solution carries this division of matter probably still farther. Thus it has been demonstrated that an atom of lead must weigh less than the one three hundred and ten thousand millionth part of a grain, and an atom of sulphur less than the one two trillionth part of a grain. The bulk of the atom of lead must be less than the eight hundred and eighty-eight trillionth part of a cubic inch. But it seems almost useless to make such statements; for who can form any correct idea of things so inconceivably minute? *

If, however, we regard light as a material substance, results still more astonishing follow. It can be shown that, in such a case, the particles of light cannot weigh more than one million millionth part of a grain; for if larger, they would destroy the organs of vision.† On the same principle, it has been calculated that the particles of light that flow from a candle in a second are more than six billion times as many as the grains of sand in the whole earth, if each cubic inch contains one million.‡ The opinion that light is material, however, has given place to what is called *the undulatory theory*. This supposes the universe to be filled with a very subtle elastic fluid, called the luminiferous ether, and that the vibrations of this ether communicate the impression of light to the eye just as the vibrations of the air convey to the ear the idea of sound. But, upon this hypothesis, the inferences are no less wonderful than upon the supposition that light is material. It is a demonstrated fact, for instance, that light moves at the rate of nearly 200,000 miles (192,500) per

* Prout's Bridgewater Treatise, p. 36.

† Turner's Sacred History, Vol. I. p. 24.

‡ Ferguson's Lectures, Vol. I. p. 228.

second; and who can conceive of vibrations spreading on all sides of a luminous body with such a velocity? Take, for an example, one of the fixed stars. Astronomers have demonstrated that the distance of the nearest star cannot be less than twenty billions of miles, while stars of smaller magnitude must be situated at a distance immensely greater. Now, it has been shown by Dr. Wollaston that the light of Sirius is only one twelve thousand millionth part (11,839,-530,000) as great as the light of the sun; and the light of the star Vega, of much smaller magnitude, is 180 millions of times less than that of the sun. Yet, if the eyes of the ten thousand millions of animals on the globe were all turned towards this star at the same instant, each one would have a distinct image of it formed upon the retina. And if the millions of millions of other worlds, scattered through space, are peopled as thickly as our own, and every eye there were directed to that star at the same time, each eye would see it as distinctly as if no other one were gazing upon it. What an astonishing power, then, is light! Who does not feel himself lost in attempting to comprehend its nature!

But, still further, philosophers suppose they have demonstrated that the different colors in nature are produced by a difference in the number of vibrations in the luminiferous ether, and that, in a single second of time, the eye is affected by these movements as follows: —

In red, . . 477,000,000,000 of times;
In orange, . 506,000,000,000 of times;
In yellow, . 535,000,000,000 of times;
In green, . 577,000,000,000 of times;
In blue, . . 622,000,000,000 of times;
In indigo, . 658,000,000,000 of times;
In violet, . 699,000,000,000 of times.

Is it strange that man looks upon light with an awe approaching devotion, and that Milton should exclaim, —

> "Hail, holy light! offspring of Heaven, first born,
> Or of the eternal, coeternal beam"?

I will only add, in this connection, a statement of La Place respecting attraction: "I have ascertained," says he, "that between the heavenly bodies all attractions are transmitted with a velocity which, if it be not infinite, surpasses several thousand times the velocity of light." His annotator estimates it as eight million of times greater than that of light.

Were there time for the details, the science of optics would furnish many other illustrations appropriate to my object — such as the diffraction of light, the splendid colors of their films, and the phenomena of polarization and double refraction. But I must hurry forward. Nor can we be long detained even upon the sublime developments of astronomy. Since the most common and striking of these have been so often and familiarly described in public lectures, and even in the primary school manual, I shall confine my remarks to some principles that are less generally known, or to recent discoveries.

I have always regarded it as one of the greatest achievements of astronomers that they have been able to weigh the bodies of the solar system, so as to state how many pounds avoirdupois they contain, and to ascertain their relative weight compared with that of water. It is certain, for instance, that the mass of Jupiter is more than 322, and less than 323, times the mass of this globe — so accurately has this work been accomplished. The mass of the sun is 359,551 times greater than that of the earth and moon, and 700 times greater than the united masses of all the planets. The weight of the most important bodies of the solar system, compared with water, is as follows: —

Sun, . . .	1.40	Mars, . .	0.71
Moon, . .	3.37	Jupiter, . .	1.42
Mercury, .	15.24	Saturn, . .	0.56
Venus, . .	5.15	Uranus, .	1.53
Earth, . .	5.48		

From this statement we learn that Saturn is composed of matter only half as heavy as water; while Mercury is considerably heavier than quicksilver, and a third heavier than lead. Our own globe, also, taken as a whole, is twice as heavy as common rock, and half as heavy as lead — a fact which shows the great density of its internal parts.

The disturbances that take place among the heavenly bodies in consequence of their mutual attraction constitute a branch of knowledge the most profound, it is said, in the whole circle of human science — requiring all the aid of the most difficult and subtle mathematical analysis. In this field such men as Newton and La Grange, La Place and Bowditch, have won their noblest honors; and I may add, it is only such minds that can disentangle the mazes of this labyrinth. The problem to be solved was this: given the directions and velocities of about thirty mutually-attracting bodies, to find their places after any number of ages. And to give some idea of the complexity of the problem, it may be stated that one of these bodies, the moon, is subject to no less than sixty perturbations in her longitude. And to show how successful astronomers have been in estimating these, it may be stated that the lunar tables actually contain twenty-eight corrections, or equations, to be applied to her mean place to obtain her true place; and the result never varies from the truth more than five seconds of a degree. But the most interesting result to which these investigations have led is the great truth, that, in spite of these perturbations, the permanence of the solar system is secured ; nay, that these very disturbances are the means of preserving it from ruin. Formerly, astronomers thought they saw in the motions of the heavenly bodies a tendency to ruin. The moon, for instance, has been for thousands of years coming nearer and nearer the earth in every revolution ; and the eccentricity of the earth's orbit has been diminishing, as has also the obliquity of the ecliptic to the equator. But it is now shown that all these irregularities are periodical ; and that after having proceeded in one direction for a time, — it may be for hundreds, or thousands, or even millions of years, — they will reach a limit which they cannot pass, and oscillate in the opposite direction ; and the limits of oscillation are too narrow seriously to affect the stability of the system or the comfort of its inhabitants. This demonstration, first wrought out by La Grange and La Place, and afterwards corrected by Bowditch, is one of the proudest achievements of modern science, and proves that our system, in itself considered, is eternal.

But a question has long been agitated whether all space is not occupied with very thin and subtle matter, which must offer a resistance to the motions of the heavenly bodies, and bring the system to ruin at last. And modern astronomical discoveries seem nearly to have settled this question in the affirmative. The universal diffusion of light, heat, and electricity, especially if the undulatory theory of light be true, render such an opinion probable. But the observations that have been made upon what is called Encke's comet, which revolves round the sun in three and a half years, make it almost certain that this medium does exist. That comet, being nothing but a mass of thin vapor, is retarded much more than the planets, which are solid, and has actually advanced in its orbit, since its discovery, ten days more than can be explained by the laws of gravity, exclusive of a resisting medium. Some thirty thousand years will elapse before it will fall into the sun, and many millions of years before the same cause would precipitate the planets to the centre ; but it is an interesting conclusion that, ultimately and inevitably, if such a cause exist, ruin must ensue.

Modern discoveries respecting the nature of comets in general open a wide field for the play of the imagination. It seems now to be proved that nearly all of them (say, perhaps, 800) are nothing but thin vapor ; for the fixed stars are visible directly through their centres. They must, of course, be far less dense than the thinnest cloud. And yet these bodies move round the sun in obedience to the same laws as the planets, though liable to greater irregularities. The trains which accompany them, and which are sometimes, as in the comet of 1811, more than 130 millions of miles long, are evidently produced by the action of the sun, but in what way it seems difficult to conceive. In all ages, great anxiety has been manifested lest a collision should take place between the earth and one of these bodies. But the knowledge we now have of their nature teaches us that, even should one of them be encountered in the earth's annual circuit, it is not probable that matter so tenuous could pass through the atmosphere, and that the only effect of such an occurrence would be some slight meteorological change, or perhaps, as one of our countrymen suggests, who has distinguished himself by attention to this and kindred subjects, another splendid meteoric shower might signalize the event.*

* Olmsted's Astronomy, p. 242.

The comet called Biela's, from its discoverer, which revolves around the sun in about seven years, in one of its recent returns, divided into two parts, which moved on together, with no apparent mutual influence. This fact proves, if proof were wanting, the extreme tenuity of the matter. The parts move along together just like two wreaths of smoke or vapor, and have occupied the same relative position for at least one revolution, except that they are receding from each other.

So successful have Lord Rosse and others been in resolving nebulæ, of late, that some astronomers are confident that all of them will be found, at length, to consist of stars. But such masses as the Magellanic Clouds of the southern hemisphere, and especially the facts respecting spiral nebulæ, make it more probable that some of them consist rather of diffused patches of self-luminous vapor, analogous to comets. On the hypothesis that they are made up of fixed stars, it is quite impossible to account for their spiral form. But if the matter has been in motion in a resisting medium, it would have assumed a spiral form, and be disseminated all along its course towards the centre of attraction.

The curious facts that are established by modern astronomers respecting double stars prove that the great law of gravitation extends to other systems beyond the solar. More than one quarter of the stars, according to Struve, are double; and, in several instances, it is proved that these stars revolve about each other in elliptic orbits, in periods between 43 and 1200 years. Taking these facts in connection with the periodical disappearance and reappearance of some stars, with the occasional sudden bursting forth of a new star, and the total extinguishment of others, we are led to doubt whether our solar system is a type, in all respects, of the entire universe, though probably the same general laws prevail in all worlds. But how difficult to conceive of revolving planets in a system that has two suns, one of which revolves around the other! Infinite wisdom may have plans and objects in the collocation, movements, and physical condition of worlds totally inconceivable by human powers.

Even as long ago as the time of Halley, that astronomer suggested that probably the solar system had a motion in an orbit around some remote centre; and the idea has been frequently revived in more recent times, and subjected to the test of observation. And though some still profess to be sceptical on the subject, it seems difficult to resist the conviction that it is true. For the stars in one part of the heaven gradually approximate towards one another, while in the opposite part they recede. In what other way can we explain such a fact, but by supposing that we are approaching the stars in one direction, and receding from them in the other? The point towards which we seem to be tending is in right ascension about 260°, in declination 34° north, corresponding to the constellation Hercules. Astronomers even profess to have determined the velocity approximately with which we are moving — which is 154,185,000 miles in a year, 422,000 in an hour, and 57 each second. Whether the remote centre that regulates this movement may be occupied by a vast sun, or the attraction may be but the aggregate of the influence of a vast number of smaller bodies embraced in the same system, it may never be possible to know; yet possibly the discovery may one day be made.

The rapidity with which the new planets, denominated asteroids, have been discovered of late, is one of the most remarkable features of modern astronomy. These all move between Mars and Jupiter; and though forty are now known, their united mass is less than a quarter part of the weight of the earth. The hypothesis, that they have all originated from the bursting asunder of a planet that once revolved between Mars and Jupiter, is gaining strength, notwithstanding the powerful attack upon it by Leverrier. Professor Alexander, of this country, suggests that the form of this original planet was a mere flattened disk, that flew asunder from its centrifugal force. If so, it is not improbable that those much smaller masses that not unfrequently fall from the heavens, called meteors, had the same origin. If they had, the great problem for astronomers and meteorologists to solve is to make out the series, by discovering asteriods of less and less size, and meteors of larger size. Leverrier suggests that, probably by the close of this century, 100 of the asteriods will have been discovered and described.

Astronomers had demonstrated that the nearest fixed star could not be less than 20 billions of miles from the earth. But they were not satisfied till they could determine the actual distance. I believe that Bessel, of Prussia, was the first who ascertained the annual parallax of a star, viz., 61 Cygni, and found it to be 0''.3136; that is, the diameter of the earth's orbit, equal 190 millions of miles, as seen from this star, subtends an angle of one third of a second only. From this he deduced its actual distance to be more than 62 billions of miles, (62,481,500,000,000.) Light, travelling from this star at the rate of 200,000 miles per second, would require more than seven years to reach the earth. The parallaxes of other stars have since been ascertained, and some of them are much smaller — not more than the 0.027th of a second. This would make the distance of this star 731,136,000,000,000 miles, and light from it would require 120 years to reach us. What, then, must be the parallax and distance of the telescopic stars! A flash of lightning on the earth would be visible on the moon in a second and a quarter; on the sun, in eight minutes; on

Jupiter, when farthest from us, in 52 minutes; on Uranus, in two hours; on Neptune, in four hours and a quarter; on the star Vega, of the first magnitude, in 45 years; on a star of the eighth magnitude, in 180 years; on a star of the twelfth magnitude, in 4000 years; and such stars are visible through the telescope. One of these remotest stars, therefore, may have been struck out of existence as long ago as man's creation, and yet be still visible in our telescopes. What prodigious demands does science make upon our faith, and upon our powers of conception too!

The rapid progress which has been made within a few years past in the sciences of galvanism and electro-magnetism has made it nearly certain that electricity, magnetism, galvanism, and electro-magnetism, are all but modifications of one great power in nature, and that is the electric fluid. In common electricity, we witness this fluid in a state of uncontrollable intensity. In galvanism, we see it flowing in an uninterrupted current. In electro-magnetism, we see that magnetism is produced whenever a constant current of electricity can be made to pass through a body; and if those currents can be made to flow permanently, then permanent magnets will be produced. On the other hand, currents of electricity, which may be made visible, may be induced in coils of copper wire, by making and breaking the connection of a bar of soft iron with a permanent magnet; that is, electricity may be produced by magnetism, and it seems almost certain, therefore, that magnetism is only a modification of electricity.

These discoveries have thrown a flood of light upon many of the most curious and recondite operations of nature. The astonishing effects of the galvanic fluid upon animals recently killed, although it does not demonstrate that the mysterious principle of life is identical with electricity, yet proves a very intimate relation between the two things. By the application of galvanism, for instance, to the head of an ox recently killed, his mouth opened with a bellowing noise; a linnet, that had lain dead for some minutes, was made to spring up, flutter its wings, and breathe six or eight minutes; and several times, criminals, after hanging by the neck until they were dead, have had all the muscles of their bodies put in violent motion, full and laborious breathing has been produced, and every muscle in the murderer's face has been thrown into fearful action, so that rage, horror, despair, and ghastly smiles were exhibited in his countenance in such a hideous combination as to produce sickness and fainting among the spectators.

Physiologists have in vain endeavored to explain by what principle the numerous distinct parts, solid and fluid, that are found in animals and plants, can be separated from the blood and the sap. They could see that most delicate and complicated chemical operations must be concerned; but the question was, by what secret power these operations were accomplished. Galvanism throws at least a glimpse of light upon the subject. The galvanic fluid, when passing through bodies, especially those in solution, exerts an astonishing power of decomposing or separating them into their elements, and thus giving those elements an opportunity to form new combinations. And, indeed, I know of nothing more wonderful in the whole records of science than this mysterious power. Now, may it not be that every animal and every plant contains within its organization a galvanic combination, sufficiently powerful to elaborate all the secretions which its nature requires? Indeed, the most distinguished philosophers of our day have suggested that in animals the brain may be this electric pile, which sends along the nerves, as conductors, its successive shocks, whereby the pulsations of the heart are produced, and the proximate principles found in animals are secreted from the blood. Hypothetical as this idea may seem, when first announced, there is one fact that throws over it an air of probability. We do know that several species of fish, by means of a galvanic arrangement in their heads, have the power of giving powerful electric shocks. The *gymnotus electricus*, or electric eel, for instance, gives a shock, according to Humboldt, powerful enough to kill a man, and by repetition even a mule, horse, &c. May not a weaker power of this sort, which is all that is necessary, be found in every animal and plant?

Galvanism, also, shows us how many metallic veins may be formed even now in the solid rocks, and how the crystals and gems dug from thence may be produced. Electro-magnetism shows us that it is only necessary to suppose the revolution of electric currents around the earth, in order to show why the magnetic needle takes a north and south direction; while thermo-electricity gives us a reason why that needle has a daily variation. In electro-magnetism, also, we find a probable solution for that most remarkable phenomenon, the aurora borealis and australis. That it is an electro-magnetic phenomenon seems proved beyond all doubt by the fact that its beautiful coruscations all radiate from one of the magnetic poles, though the precise manner in which electro-magnetic currents operate to produce it is still involved in obscurity.

After all, the instantaneous development of a very great attractive force in some electro-magnetic experiments seems to me the most marvellous effect exhibited by this science. Take, for instance, the electro-magnet, which is nothing but a bent piece of soft iron, coiled with several hundred feet of copper wire. This iron has no magnetism till the extremities of the wire are connected with the poles of a very feeble galvanic battery, when instantly, as if by magic, a prodigious magnetic force is communicated to the iron — even a force of two thousand or three thousand pounds, which vanishes as soon as the connection with the battery is broken. Now, is it not amazing that this powerful force should be communicated in a moment through a wire not more than one twentieth of an inch in diameter? Do we not here catch a glimpse of a prodigious natural force, which lies hidden and silent all around us, and which, if it could only be fully developed, would arm man with an energy almost irresistible? I confess I do not yet despair of his being one day put into full possession of this power.

The next wide field that opens before us is chemistry: and how many marvellous things invite our examination! But I must not forget that my first object should be to hurry forward. Yet I must linger long enough to point out a few flowery spots.

The atoms, or particles, of all matter, are subject to the influence of two forces — attraction and repulsion. When the first predominates, solid bodies are formed; when the latter prevails, elastic gas, or air, is the result; when both are equally balanced, liquids are produced. The antagonist to affinity, or attraction, is heat; and it is always because bodies contain this principle in different degrees, that some are solid, some liquid, and some gaseous. Men are accustomed to think of heat only in that state in which it affects our senses; but in fact the greater part of it is in a hidden or latent state, and no body is so cold but a great amount of heat can be elicited from it, either chemically or mechanically. If, for instance, all the heat contained in the snow and ice that has mantled New England during the past winter had been suddenly extricated, there can be hardly a doubt but a general conflagration of the surface would have been the result.

The operation of latent heat in changing the forms of bodies produces some very paradoxical results. Thus, in freezing, water gives out 140° of heat, which becomes sensible; and the great amount of congelation in cold climates is doubtless one of the principal causes that render them habitable and comfortable; for the harder the frost, the greater the amount of heat given out. On the other hand, when water evaporates, it takes up into a latent state nearly 1000° of heat; and this probably it is, chiefly, that renders the torrid zone tolerable, since the heat of a vertical sun must produce a vast amount of evaporation. Once more, by a singular exception to a general law, that cold contracts all bodies, it is well known that water, in freezing, expands, so that the ice swims in it; and being an almost perfect non-conductor of heat, it prevents the water beneath from giving off its heat, and so it will not freeze.* Were it not for this singular anomaly, — this interference of one law with another, — all the streams and lakes in such a climate as ours would be frozen to their bottoms, and the summer would hardly suffice to thaw them out.

Not less wonderful are the effects of affinity, or the power by which the elements are combined, so as to form compound substances. In these combinations it has been found that the elements unite only in definite quantities, and each substance has its peculiar combining proportion, — a law which forms a mathematical basis for chemistry, — and exhibits strikingly the wisdom of the Deity, showing us that perfect system prevails in the minute, as well as in the most extensive operations of nature. But it is impossible for me to do any justice at this time to a subject so difficult as that of definite proportions. He only can fully appreciate its beauty who has long

* This is rather a new law coming in than an exception to a law; for it is not confined to water, and seems to be the result of a new arrangement of the particles in the act of crystallization.

been devoted to the delicate and difficult department of chemical analysis.

The vast variety which nature produces by the union of a few elements is one of the most wonderful results of chemical affinity. It is true chemists describe a little over sixty of these elements; but sixteen of these constitute almost the entire mass of the globe, and scarcely more than four are essential to form the vast variety of the animal and vegetable kingdoms. It is amazing, also, to see how very great a difference between two compounds is often produced by a slight variation in the proportion of their ingredients. Oxygen and nitrogen, for instance, mixed in the proportion of one of the former to four of the latter, constitute the atmosphere, the very *pabulum* of life to animals and plants. But combine them in the proportion of fourteen parts nitrogen and eight parts oxygen, and you form the exhilarating gas, little better adapted to respiration than the vapor of alcohol or ether. Add eight parts more of oxygen, and a gas results, which, taken into the lungs, would be almost certainly fatal. Add successively eight, sixteen, and twenty-four parts more of oxygen, and three distinct acids would be formed, eminently hostile to life. What perfect wisdom and perfect benevolence must have arranged the chemical constitution and agencies of this world, to adapt them to the delicate organization of animals and plants! And how very slightly the elements of life differ from the elements of death! The most delicious fruits of the vegetable kingdom, for instance, are composed of oxygen, hydrogen, and carbon, and sometimes nitrogen; and the most fatal vegetable poisons have the same composition, differing only in the proportion of the ingredients.

The magic power of chemical affinity is still more manifest in the entire change of properties which takes place in substances upon combination. Suppose you should direct your cook to provide an entertainment of all the varieties of food which the market and the culinary art could furnish, and he, taking a chemical fancy into his head, should set before you and your guests a dish of charcoal, and a vessel of water, telling you that if you wanted any nitrogen in addition, the atmosphere would furnish it. Now, he could truly plead that he had set before you oxygen, hydrogen, nitrogen, and carbon ; and that if he had loaded your table with the most costly viands and fruit, it would have added little more. But you would think his chemistry a poor substitute for a good dinner.

Once more : a mere difference in the arrangement of the particles of a substance makes a world of difference in its properties. Suppose, for instance, that when Messrs. Bundell and Bridges received orders to prepare Queen Victoria's crown for coronation day, instead of surmounting it with diamonds, they had covered it with charcoal points, and presented a bill of £1, instead of £100,000, or half a million of dollars. It would probably have hardly quieted the royal displeasure to have been informed that the chemical constitution of charcoal is precisely the same as that of the diamond, and that a slight difference in the arrangement of the particles could be of no consequence.

The complete neutralization and concealment of the most powerful substances, by means of strong chemical affinity, is another remarkable effect of this agency, and a striking example of divine beneficence. For had these substances been left free, the destruction of organic beings must have been certain. Almost every one knows, for instance, how fatal a poison is phosphorus, and how eminently and powerfully combustible it is. But this substance abounds through all nature —in the solid rocks, in the soils, in plants, and especially in the bones of animals; nay, it is found even in the brain. A middling-sized man, for instance, contains a pound of it, which, if in a free state and inflamed, would burn him up and every thing around him. But now, nothing is more incombustible than a bone. No one suspects what a terrible agent he carries within him; nor has any one reason to fear it, because it is disarmed. And so it is throughout nature — so concealed, indeed, that nothing but delicate chemical tests can discover its existence. The same is true of chlorine, which, in a free state, is eminently terrible. And were all of this element that is now chained in the ocean to be liberated in one day, it would sweep this fair world of all its tenants, and its beauty. In short, modern chemistry has afforded us a glimpse of a multitude of agents within us and around us, which, in a free state, are of terrific power. But the lion is converted into a lamb by the strong chain of affinity.

In meteorology, although prolific in remarkable phenomena, I shall notice but two or three. In the first place, consider what a remarkable envelope of our globe is its atmosphere! We have first an atmosphere of gas, a mixture of oxygen and nitrogen, decreasing in density upwards in a geometrical ratio. In the second place, we have an atmosphere of vapor equally extensive; for the gas is a solvent of water, and the average amount of vapor in the air would form a stratum of water on the earth's surface five inches thick; and the amount of water annually deposited in the form of dew actually amounts to four inches in depth. In the third place, we have an atmosphere of that subtle ether which probably pervades all space, and occupies the interstices between the particles of matter, and gives rise to the phenomena of light, heat, and electricity. And yet this atmosphere, so complex in its character, seems to us the most simple of all things.

The power of natural evaporation possessed by the atmosphere is very surprising. From experiments made in Europe, it appears that the quantity of water evaporated from the surface of Great Britain amounts to 32 inches, or 142 thousand millions (141,832,558,752) of tons annually, while the quantity of rain that falls is 36 inches, or 160 thousand millions of tons, (159,561,628,596.) *

In order to prevent universal stagnation and death, it was necessary that the atmospheric elements should be allowed some degree of motion. But the limits of their oscillations must be very narrow, or desolation would follow their movements. And how perfectly is this object accomplished, though seemingly impossible! for when Eolus has once escaped from his cave, who shall bind him again? Almighty wisdom and power are alone adequate; and though occasional ruin follows the elemental strife, yet security is the law, and desolation the infrequent exception.

In advancing to those sciences that relate to the animate part of creation, anatomy and physiology, the first of which treats of the structure, and the latter of the functions, of organized beings, first arrest our attention; and they so abound with wonders, that the remaining time which your patience will allow me might be all profitably devoted to them. But so many familiar and popular works have been published upon anatomy and physiology, that I may fairly presume every person of good education has some acquaintance with many of the most striking facts in these sciences. Who, for instance, has not some knowledge of the structure of that most exquisite of all organic contrivances the eye? Who cannot tell something of the mechanism of

* Thomson on Heat and Electricity, p. 267. Turner's Sacred History, Vol. I. p. 32.

the ear? of the bones, especially the vertebral column, — of the organs of digestion and assimilation, — of the muscles, and their mysterious power of contraction, — and above all, of the circulation of the blood, with the structure and functions of the heart and the lungs? Who knows not that his five senses depend chiefly upon distinct sets of nerves, all proceeding from one great centre, the brain, and yet incapable of performing the functions of one another? And who does not remember what thrilling impressions the first development of these subjects made upon him? how he trembled to hear his heart beat, and to feel his lungs heaving, and almost feared to move, lest the harp of thousand strings should be untuned?

But there is a department of these sciences, called *Comparative Anatomy and Physiology*, which has of late been cultivated with extraordinary success, and whose marvellous results are less known. I cannot, therefore, entirely neglect them.

When a man, not conversant with anatomy, looks upon the bones of an animal promiscuously mingled together, he does not perceive any striking harmony and relation between them. But a careful and extensive comparison reveals the astonishing fact, "that from the character of a single limb," (I use the words of an able comparative anatomist,) "and even of a single tooth, or bone, the form and proportion of the other bones, and the condition of the entire animal, may be inferred." "Hence, not only the framework of the fossil skeleton of an extinct animal, but also the character of the muscles, by which each bone was moved, the external form and figure of the body, the food, and habits, and haunts, and mode of life of creatures that ceased to exist before the creation of the human race, can, with a high degree of probability, be ascertained."* These statements have been established by the severest tests. For a single tooth or bone of an unknown animal has been put into the hands of the anatomist, and from it he has constructed the entire skeleton and a description of the whole animal. Afterwards a complete skeleton has been discovered, and found to correspond with the one described by analogy. Truly, there is mathematics in bones, as well as in lines, angles, and numbers.

It is an interesting process to take a particular organ of the human frame and compare it with the analogous organ in the lower classes of animals, and to see how its functions and structure gradually change; but always in such a manner as will adapt it more perfectly to the condition and wants of the animal. So manifold and striking, for example, are these adaptations in that most remarkable organ, the hand, that a distinguished anatomist has made it the entire subject of one of the famous Bridgewater Treatises. Or take the organs of motion, and compare the movements of the sloth with those of the deer, the antelope, the hare, the grasshopper, or the flea. The sloth consumes several days in getting from one tree to another — which he never does till nearly starved. But such a change is rarely necessary, and therefore the muscles are not adapted to it. Yet the *cicada spumaria*, a species of locust, can leap two hundred and fifty times its length. If a man could leap the same distance in proportion to his size, he would be carried a quarter of a mile; and an ox or an elephant still farther — far enough, indeed, to dash him in pieces. A flea weighs less than a grain, and can leap an inch and a half. A man, at the same rate, would pass over 12,800 miles, or half round the globe! The legs of one

* Buckland's Bridgewater Treatise, Vol. I. p. 109.

insect, the water boatman, (*notenecta*,) are so fitted that he always swims upon his back. Another, the bat-mite, (*pteroptus*,) has the power of instantly throwing its legs upwards so as to walk upon its back. Another, the dragon fly, can project a stream of water from its body, and thus be driven forward on the principle of the rocket.

Not less variety exists in the organs of respiration. We are apt to feel that breathing can be performed only by lungs. But the membranous air bags of reptiles are quite different. Frogs and tortoises swallow air, and hence have been known to live more than a month with their mouths and nostrils closed; although there is reason to believe that the common opinion that frogs live for centuries without air, enclosed in stone, is unfounded. Fishes breathe by their gills, and insects by means of tubes in various parts of their bodies.

Man, too, finds it difficult to conceive how animals can exist without heads. But a large class that inhabit sea shells are called *acephala*,—that is, headless animals,—and the skill which they discover in the formation of those beautiful structures which form their habitations throws into the shade the architecture of that biped race who not only have heads, but boast that they constitute the head of this lower creation.

The delicate changes in the organs of vision to adapt them to the condition and wants of animals are among the most remarkable provisions of divine wisdom for their comfort. We cannot see well in water, because our eyes are fitted for the air; nor can fish see well in air, for the same reason. By using very convex spectacles we might have distinct vision in water; and so, were a whale disposed to take an excursion on land, the optician might doubtless provide him with a pair of spectacles through which he could see as well as many travellers of our own species have done. But his glasses must be concave. Some insects, as the *gyrinus*, which live chiefly upon the surface of the water, have two pairs of eyes, or perhaps a division of one pair into an upper and lower part — one set for looking into the water, and the other for looking into the air. The eyes of insects generally are fixed immovably in the head, and, therefore, they need some provision to enable them to see on all sides. This is accomplished by making their eyes polygonal, like a multiplying glass, which, in fact, amounts to giving them as many eyes as there are facets; for each plane will produce a separate image on the retina. In this sense the house fly has 14,000 eyes — that is, 7000 facets to each eye; the dragon fly, 25,000; the butterfly, 35,000; and the mordella, 50,000. How perfect must be the structure of the eye to keep so complex an organ in repair! Another fact in relation to the eye of the cod fish is still more striking in this connection. The crystalline lens in that fish, which is never half an inch in diameter, has been proved to be made up of more than 5,000,000 fibres, which are united together by more than 62,500,000,000 teeth!

The instincts of animals afford a prolific source of examples appropriate to my object. But presuming that many marvellous facts on this subject are known to all, I shall pass rapidly over it. Perhaps, however, no department of science presents facts so nearly approaching to romance as this. Indeed, the earlier works on zoölogy contain not a few statements that are really fictitious. Many, for example, still suppose that serpents have the power of charming their prey, and even man, within the reach of their fangs; a notion which is of a piece with the ancient stories about the sirens, — the *dulce malum in pelago*, — or with the modern notions about the conversion of a horsehair into a snake. But making all due allowances for such fancies, there still remains in the history of animal instincts a vast mass of facts that are truly marvellous. Perhaps in nothing do these instincts seem more like perfected reason than in the construction of the habitations of animals. Who does not know what geometry as well as perfection of government there is in a beehive? Nor are they less striking in a vespiary. Indeed, the queen of the wasps is far more enterprising and energetic than the queen of the honey bees. For during the winter nearly all the wasps die, and the queen has to rear up an entirely new colony, and provide for them. But before autumn she not unfrequently rules over no less than 30,000 subjects — and all her own children. I must not, however, go into details on these points. But there is one fact connected with the history of bees, though not very relevant to my subject, which I mention for the special benefit of young men. Naturalists admit that the most satisfactory account of the instincts and habits of bees was furnished by the elder Huber, who constructed glass hives, and other apparatus, so that he could watch their movements. But of what use were glass hives to him? for he was stone blind. The mystery is easily explained. "He saw the bees," says his biographer, "through the eyes of the admirable woman whom he married." Now, I wish the young gentlemen who hear me to understand that it is no uncommon occurrence for a man to find his wife as great a blessing as a good pair of eyes.

The instincts of the spider are quite as remarkable as those of the bee, the wasp, and the ant. Though the most ferocious of all animals, she will fight with desperation in defence of her young; but when the cocoon containing them is torn from her, she will simulate death so perfectly, that her limbs may be torn off one by one, and yet she will show no sign of life; but let her cocoon be brought within her reach, and she will seize it with desperate strength. The process by which the spider weaves its web is as remarkable as any thing in the animal kingdom; but the description would be too prolix.

I must not leave the comparative physiology of animals without adverting to the subject of their transformation, or metamorphosis. Every animal, in the successive stages of its existence, undergoes more or less of change. It is said that, in man, the particles that compose the infant are several times entirely replaced by others before the period of old age. But some animals undergo sudden and remarkable changes. Serpents cast off their skins, and crustaceans, such as the lobster, their shells, annually. The frog is first hatched in the form of a tadpole,—or, as we more commonly say in New England, a *polliwog*,—which has the form of a fish with a large head, but without legs or fins. Gradually this creature becomes a frog, with four legs. But the most perfect example of metamorphosis is that of insects, especially the winged species. They are hatched as a caterpillar, or grub, which is called their larva state. Next they enclose themselves in a cocoon, and become torpid. This is their *pupa* or chrysalis state. From this condition they emerge into their imago or perfect state, as elegant, lively, winged insects. Such cases have been beautifully denominated *emblems of immortality*. The larva state, in which the animal is in an active, but depressed and imperfect condition, may well be likened to the present life. The torpidity and confinement of the pupa state well represents our detention in the grave; while the imago or perfect state beautifully typifies our condition when *this corruptible shall have put on incorruption, and this mortal shall have put on immortality.*

Among the lowest tribes of animals, the polypi are distinguished for their anomalies. The simplest form of one of these animals is a fleshy tube, open only at the top, and the opening surrounded by flexible arms, called tentacula. On each side of the tentacula are usually fine fibres, like hairs, called ciliæ. These are capable of such rapid motion that the eye cannot follow them; and the object of their movements usually is to produce eddying currents of water around their mouths, in order to bring food within their reach. A good example of these animals is the hydra, which is found in fresh water. It may be described as consisting of nothing but a stomach, with tentacula around its mouth to draw in its prey. It is an enormous glutton when it can obtain food, yet it will live four months without it. When two hydras contend for a worm, the stronger not only swallows the morsel, but also his antagonist and his own tentacula; the two latter, however, usually escape without being digested. When this animal is turned inside out, as it may be, digestion goes on equally well — a power which would be very convenient for the biped gormands of the Caucasian race. But the most remarkable fact relating to these animals is, their power of repairing almost any injury which they receive that does not absolutely annihilate them. If they be divided lengthwise into several strips, each piece will in a few hours become a tube; and in a day new tentacula will be produced and ready for taking in food. Or, by cutting up several hydras, different parts may be made to grow together, and become one animal. In this way, every variety of monster which "fancy yet has feigned or fear conceived" may be originated; and this is actually the way in which the hydra with seven heads, which has often been the occasion of gross imposition, has been formed.

In the greater number of cases, the simple polypi, that have been described, are attached to a stony or horny axis, which they themselves secrete and build up. And it is remarkable that multitudes unite to build up a habitation with the same regularity as if a single will guided them. It is a question among naturalists whether, in such a case, the individuals that thus combine ought not to be regarded as a single animal. In a single specimen of flustra there are sometimes more than 18,000 polypi. Each polype has 22 tentacula and 50 ciliæ; so that in the whole specimen there are 396,000 tentacula and 39,600,000 ciliæ. In another species, Dr. Grant calculates that there are 400,000,000 of ciliæ. And these are all busy upon that one specimen, of only a few square inches. How immense, then, must be the number of polypi and their ciliæ upon those vast coral structures which, in the tropical seas, form reefs several hundred miles long!

I shall mention here one other physiological fact relating to the lower orders of animals, because I believe it to be extremely rare, and I happen to have a few specimens to illustrate it. A very few examples are on record in which plants of the fungus tribe, such as sphæria and isaria, have been known to grow out of the bodies of insects or their larvæ, in the West Indies and South America, even while they were yet alive. I have specimens from Wisconsin, in which a species of sphæria has grown two or three inches long from the head of a small grub.*

In proceeding onwards through the fields of science, just on the borders of the domains of physiology and psychology,

* For details on this curious subject, see Griffith and Henfrey's Micographic Dictionary, article *Parasites*.

two gateways open laterally, through which we catch a glimpse of scenery the most enchanting, though the fogs of night still rest upon much of it, and the sun, yet but a little above the horizon, has not been able to dissipate it. Over these gateways is written *Phrenology*, *Mesmerism*, and *Spiritualism.* Shall we pass through them? I answer, No; for around the entrance I see not a few, whom I recognize as veterans in science, arrayed in opposition to one another in earnest controversy. On the one side it is maintained that these passages lead into regions of knowledge, not only smiling with flowers, but clustered with golden fruit; that, in fact, here, and here only, are found the clear fountains of intellectual science. On the other hand, it is said that these passages lead only into the regions of fancy and romance; that nothing here is fixed and settled; and that a few parhelia and rainbows, painted on the clouds and fogs that hover on the outskirts of physiology and metaphysics, have been mistaken for golden mountains; in short, that nothing can be found in those regions of morass and fog deserving the name of science.

Now, it is not my intention, in this lecture, to enter into a discussion of contested principles and facts, but only to state those in which the highest authorities are agreed; and therefore we will pass by phrenology and mesmerism. But I must be allowed to make one or two remarks upon the manner in which these and some other subjects of a scientific nature have been treated both in this and other countries. As to the truth or falsehood of these subjects, I pretend not to decide. I have not studied them thoroughly enough, either to advocate or oppose them. But, unless we must discredit testimony which would be deemed sufficient to establish the truth in any other science, they do present us with many curious and remarkable facts, which, to say the least, are explained with great difficulty by ordinary scientific principles. Now, what, in such a case, is the course which every true philosopher ought to take? Evidently, if he follow Newton and Bacon, he ought to examine those facts calmly, and with a scrutiny proportionate to their anomalous and marvellous character. The philosophy of those facts is a subsequent matter, and should be left untouched till facts enough are collected to force the mind to theorize; and very possibly, in this case, the real philosopher would decide that he could do nothing more than to collect facts, and leave posterity to form the theories. But how different from all this has been the course pursued in respect to phrenology, mesmerism, and spiritualism! On the one hand, many have become violent partisans for the theories before they could be half acquainted with the facts, and have set themselves up as leaders and oracles in these sciences before they had strength enough to sustain for a moment the panoply of philosophy. On the other hand, it has been maintained that the facts respecting these sciences could not be true, because they conflicted either with the principles of sciences already established or with those of religion — thus virtually declaring that nothing new can be learned respecting mind or matter. On these grounds, an appeal is made to the strongest prejudices and passions of human nature against the claims of the new sciences; and a popular odium is thus excited against those who cultivate them. The mass of men become afraid of such as innovators and enemies of religion; and it requires not a little moral courage and attachment to science to induce a man to pursue his investigations in the face of so much obloquy and illiberality.

But to return from this digression. In treating of comparative anatomy and physiology, already have I glanced at the domains of zoölogy, and brought before you some objects from the great menagerie of nature. A few statements, therefore, respecting the number of species and individuals which her zoölogical gardens contain, with a short description of one most remarkable class, will be all that I shall attempt.

It is impossible to give an exact estimate of the number of species of animals on the globe that have been actually named up to the present moment, because I cannot have access to all the works where new ones are being continually described. A few years since, however, the number was as follows: —

Vertebrata.	Mammalia,	2,030
	Birds,	7,000
	Chelonians, (tortoises,)	120
	Saurian Lizards,	460
	Serpents,	300
	Batrachians, (frogs, &c.,)	175
	Fishes,	8,000
Articulata, or Entomozoa.	Vermes, (worms, &c.,)	770
	Crustacea, (lobsters, &c.,)	792
	Hexapoda, (insects,)	65,000
	Mollusca, (shells,)	11,482
	Radiata, or Phytozoa,	4,818
		100,947

Now, it is certain that this estimate must be very far below the actual number of species on the globe, especially in respect to the smaller animals. Thus it is stated by a late distinguished entomologist, Dr. Harris, that there are six species of insects to every species of plants. And since the number of species of flowering plants already described amounts to at least 60,000, the species of insects must approach half a million. Indeed, judicious naturalists suppose that the species of animals existing on the globe cannot be less than a million — perhaps more.

A few facts respecting the numbers of individuals in particular species of animals may give a still deeper impression of the extent of the animate creation. And here the recollection immediately recurs to those vast swarms of locusts that have sometimes laid waste entire kingdoms — shut out the sun, as their armies, several feet thick, and miles in width, flew through the air. Among fishes, perhaps the shoals of herring which annually migrate southward from the arctic seas are the most incredibly numerous. Often these vast bodies move in columns that are several leagues in width and many fathoms thick, and so close together that they touch one another, and sensibly impede ships; and this stream continues to move past any particular spot nearly all summer. In Norway, 400,000,000 are annually taken; near Gottenburg, 700,000,000; and by other nations, "numbers without number."

No less numerous are the tenants of the air. Captain Flinders saw a flock of sooty petrels pass over him, in Van Diemen's Land, which could not have contained less than 150,500,000.* But a flock of pigeons which passed over Mr. Audubon, on the banks of the Ohio, he estimates at no less than 1,000,115,000,000 individuals — which would require for their support 8,712,000 bushels of grain per day.† The gelatinous animals, called medusæ, often small and even

* Quarterly Review, 1814, p. 27.

† Jardine's American Ornithology, Vol. II. p. 196.

microscopic, swarm in the arctic seas, so as to give a color to the water for hundreds of miles; and a cubic foot of water, taken up indiscriminately, was found by Captain Scoresby to contain 100,000.* And he estimates that, if 80,000 persons had been counting since the creation, they would not yet have been able to number those that exist in the arctic seas at the present moment.† I have already stated that the wasp will multiply 30,000 fold in one summer. The queen of the termites, or African ant, will deposit 80,000 eggs in 24 hours. A cyclops, a species of insect, is capable of multiplying so prodigiously, that in four months her descendants would amount to 4500 millions. A single herring is capable of depositing from 20,000 to 37,000 eggs; a carp, 200,000; the tench, 383,000; and the flounder, 1,000,000. But the common oyster might produce 1,200,000; and if these were each to become a full-grown oyster, they would fill 1200 barrels.

The last tribe of animals, called animalcula, or infusoria, which are all microscopic, present examples of increase still more surprising. Indeed, the splendid discoveries of the Prussian naturalist Ehrenberg have disclosed a world of wonders in the microscopic department of nature no less astonishing than those brought to light by the telescope. He has described no less than 1000 species of animalcula, which swim in salt and fresh water, in many of the fluids of the living and healthy animal — in short, in all vegetable and animal substances, and in the atmosphere. The smallest of these animals are not more than one forty thousandth of an inch in diameter; and so thickly are they sometimes crowded together, that a small drop of fluid contains 500,000,000, or

* Roget, Vol. I. p. 143. † Kirby, p. 450.

nearly as many as the human beings on the globe. Formerly it was supposed that these animals were little more than simple particles of matter, endowed with vitality. But Ehrenberg has ascertained that they possess mouths, teeth, stomachs, muscles, nerves, glands, eyes, — and in short, all the important organs of the more perfect animals. Some species have from one hundred to two hundred sacs or stomachs connected with an intestinal canal; and the thickness of the membrane that lines these stomachs he estimates at one fifty millionth part of an inch.

The rate at which these animals multiply is prodigious. An individual of the *hydatina senta* had increased, in ten days, to a million; in eleven days, to four millions; and in twelve days, to sixteen millions. But this is moderate, compared with another species, which is capable of multiplying, in four days, to one hundred and seventy billions!

But perhaps the most remarkable facts remain yet to be mentioned. Minute as these animalcula are, they are covered with a case or shield, composed either of pure silex or oxide of iron; and when the animal dies, these shields are deposited at the bottom of the water. In this way, incredible though it may appear, have beds of silicious or ferruginous matter been accumulated, many feet thick, which has been sometimes changed in part into solid rock. The polishing slate, for instance, a kind of rotten stone near Bilin, in Germany, is entirely composed of these skeletons, 14 feet in thickness; and another bed of infusorial earth, near Lunenburg, is more than 28 feet thick. Yet it requires 41,000 millions of these skeletons to make a cubic inch, which weighs 220 grains. So that a single skeleton weighs the 187 millionth part of a grain. Many of the hardest minerals, such as flint and opal, have been found to be composed of the same remains; and bog iron ore is said to have a similar origin. A kind of silicious marl, similar to that from Bilin, exists probably in almost every town in New England, beneath peat bogs. In some places, in Massachusetts, this deposit, mixed with a little clay, is fifteen feet thick; and in Virginia are beds of fossil animalcula from twelve to twenty-five feet thick.

We have now arrived at the *ne plus ultra* of the animal kingdom, and yet who can tell what new mysteries will be unfolded by future improvements in optical instruments? I turn, therefore, to the vegetable world, — literally a flowery field, — and yet I shall have time to refer to only a very few facts, abundant as they are.

A moderate estimate of the number of species already described in the vegetable kingdom makes it 69,403. Of these, 9100 are flowerless, and their structure is cellular; such as mosses, lichens, fungi, and sea weeds. 60,303 have regular flowers, and they have a vascular structure. Of the latter class, 10,629 are monocotyledons, and 49,674 are dicotyledons.

The largest known flower is the *Rafflesia Arnoldii*, a parasitic plant, a sort of vine, that bears a flower three and a half feet in diameter, growing in Sumatra.

Microscopic plants are no less abundant and remarkable than microscopic animals. Indeed, many of those which I have described as belonging to the infusoria are regarded as plants by some of the ablest naturalists.

In the Alps, as well as in high latitudes, the snow has sometimes a red color; and it is found to proceed from the presence of a minute fungus, the *hæmatococcus nivalis.* The snow seems to be the soil natural to its growth. It is said to be associated with living infusoria, which die when the snow melts.

A still more remarkable fact is, that fermentation is, in most cases, the result of the growth of a fungus called the *yeast plant*, the *vinegar plant*, &c., or *torula cerevisiæ*. The cells of this plant multiply rapidly by the decomposition of the substances in a state of fermentation, and hence the evolution of carbonic acid. The cells of this yeast plant are from one twenty-four hundredth to one three thousandth of an inch in diameter. Whether the process of digestion in the animal stomach consists of the same process, does not yet seem to be determined; but there is certainly great similarity in the processes. Should digestion come into the same category, it would be indeed a marvellous development.

Crystallography and mineralogy might furnish abundant materials for my subject; but want of time compels me to pass them by; and I can only add a few things from geology — a science so abounding in marvels that a late popular writer denominates his work on that subject the Wonders of Geology.

A careful examination of all the rocks in the earth's crust, accessible to man, results in the conclusion, that the whole crust of the globe — at least several miles thick, and probably to its centre — has undergone an entire change, and most of the rocks several changes, since their creation. The unstratified rocks, which probably form the whole of the interior of the globe, have been melted, as all admit. The stratified class, lying above the unstratified, have been worn from the latter, and then deposited in water. Afterwards, they have been solidified by heat, and some of them so nearly melted as to become crystallized, constituting the metamorphic rocks. The loose materials now covering the surface have also been subsequently worn off by atmospheric and aqueous agencies, from whatever rocks were exposed. So that probably no particle in the earth has now the form in which it was originally created. How different this from the common views of the earth's condition!

A second conclusion, forced upon the practical geologist, is, that the continents of our globe have been for long periods, and most of them several times, beneath the ocean, and have been subsequently elevated from thence, or the waters have been drained off. At least two thirds of these continents are covered by rocks, thousands of feet thick, abounding in the remains of sea animals and plants, which lived near where they are now found, and could not have been drifted far. To accumulate materials, with their fossil contents, several miles thick, must have required immense periods of time. The fractured and upturned condition of most of the older rocks proves that they have been elevated by some internal force, acting vertically or laterally, to form continents. But in some places the strata, especially the newest, have never been disturbed, and in such cases it seems most probable that the waters have been drained off. Again, we have evidence often of the subsidence of the same continent that had long been above the waters, and then a second emergence. Nay, three, and even more vertical movements of this sort are sometimes shown by the geological monuments. Indeed, we have proof that existing continents are now experiencing similar changes, in some places rising, and in others falling, yet so slowly as to be unnoticed, save by the most careful observation.

These vertical changes have not been effected without causing a vast amount of erosion at the earth's surface. While the continents were below the ocean, this work was aided in high latitudes by enormous icebergs, charged with boulders, and driven by the currents along the surface, grinding down its salient parts, and sweeping along the abraded materials, even hundreds of miles from their original beds. The grooves and polished surfaces thus produced still remain in such countries as the northern parts of the United States, Scotland, and Scandinavia, wherever the rock has not been decomposed, and the huge boulders lie every where strewed along the course of these ancient icebergs.

As the continents rose, lakes and rivers would be formed, whose currents would bring together and accumulate those large deposits of sand and gravel, which in our country show themselves in the form of old beaches, ridges, and terraces, which can be found at least two thousand feet above the present ocean, and which attest unequivocally the former presence of the ocean, and the gradual drainage of the land.

The amount of abrasion by these various causes has been very great. In Great Britain, — in South Wales, for instance, — nearly ten thousand feet in thickness have been worn away. Indeed, it is a moderate estimate to say that more matter has been swept into the ocean from England and Scotland than now remains above the waters. The same is doubtless true in this country, although the observations here have not been so accurately made.

How deeply interesting to every ingenuous mind must it be to trace out on the earth's surface the marks of these stupendous and wonderful changes! They lie scattered along every man's path; yet how few have an eye open to see them! How many would prefer the baseless visions of romance to these mementos of the earth's wonderful history!

But geology has other wonders. Wherever on the globe the temperature of deep excavations has been ascertained, — and the experiment has been made at hundreds of places in Europe and America, both in mines and Artesian wells, to the depth of two thousand feet, — the heat has been found to increase at the mean rate of one degree for every forty-five feet. At this rate, water would boil at the depth of a little more than a mile, and all rocks would be melted at the depth of sixty miles. Shall we, therefore, conclude that all the internal parts of the earth are actually in an incandescent, melted state? Many of the ablest geologists have not seen how they could escape this conclusion, especially when they see how it explains the spheroidal figure of the earth; also the phenomena of active and extinct volcanoes; the protrusion of the unstratified rocks; the numerous elevations of mountains and continents that have taken place, and the fact that a tropical climate once prevailed in the northern regions of the globe, even to the arctic circle. Besides, it has been proved by the profound mathematical researches of Baron Fourier, that even though all the internal parts of the earth, below the depth of eighteen or twenty miles, are five hundred times hotter than boiling water, — that is, in a melted state, — it would not increase the temperature at the surface more than one degree in two hundred thousand years. So that even if such be the case, it cannot sensibly affect the climate. Although, therefore, it would be presumptive to say that this doctrine of internal heat is as well established as the Newtonian doctrine of gravitation, yet every candid mind will acknowledge that it bears the strongest marks of probability, and that it lacks but little of being placed among the settled principles of science. And yet what an immense and startling conclusion!

Still more certainly demonstrated is another related conclusion, viz., that the whole globe in early times was in a melted state, and has been slowly cooling ever since. It is certain that its internal parts are now at a higher temperature than the surface, and that the planetary space around the earth is as low as 70° below zero on Fahrenheit's scale. The laws of heat show, therefore, that the process of refrigeration must be now going on, and however little heat now escapes, it increases as we run backward through past ages, until we reach a period when it must have been great enough to have melted all known substances. And that such a state of things once existed, the character of the rocks demonstrates. For it is agreed on all hands that all the unstratified formations were once melted. Almost equally unanimous is the opinion that the stratified rocks, whether crystalline or sedimentary, were derived chiefly by abrasion from the unstratified. The spheroidal figure of the earth, exactly such as would be taken by a fluid globe revolving with the velocity of the earth, confirms this conclusion. And so do the facts as to the tropical and ultra-tropical character of the organic remains in the older rocks in high latitudes. Original fluidity and subsequent refrigeration are seemingly the only theory that will explain the elevation and subsidence of continents and mountain ranges. Moreover, the slow passage of worlds from a liquid and even a gaseous to a solid state, seems to be a law of the material universe. So that really the evidence appears to be overwhelming, to prove the early igneous fluidity of the earth. And scientific men will not long hesitate, if some of them now do, to place this among the demonstrated verities of philosophy, as the basis of reasoning in physics and in religion.

But after all, probably the history of the remains of animals and plants, found buried hundreds and thousands of feet deep in the rocks, and often converted into stone, is generally regarded as the most interesting part of geology. In Great Britain the rocks containing these relics are from ten to eleven miles thick, and in this country much thicker. Not less than 30,000 species of animals and plants have already been found in the rocks; and with the exception of a few near the top of the series, chiefly in clay and marl, they are different, often widely, from those now living on the globe; and hence the conclusion seems irresistible, that the fossil species must have lived and died before the present races had a being. Moreover, on comparing together the remains in the different groups of rocks, they are found to be so entirely unlike as to prove that they could not have been contemporaries; and hence the conclusion is, that several successive groups of animals and plants have been created, and after occupying the earth for a long period, have been destroyed to make room for another group, better fitted to the altered condition of the surface; and that at least five or six changes of this sort took place before the creation of man and his contemporaries. Nor do geologists suppose that this view conflicts with revelation. For although Moses fixes the date of the creation of the present races of organic beings on the earth, which appeared about 6000 years ago, he does not fix the time of the creation of the globe; which he says took place in the beginning, — a term perfectly indefinite as to time, — and therefore between that event and the appearance of men upon it, immense periods might have rolled away, during which the fossil races might have lived and died. And that those periods must have been immensely long, no one conversant with the details of geology can doubt, although the proof cannot be here given. What enlarged and refreshing views does this theory exhibit to us of the plans and benevolence of the Deity!

Another interesting conclusion on this subject is, that when these fossil animals and plants lived, the climate of these northern regions must have been tropical, or even ultra-tropical. They are often much larger than their representatives of the same races that now live between the tropics ; and often perfect giants compared with the pygmy races that are now found in northern regions.

Perhaps the most remarkable animal of the saurian tribe was the iguanodon — an enormous reptile that lived on land and fed on vegetables, and resembled the iguana of the West Indies. The average length of this animal was thirty feet, and its circumference fourteen feet. I thought it might give a more impressive idea of this reptile to exhibit a drawing of it of the natural size. (*Exhibited in the lecture.*)

I have no doubt but this drawing gives a tolerably accurate idea of this huge animal, although of course less perfect than if the living specimen had stood before the artist. It shows you what sort of inhabitants had possession of Great Britain before the Anglo-Saxons. The largest analogous reptile now living there is only a few inches in length. How different must have been the climate and vegetation of that country from what they now are, to nourish such monsters ! I do not think there is any evidence that this animal was very ferocious and savage, and therefore I have had his organ of benevolence drawn large. Nevertheless, I confess that the drawing strongly reminds me of Milton's description of Satan : —

> "With head uplift above the waves,
> That sparkling blazed, his other parts besides
> Prone on the flood, extended long and large,
> Lay floating many a rood, in bulk as huge
> As whom the fables name of monstrous size,
> Titanian or earth-born, that warred on Jove ;
> Briareos, or Typhon, whom the den
> By ancient Tarsus held, or that sea beast,
> Leviathan, whom God of all his works
> Created hugest that swim the ocean stream."

In the valley of Connecticut River especially, but also in

several other places in this country, and in Europe, the tracks of a large number of animals have been found in the sandstone, and some of them are of an extraordinary character. In Massachusetts and Connecticut, not less than sixty species have been brought to light, twelve or fifteen of which were made by four-legged, but the rest by two-legged animals; and some of these must have been as gigantic and heteroclitic as any that have been disinterred in any country. Some of them appear to have been three-toed birds, with feet sixteen to eighteen inches long, with a stride from four to six feet. Another was a biped, with four toes, and a foot about twenty inches long — apparently a two-legged frog, with a foot two or three times as large as that of an elephant! Another track indicates an animal with three forward toes some fifteen inches long, and a small hind toe; and though a biped, its tail has left a distinct trace on the rock. Such animals have no representatives among living races, yet they were once common along this river.

With what interest and enthusiasm does the antiquary open and attempt to decipher and arrange the mutilated rolls of some ancient papyrus that has just been brought to light, and whose contents reveal a new and an earlier chapter in a nation's history, or tell of the former existence of some race before unknown! Shall not the geologist be pardoned if he indulges some of the same feelings when he discovers and can read, even though imperfectly, archives of far more ancient date, bring fresh before his mind races of animals, new and peculiar, that tenanted the globe untold ages before man became its possessor? If an event becomes more interesting the farther it is thrown back into the past, geological facts must in this respect take the precedence of all others. For the most ancient event in chronology — the six days' work of creation — I had almost said is the most recent in geology. From thence we wander back through a duration which can be measured only by the succession of events, and not by chronological cycles, except to ascertain from existing agencies that the intervening periods have been vastly long. Then, too, the records, which the geologist digs from the rocks, of animal and vegetable existence at immeasurably remote periods, are often as fresh as if intombed yesterday. Their most delicate parts — even the eye in some instances — are as perfect as when the animal was alive, and the footmarks, which he sees following one another in succession, are as distinct as those of living animals passing over the mud or snow before his eyes; while the pattering of a shower, that fell on the same surface thousands of ages ago, is as fresh before him as if every drop had been instantly petrified.

How many millions of men have spent their days, and finally sacrificed their lives, in order to leave some memento of their labors that would go down to posterity! and yet not a vestige of their existence remains upon the earth! But the birds and reptiles that passed over the surface long before the globe was fit for the residence of man, have left marks of their transit which can never be effaced. The proudest monuments of human art will moulder down and disappear; but as long as there are eyes to behold them, the sandstone of the Connecticut valley will never cease to remind future generations of the gigantic races that passed over it when in a half formed state.

> Reptiles and birds, a problem ye have solved
> Man never has — to leave a trace on earth
> Too deep for time and fate to wear away.

It would be appropriate to my subject to indulge the imagination, for a few moments, in viewing science prospectively; that is, in predicting from its past history its future triumphs. But I am admonished that your patience has already been severely taxed, and can, therefore, only allude to a very few prospective applications of science to the welfare and happiness of society.

Notwithstanding the wonders which steam is accomplishing in our day, whoever will compare the description of tho first steam engine invented by the Marquis of Worcester, in 1663, with those which now sweep with giant strength over land and sea, will be satisfied that it has still greater triumphs to achieve. But the chemist is conversant with several agents of analogous character, but of far greater power; and he cannot but confidently expect that the time is not distant when some of these will take the place of steam; because safer, more powerful, less costly, and more easily managed. Indeed, I know of but one thing, and that is the resistance of the air, that will prevent the attainment of a velocity by the locomotive and the boat indefinitely greater than that now attained.

If a lecturer twenty years ago had predicted what is now daily witnessed in hundreds of electric telegraph offices, he would have been looked upon as a visionary dreamer. I well remember how I trembled for my reputation as a sane man, when I uttered the following sentence, in a lecture written about the time of the earliest experiments with the telegraph by Professor Wheatstone in England, and Professor Morse in this country: "There is every reason to believe," I said, "that by Professor Morse's telegraph, which he has already tried over an extent of a mile or two, information will be conveyed as fast as a printer can set up types. So that were such a train laid between Washington and this place, [Salem,] the president's message, or any interesting speech, might be in print at an office here within an hour or two after its delivery." Such a result is now so constantly realized, that it has ceased to excite any special attention, and the civilized world are now confidently anticipating the time as near at hand when these marvellous wires shall encircle the globe, and two or three hours suffice to bring intelligence from the antipodes.

What we may reasonably anticipate from the extraordinary developments of photography, it is difficult to say. It would not be very strange, however, if by combining galvanism with photography, the same picture, which is sketched by the sun's chemical rays, should be engraved by electricity. Indeed, an approximation to such a result has already been attained.

Since chemists can ascertain the elements of the most useful substances, the prospect seems fair that they will be able to unite these elements yet more extensively than they have done, so as to form the substances. And, indeed, within a few years they have ascertained that linen rags, by the action of a cheap acid, will produce more than their weight of sugar, and that a coarse but palatable bread can be made of saw dust. Who can tell how soon the time may come when the poor man will only need to purchase a cord of wood to supply his family with bread during the winter? *

The fear has often been indulged that many of the colder countries of the globe must ultimately become nearly uninhabitable, from a failure of fuel. An application of a geological discovery in Germany has, it seems to me, thrown a gleam of light on this point. The rapid increase of heat as we descend into the earth, and the ease with which Artesian wells are formed to a great depth, led a manufacturer to bore

* Herschel's Discourse, &c., p. 48.

one, that he might bring warm water to keep his machinery free from ice during the winter. Not only did he succeed in this object, but by conducting the water in open pipes through his whole establishment, it gave off heat enough to render fires unnecessary. Is not here an inexhaustible source of heat accessible to human industry and ingenuity?

In my view, the most interesting thought connected with anticipated improvements in science and art, is the large amount of leisure which will be thereby afforded to the great mass of mankind for intellectual and moral improvement. But I do not believe that Providence will allow these discoveries to come out fully till men learn how to improve that leisure aright. For if they only foster idleness, they will prove a greater curse than a blessing.

But I forbear, lest I should seem to be venturing too far into the regions of the uncertain and the fanciful.

I have now presented before you specimens, selected from the different sciences, of the wonders which they can offer to the youthful mind, as a substitute for the wonders of romance. And can I doubt what will be the choice of every noble and ingenuous soul? Does it need any analysis of the labors of the most celebrated writers of fiction to make every one feel how infinitely superior is nature to all their fancies? And science is the history of nature — the history of the works of the Deity. And shall the inventions of man come into competition with the inventions of the Deity?

"O Nature! how in every charm supreme!
 Whose votaries feast on raptures ever new!
O for the fire and voice of seraphim,
 To sing thy glories with devotion due!"

It has not been my intention to make this audience acquainted with the sciences upon which I have touched. But I wished to give a sample of the wonders that will meet him at every step, who resolutely engages in the study of any department of science. I say a sample only; for the farther he advances, the more enchanting will the prospect become, and the richer and more plenteous the gems that will reward his search. But not so with the devotee of romance. Though for a time he may seem to be quaffing nectar, yet, ere long, to use the graphic language of inspiration, *it shall even be as when a hungry man dreameth, and behold he eateth; but he awaketh, and his soul is empty: or as when a thirsty man dreameth, and behold he drinketh; but he awaketh, and behold he is faint, and his soul hath appetite.*

Will it not be pardoned if one who for thirty years has been almost constantly engaged in the examination of nature should bear testimony, from his own experience, to the charms and pleasures of science? I know it would be vanity for me to pretend to a profound acquaintance with science, or to distinction in it. But I cannot feel that it is vanity to profess a strong attachment to it. Indeed, how ungrateful in me not to recommend with enthusiasm that which has spread before me so many and such delightful prospects along the path of life; which has furnished a delightful retreat from the agitations and vexations of the world; which has thrown so many gleams of light into the darkest part of my path; which has led me to many a clear and sparkling fountain, and permitted me to breathe an atmosphere of peace and happiness! Often have I known the time, when, through feeble health, the languid eye looked out with indifference, if not absolute disgust, upon all the ordinary objects of life; but never has a view of nature, dressed in the garb of science, failed to rally back the sinking powers, relume the leaden eye, and diffuse animation and joy through the soul. A distinguished writer of fiction and false philosophy, in chagrin and disgust, expressed a regret that he had ever been born. But leaving every thing else out of the account, I can bless the day in which I was born, because I have enjoyed so much in studying the works of nature. And when I see so many noble-minded youth placing all their hopes of earthly happiness, some in the hot strife after political distinction, some in the possession of wealth, equipage, and power, some in following the tasteless round of fashionable amusements, and above all, when I see some whose chief source of happiness lies in a devoted attachment to fictitious literature, how gladly would I win them into those fields of science, at which we have this evening glanced, and thus save them from the disappointment and disgust which I know they will ere long experience, and which may lead them also to lament that they were ever born!

Many, many are the bright eyes that are turned upon me at this moment; eyes sparkling with health and hope. Must any of these be palsied by the withering touch of such disappointment? O, if their possessors will not place their hopes of happiness in factitious and unnatural pursuits, but in a knowledge and a love of nature, they will have a refuge amid all the storms and fluctuations of life, and those eyes may be bright and sparkling even amid the frosts of age.

"O, how canst thou renounce the boundless store
Of charms which Nature to her votary yields ? —
The warbling woodland, the resounding shore,
The pomp of groves, and garniture of fields;
All that the genial ray of morning gilds,
And all that echoes to the song of even;
All that the mountain's sheltering bosom shields,
And all the dread magnificence of heaven: —
O, how canst thou renounce and hope to be forgiven!"

I would not undervalue other sources of happiness, which are mercifully provided for us in this world. I only wish to show that the pursuit of science, as a means of happiness, has strong claims upon the attention ; that it does not interfere with any other innocent enjoyment ; that it is able effectually to overcome that appetite for artificial excitement and dissipation which makes so many miserable ; that it furnishes in youth a rich fund of happiness ; to the man in middle life, a delightful relaxation from business and professional duties ; and that, unlike most other sources of enjoyment, the relish for it grows stronger by age, so that in advanced life, when the common objects of life cease to interest, those of science still possess the charm of novelty.

Let me not, however, be understood to imply that there are not pursuits and pleasures of a more noble and satisfying character than even those of science. I would not bring them into competition with the results of active benevolence and piety. But the two pursuits are not inconsistent with each other ; and he who chooses can make the pleasures of both his own. Such a man has reached the highest point of earthly happiness. For every wonder of science now becomes invested with the double interest of being beautiful in itself and an exhibition of divine wisdom. And then, what delightful anticipations crowd upon his mind ! He soon learns that even the veteran in science can obtain but little more than a glimpse of nature in this world, and that much cloud and darkness rest upon the brightest spots. Yet he knows that the works of the Deity will form objects of study in a future state, where nothing intercepts the pure rays of truth, and that those works are vast enough to fill and feast the soul through the round of eternal ages. Such hopes as these constitute the true nobility of man : —

"For how great
To mingle interests, converse, amities,
With all the sons of reason scattered wide
Through habitable space, wherever born!
To call heaven's rich, unfathomable mines
Our own! To rise in science as in bliss!
To read creation, read its mighty plan,
In the bare bosom of the Deity!
In an eternity, what scenes shall strike!
Adventures thicken! novelties surprise!
What webs of wonder shall unravel there!
What full day pour on all the paths of heaven,
And light th' Almighty's footsteps in the deep!"

YOUNG, N 6.

THE RELIGIOUS BEARINGS OF MAN'S CREATION.

And the Lord God formed man of the dust of the ground, and breathed into his nostrils the breath of life, and man became a living soul.
Genesis ii. 7.

SCEPTICAL minds are fond of selecting and giving prominence to those facts, historical or scientific, that have an unfavorable bearing upon religion. This is natural; and why should not the friends of religion sometimes illustrate subjects derived from the same fields, which strengthen our faith, and clarify our views of the great principles of natural and revealed truth? Guided by this principle, I propose this morning to discuss the religious bearings of man's creation.

Of this event we have two records; the one revealed, the other scientific. Let us look at the details of both, and then we shall be able to see the religious relations of the subject.

The scriptural account of man's creation is full, explicit, and peculiar; more so than any other event of the six days' work. I shall call your attention to a few only of the prominent facts therein developed; particularly such as have a parallel in the scientific history of our world.

1. *Revelation teaches us that man was the last of the animals created.*

None of them were produced till the fifth day, when the

waters were commanded *to bring forth abundantly the moving creature that hath life, and fowl that may fly above the earth in the open firmament of heaven. And God created great whales, and every living thing that moveth, which the waters brought forth abundantly after their kind, and every winged fowl after his kind.* At the beginning of the sixth day, *God* also *said, Let the earth bring forth the living creature after his kind, cattle and creeping thing and beast of the earth after his kind.* Next follows, as the closing act of the demiurgic week, the introduction of man.

If we turn now to the scientific history of our race, we shall find essentially the same account of its origin as revelation presents. If Science cannot say positively that man was the very last of the animals created, she can and does say, that he was among the most recent. The arguments to prove this point are exceedingly simple and satisfactory. The chief one is this: —

We find rocks in various places on the earth to have accumulated in the course of past ages, to the depth of eight or ten miles, and in them we find buried the remains of the animals and plants that lived at the different periods when the successive strata were formed. Many new species were introduced from time to time, but nowhere on the globe do we discover human remains till we rise to the newest formations; not in fact till we reach the loose covering of soil, clay, and gravel spread over the surface, and called alluvium, whose lower part has been more usually denominated drift, or diluvium. This deposit is never more than a few hundred feet thick, usually not over one or two hundred; and I know of no example in which it is pretended that human bones occur as deep below the surface as one hundred feet. Yet the whole depth of rock from which animal remains have been dug out is between 50,000 and 60,000 feet, and at least 30,000 species of animals differing from any now alive have been disinterred in the rocks. Yet man is not among them. But no reason can be given why he is not, had he lived in any of the periods before the alluvial; for his bones, being composed of the same materials as those of other animals, would be no more subject to decay than theirs; as is proved, in fact, by their appearance upon ancient battle fields, where they lie mingled with those of horses and elephants.

The precise period when man first appeared on earth has been a question of deep interest among scientific men, and their eyes have been wide open to every fact bearing upon the subject. In earlier times, when comparative anatomy was in its infancy, the bones of other animals were mistaken for those of man, and in one case a fossil man was announced quite deep in the rocks, which turned out, beneath the scrutinizing glance of Cuvier, to be a gigantic salamander; and the bones of mammoths were in Switzerland regarded as those of giants, and in England as those of the fallen angels. But since comparative anatomy has applied to fossil bones principles and modes of investigation little less certain than those of mathematics, every able geologist has abandoned the expectation of finding human remains below the superficial deposits, the lowest of which are, in a geological sense, very recent. In the words of Sir Charles Lyell, "If there be a difference of opinion respecting the occurrence in certain deposits of the remains of man and his works, it is always in reference to strata confessedly of the most modern order; and it is never pretended that our race coexisted with assemblages of animals and plants of which all, or even a large proportion of the species, are extinct."

It is well known that geologists have divided those loose

deposits that cover the surface, and are more or less confusedly mingled together, into two formations, the lowest called drift or diluvium, and the highest called alluvium. That human remains exist in the latter no one doubts, though it may be a question whether they fall into the class properly called fossils. But the main question is, Do any of these remains occur as low as the drift? On this question we shall find some diversity of opinion. But here let me make one or two preliminary remarks. The first is, that geologists are not at all agreed where drift ends and alluvium begins; so that what one calls drift, another calls alluvium. Nor do I believe it possible to fix a line of demarcation between them, just because no such line exists in nature. With Professor Pictet, Sir Charles Lyell, and others, I believe that we ought to consider drift and alluvium as forming a single series, and that life has not been interrupted, or entirely renewed, but only some species destroyed during its deposition.

Another remark is, that in my own opinion, the causes producing drift are still in operation, as well as those producing alluvium; and that, in fact, the two classes of causes have had a parallel operation from the first; and, therefore, the two formations should be regarded as contemporaneous, rather than successive. From the earliest times, glaciers, icebergs, waves of translation, and landslips have been forming drift, and are still forming it. And so the oceans, lakes, and rivers have ever been at work to deposit alluvium. I admit that these causes have not always acted with equal intensity, and that the greater part of drift is anterior to the great body of alluvium. But admitting any degree of parallelism in the operation of these causes, the discovery of human remains in drift does not necessarily show them to be of great antiquity. Their age can be settled only by settling that of the deposit in which they occur. Moreover, from this unsettled state of opinion as to these formations, it does not follow, because one observer announces human remains in drift, that others would admit them to belong to that deposit. When such announcements, therefore, are made, we should draw no inference as to the antiquity of the remains till the discoverer has told us what he means by drift.

I ought, perhaps, to add, that there is a like want of agreement among able writers in the meaning which they attach to the term *fossil.* Originally it included every thing, mineral as well as organic, dug from the earth. Says one distinguished writer, "Geologists now use the word only to express the remains of animals and plants found buried in the earth." — *Lyell.* Says another, "An organized fossil body is one which has been buried in the earth at an undetermined epoch, and has been preserved, or left there unequivocal traces of its existence." — *M. Deshayes.* A third defines a fossil as "every organized body, or vestige of it, found naturally buried in the earth's strata, in a state different from the normal and actual conditions of existence." — *M. D'Orbigny.* A fourth applies the word fossil to "every organic body found naturally buried in the earth, which has been preserved, or has left traces not doubtful of its existence; provided that the deposit in which it occurs has been formed under the influence of circumstances different from those now passing before our eyes." — *M. Pictet.**

Now, some writers have taken it for granted, that if they can only make out that man is found in a *fossil* state, he must have lived before Adam. But until the meaning of this term

* Traite de Paleontologie, par Professeur F. J. Pictet, Tome Premier, p. 17. See also *Lehrbuch der Geognosie, von Dr. Carl Friedrich Naumann, Erster Band,* p. 812. Dr. Naumann's views correspond essentially with those of Sir Charles Lyell.

can be made more definite than it now is, a fossil man is not necessarily preadamic. He may not even be antediluvian.

Let us now look briefly at the most remarkable examples of organic remains that have been thought to prove the great antiquity of the human race, if not geologically, yet chronologically considered.

In the British Museum, and the Royal Cabinet in Paris, are specimens of human skeletons from Guadaloupe, in solid rock, hard as marble. To a person unfamiliar with rocks, these seem very striking examples of fossil men. But in fact this rock is daily forming in all the West Indian Archipelago, by the cementation of fragments of corals and shells worn off and collected by the waves; and it is not probable that these individual specimens are more than a few hundred years old — the skeletons perhaps of Caribs or Galibis, who fought a battle on the spot where they were found, about the beginning of the eighteenth century.

The most numerous examples of human bones, supposed to be fossil, occur in limestone caverns, buried in mud, or stalagmite, with the bones of other animals, recent and extinct. Such cases are described in Greece, in several places in the south of France, in Belgium, in England, and in Brazil. The bones are usually separated from one another, and mixed up with those of extinct species of rhinoceroses, hyenas, bears, and other terrestrial quadrupeds, as well as with those of living species. Still more recently human remains have been found in the Suabian Alps, in connection with those of the mastodon, though I cannot say whether these occur in caverns.

Now, in regard to all such cases, several considerations should lead us to be very cautious in inferring that man, and the extinct animals found in such circumstances, were contemporaries. For, in the first place, these caverns were, for the most part, formed by subterranean streams, which carried the bones into them from without, and, therefore, those of widely different periods might have been mixed together. Again, earthquakes often produce great changes in these streams, and mix up confusedly alluvium and drift. Once more, such caverns have in various periods been tenanted by man; and there has he buried his dead, while succeeding generations have dug up their bones, and mixed them with those of the extinct animals. We need not wonder, therefore, that the most cautious geologists have hesitated to admit that in any of the cases yet described, the evidence compels us to believe that the human remains were deposited at the same time with those of extinct hyenas, bears, and mastodons. In the language of Sir Charles Lyell, "It is not on the evidence of such intermixtures that we ought readily to admit, either the high antiquity of the human race, or the recent data of certain lost species of quadrupeds."

In our own country several examples of fossil men have been announced, of late, with much confidence. At Natchez, it is said that a human pelvis was found in clay, beneath "a diluvial deposit;" in Florida, a jaw and foot in a conglomerate coral reef, limestone, said to be at least ten thousand years old; another beneath four ancient cypress swamps, near New Orleans, sixteen feet below the surface, whose period of sepulture has been put at 57,600 years ago.

Every practical geologist knows well how extremely uncertain are all such calculations of the time requisite to form an alluvial deposit of a given thickness; first, because we have so very few data for comparison, and secondly, because the work is so very different in some places from what it is in others. Moreover, the many causes by which the remains of recent animals might become mixed with the extinct ones, render it necessary to scrutinize all such cases as the above, with extreme care, before we can confidently assign a very high antiquity to these supposed fossils; and accordingly, most of the ablest geologists, who have carefully examined the facts in these examples, are not convinced of their reliableness.

But suppose we admit all that is claimed in the cases that have been stated, viz., that human remains do occur in such situations as to prove that man was a contemporary of some of the extinct races of animals — will this prove a higher antiquity to man than the Bible allows?

Not necessarily, I reply; for we have undoubted proof that since the biblical epoch of man's creation, several large animals have disappeared from the globe. In New Zealand, for instance, no less than eleven species of gigantic birds, and several other species in Madagascar, Rodriguez, and Bourbon, have become extinct, probably within a few hundred years. For we find their half burned bones mixed with those of man on spots which were once the scenes of cannibal feasts. How false the inference which should hence make these human bones of very great antiquity, because found among extinct animals! Again, the great mastodon of this country often occurs buried in our peat swamps, as at Newburg, only a few feet below the surface; and apparently, therefore, this animal did not perish till a very late epoch in the alluvial period; nor is it possible to show that it may not have been alive since the fifth day's work of creation. Should we then even find a human skeleton in the same deposit as that of the mastodon, we might still reasonably doubt whether it had a preadamic existence.

I trust that these details will not be regarded as inappropriate on the Sabbath, when it is recollected how important to my object it is to show from science the recent origin of man, and what strenuous exertions are made at the present day to establish his preadamic existence. I only regret that I cannot go more into details, but I feel as if the following positions were incontrovertibly established.

First, that the occurrence of human remains in drift does not certainly show man's preadamic existence.

Secondly, neither is it shown by finding his bones mixed with those of some extinct animals.

But thirdly, there is too much doubt still attached to all cases of the supposed antediluvian origin of human remains found in the earth, to allow any one to conclude certainly that they occur either in ancient drift, or among extinct preadamic races, except by accident.

Yet, fourthly, admitting their occurrence in such circumstances, it is still emphatically true, that according to science, man is among the most recent of the animals created, since his remains have never been found as low as 100 feet, while in the more than 50,000 feet of rock below, abounding with other animals, they are not found.*

* It may gratify some readers, if, in addition to the opinion of Sir Charles Lyell, in the text, I add that of a few other eminent geologists, whose writings happen to be at hand, respecting the time of man's appearance on the globe.

"It may be stated," says Professor John Phillips, "as a general admission, that man did not exist on the globe during the secondary and probably not during the epoch of eocene and pleiocene formations, and that sufficient evidence for his coexistence in northern climes with the mammoths and hippopotami is yet wanting; but as the races of oxen, horses, camels, &c., had then begun to exist, it is not, perhaps, an unreasonable expectation that, eventually, this question will be decided in the affirmative." — *Phillips's Manual of Geology*, p. 438. *London* 1855.

"Does man exist in a fossil state?" inquires M. Alcide D'Orbigny. "By consulting well-established facts, we have no doubt of the truth of the affirma-

2. *Man, according to the inspired account, was placed at the head of all creatures on earth.*

tive, particularly in the sense which we give to the word fossil. (See text, p. 196.) Now, since we admit man to be in a fossil condition, we may inquire to what epoch his remains belong. The last geological stages — the Subapennine and Fahlunien — which preceded the existing epoch, do they show any where traces of human remains either in marine or terrestrial deposits? We think we can reply in the negative; for no well-established fact will sustain the opinion that they do occur therein. Human remains are peculiar to caverns, or osseous breccias, or alluvions. It follows from thence that fossil human remains, whenever they have been carefully observed, are met with, in all cases, along with other beings of the existing epoch, and are fossil in contemporaneous deposits. Human bones are wanting entirely in the two last stages (geological) which have preceded our own." — *Cours Elementaire de Paleontologie et de Geologie, &c., par M. Alcide D'Orbigny. Premier volume,* p. 162. *Paris,* 1849.

"Have human fossils been found? Did man appear on the globe before the present epoch?" inquires Professor Pictet. "Such is the important question to which modern science seems to give a negative answer, although at various times it has been judged otherwise. The true question appears to me to be the following: What animals peopled Europe when man first appeared, and, by consequent, at what geological period can his origin be placed? All paleontologists, at this day, are agreed that there is no proof of his existence during the tertiary epoch or the anterior epochs. All who admit the view, which I have elsewhere exhibited, of the relations of the diluvial and modern epochs, will know also that this question may be treated without prejudice, and according to facts alone. I have shown, in fact, that we may probably regard these two periods as forming together a single series, during which life has been neither entirely interrupted nor renewed, at least in Europe; and during which partial, local, and successive inundations have deposited several formations, destroying only some species." After reviewing the facts, Professor Pictet concludes, "1. That man was not established in Europe at the commencement of the diluvial epoch; 2. That some migrations probably took place in the course of the diluvial period; 3. That the definite establishment of man in Europe, and the occupation of that continent by a numerous population, probably took place after the great inundation which deposited the rolled fragments in the caverns and on the plains of the continent." — *Pictet's Traite de Paleontologie, &c., Tome Premier,* p. 145 *et seq. Seconde edition. Paris,* 1853.

And God said, Let us make man in our image, after our likeness; and let them have dominion over the fish of the sea, and over the fowl of the air, and over the cattle, and over all the earth, and over every creeping thing that creepeth upon the earth. So God created man in his own image, in the image of God created he him, male and female created he them. And God blessed them, and God said unto them, Be fruitful, and multiply, and replenish the earth, and subdue it; and have dominion over the fish of the sea, and over the fowl of the air, and over every living thing that moveth upon the earth.

Who is not struck with the exalted character and office assigned to man in this passage by his Creator? And the features of his character that give him this preëminence are distinctly stated. It is not his physical organization; for though fearfully made in this respect, he is scarcely superior to some of the monkey tribe denominated quadrumanous, or even to the mammiferous animals. But his exaltation rests on his intellectual and moral powers. That rich sentence, *So God created man in his own image, in the image of God created he him*, is full of meaning and interest. The image of God! What is that? Who would dare apply such language to man, if God had not done it? A Being of infinite moral and intellectual attributes, immaterial and immortal, condescends to state, without qualification, that he has stamped his own image upon a creature of his hand, and therefore gives him dominion over all other creatures in the same world. If some of them show a spark of intelligence, not one discovers a single moral characteristic; and as to intellect, if any of them possess it at all, it is immeasurably inferior to man's. If the idiot and the long-degraded savage show a mental hebetude and grossness even inferior to many of the brutes, the proper inference is, not that the race are allied to the quadrumana, but that in such cases the development of mind is prevented by natural or artificial obstructions. On the other hand, the loftiest exhibition of mental and moral power which any of our race have exhibited may be taken as the measure of the intellectual ability of the whole race; because there is every reason to presume that, when man is freed from the fetters and clogs that now obstruct the full development of his powers, the mind now apparently the weakest will manifest latent powers equal to the strongest. God's own image is instamped on every soul; and though sin and sorrow may for a while mar it, or cover it with rubbish, yet when it is polished anew by a divine hand, it will shine forth in its original freshness and beauty. In a higher sphere, where the deteriorating influences of sin are not felt, it will be seen how worthy man is to wear the crown of this lower world.

If we place side by side sketches of the heads of the different races of men, beginning with the Caucasian, and passing through the Mongolian, the Malay, and the American, to the negro, we find marked and characteristic differences; and if we extend the comparison to the cranium of the orang outang, we seem to have proceeded only a little farther on a descending scale; so that, if we judge of the animal by its head, we shall be ready, perhaps, to conclude that the lowest type in the human series is only slightly elevated above the highest on the quadrumanous scale. But this is a false inference, if we look no farther than the physical organization. The most prognathous, thick-lipped Hottentot stands far above the semi-quadrupedal orang. Says one of our ablest American comparative anatomists,* "The organization of anthro-

* Professor Jeffries Wyman.

poid quadrumana justifies the naturalist in placing them at the head of the brute creation, and placing them in a position in which they, of all the animal series, shall be nearest to man. Any anatomist, however, who will take the trouble to compare the skeletons of the negro and orang, cannot fail to be struck at sight with the wide gap which separates them. The difference between the cranium, the pelvis, and the conformation of the upper extremities, in the negro and Caucasian, sinks into insignificance when compared with the vast difference which exists between the conformation of the same parts in the negro and orang."

But mere physical differences are of small consequence compared with such as are intellectual and moral. I shall not, indeed, take the ground that the inferior animals exhibit no traces of what we call mind in man — such as memory, imagination, volition, and reason. Admit, if you please, — what, in fact, seems to be almost beyond question, — that we do see evidence in brutes of the possession of mental faculties similar to those in man; yet who has so low an opinion of his own mental powers as not to see an immense disparity between the psychological characteristics of brutes and of men? The difference does not lie merely, or chiefly, in the original strength or weakness of these faculties. For if measured by such a test, we might well hesitate to ascribe a marked superiority to man; since in his infancy he is of all animals one of the most helpless, and with less of instinctive power than they, and with a tardy development of intellect, he really often appears to disadvantage by their side. But let time pass on, and while the brute makes scarcely no progress, you will see a surprising expansion and invigoration of the powers of the infant, as it rises to the stage of youth and manhood. Excepting in the case of idiocy or disease, you cannot stop, though you may retard, the expanding process; and by cultivation you may wonderfully accelerate and perfect it. But all such labor will be nearly wasted upon the brute. His instincts are capable of some improvement; but when you try your hand upon his mental powers, you will see at once that you have got no foundation on which to build. A few animals may, indeed, with great care, be taught to do some things mechanically; but their instruction consists chiefly in severe bodily inflictions, and fear and memory seem to be almost the only powers that are quickened; so that the feats which they perform manifest nothing almost of mental acumen. As to the power of abstraction, indeed, there is no evidence that the brutes are capable of it in any degree.

In order to see the immense intellectual disparity between man and the brutes, compare the attainments of the most remarkable specimens of the latter with those of the loftiest human genius in the full maturity of his powers. Suppose you call on the chimpanze, the gorilla, or the "half-reasoning elephant," to make the comparison: they are incapable even of understanding what you mean; and in that fact you see their vast inferiority. The entire field of what we call knowledge lies absolutely beyond their reach. You may subject them to the best discipline of which they are capable during their whole lives; and yet you cannot get them possessed of a single idea, either literary or scientific.

It may be said that the idiot, and even the Hottentot, or the negro of Central Africa, seem almost equally incapable of such ideas, and of drawing a comparison between themselves and the cultivated savant of civilized lands; and yet all these are men.

Of the idiot I shall speak shortly. But in respect to the Hottentot and the negro, it is not true that they cannot comprehend scientific truths. You have only to subject them to the culture that has been bestowed upon civilized man, especially if continued through successive generations, and not only shall they be able to understand science, but it may be to rise almost to the level of the Newtons, the La Places, the Leibnitzes, and the Cuviers of proud Europe. Africaner, while prowling with the lion and the hyena for his human prey, may be only a little the most sagacious brute. For, as Cicĕro says, "What is the difference whether a man take the form of a brute, or, having the figure of a man, show the savageness of a brute?"

But when Africaner has been subdued by the gospel, and learns to aspire after knowledge, he shows that early discipline was alone wanting to make him as well known for mental and moral excellence as he was for savage ferocity. But his former fellow-tigers and hyenas could neither be thus tamed nor educated. He shows himself possessed of an intellectual principle within, that exalts him far, far above them.

I admit that, as a matter of fact, a large proportion of the human family exhibit but a feeble intellectual development, and, in popular language, are justly represented as but little above the brutes. But even though the majority are thus degraded, are they to be taken as a measure of the mental power of the race, or shall we rather look upon the princes of the intellectual world as fair samples of what the whole race might become, if all obstructions were taken out of the way? I have already intimated that I am an advocate of the latter view. For we do know that the most powerful intellect is reduced to the weakness of infancy by the force of bodily disease; and that minds, seemingly weak in early life, have become strong when health was invigorated, and peculiar circumstances roused them to action. It is also true that a blow upon the head, producing some change in the brain, has been followed sometimes by an almost total loss of some of the mental faculties, and sometimes by their marked invigoration. We have cases, also, in which recovery from swoons that were supposed to be death, has been succeeded by the total loss for a time of all knowledge previously gained, until, all of a sudden, and preceded by some alteration in the brain, the mind has recovered in a moment all that it had lost.

From such facts, the inference is certainly plausible that the intellectual diversities among men may be owing to physical causes, rather than difference of original calibre. If changes of physical structure or condition do, in some cases, materially clarify and invigorate the mental powers, the presumption is certainly fair that, if all minds were brought into the same circumstances in this respect, they would exhibit equal power; and even idiocy, it may be, would be transformed into genius of the highest grade. If so, then may we take the most extraordinary developments ever made by renowned scholars as a measure of the intellectual dynamics of the race. And how immeasurably higher on the scale would such a standard place man than the most elevated point reached by the brute!

But man's chief glory lies in his moral nature — that is, in his power of distinguishing right and wrong, virtue and vice; instinctively approving of the one, and disapproving of the other; feeling a satisfaction when he conforms to the one, and dissatisfaction when he yields to the other. This power assimilates him more than any thing else to the Deity, whose approval of holiness and hatred of sin are infinitely strong.

Now, these moral faculties are entirely wanting in the brutes. They may be taught to perform certain actions, and refrain from others; but there is not the shadow of proof that they have any consciousness of right and wrong. Their actions are all prompted by instinct, or by the fear of punishment, or the hope of reward. There is no conscience within to approve or to condemn; nor have they any idea of a Moral Governor, who will reward virtue and punish vice. This, the grandest idea of which created beings are capable, is man's sole prerogative of all beings in this lower world, and it constitutes his highest distinction.

It may be said — and correctly, too, as I admit, though contrary to long-received opinions — that there are degraded races of men, who not only have no idea of any being superior to themselves, but no moral sense to accuse or excuse their actions; so that not even murder, or any other monstrous crime, will awaken the slightest self-condemnation;* and hence it is maintained that man's boasted moral nature is the result of conventional rules, and therefore not an original implanted power of divine origin. But the existence of moral feelings is too nearly universal in the human bosom, and too nearly identical in character in all hearts, to be referred to fluctuating human opinions. And the very few cases in which the moral sense seems to be wanting are explained plausibly by admitting that extreme degradation and unrestrained wickedness, committed from generation to generation, can so sear the moral sensibilities that they seem utterly dead for a time. Nevertheless, let the truth be poured in upon such a soul, with an accompanying divine influence, and moral life will be again awakened, whose cords shall vibrate to the slightest touch.

But not so with the brute. By no process can you awaken

* See Moffat's Southern Africa, pp. 89, 177, 182, &c., sixth edition.

or create moral sensibilities in his nature. Indeed, the idea of exhibiting moral truth to a brute is ridiculous. Writers of a certain school of material philosophy do, indeed, speak of the *morale*, as well as the *physique*, of the lower animals. But it is a monstrous perversion of language, and would not be employed by any one who has any just ideas of the exalted nature of the moral faculties.

3. *According to Scripture, the creation of man was a miraculous and unusually important event.*

Observe in what different terms the creation of man is described from that of the inferior animals. When God would introduce the latter, he said, on the fifth day, *Let the waters bring forth abundantly the moving creature that hath life, and fowl that may fly in the open firmament of heaven.* And God said, on the sixth day, *Let the earth bring forth the living creature after his kind, cattle and creeping thing, and beast of the earth after his kind; and it was so.* Here the command appears to be directed to the earth and the waters, to put forth a power for the production of these organic races; and it might be argued, perhaps, with some plausibility, that this power was inherent in the elements, and not communicated with the command. Thus, instead of a miracle, it might be only a development by natural laws of the germ of organic existence in elementary matter. But when we come to the creation of man, intervening agencies are set aside, and the object seems important enough to demand the direct agency of Jehovah. Nay, he uses the plural form of expression — the language of sovereigns when from the midst of counsellors they issue their mandates. God speaks as if in council, and says, *Let us make man in our image, and after our likeness.* Then he is described as having put forth his power to execute his decree: *So God created man in his own image, in the image of God created he him.* In the next chapter, where the inspired historian recapitulates the work of creation, he uses a form of expression no less dignified and impressive : *And the Lord God formed man of the dust of the ground, and breathed into his nostrils the breath of life, and man became a living soul.* One cannot but notice in all these passages how differently man's creation is described from that of the inferior animals. To produce them, God merely directs agencies already in existence to do the work; and the simple fact of their creation is stated. But to create man, he comes forth, as it were, from his hiding place, and, taking in his hand the dust of the ground, he moulds it with divine skill, and then breathes into it a portion of his own mental and moral life, and then fits up paradise to receive this emanation of his skill — this image of himself. If this was not a miracle, if it was not a stupendous miracle, revelation contains none, nor can language describe one. I am awed, when I read the lofty description of man's creation in Genesis. There is a fulness and dignity about it which I find connected with no other event in Scripture. It impresses me with a sense of man's original elevation and importance in the scale of being; and though he has fallen, I do not forget that his mental characteristics remain essentially unchanged, and that by the work of redemption his moral powers may be reinstamped with the divine image.

No less distinctly does science, or rather natural religion founded upon science, teach the miraculous origin of man.

To speak of miracles as taught by natural religion is, indeed, a new feature in theology. But it is a neology that has a scientific basis, and a most favorable bearing upon the whole system of religious truth. For what is a miracle? What else but an event inexplicable by the ordinary laws of nature, and which therefore demands special divine interference to bring it about? Now, then, the question is, Can the creation of man be explained by the ordinary laws of nature? Science shows unequivocally that there was a period when he did not exist on this globe; nay, she can nearly fix the epoch of his appearance.

Was he brought in by natural law? There is, indeed, a dreamy hypothesis that attempts to explain the origination of organic beings by the inherent force of law. But to explain thus the appearance of a moral and intellectual being as unique and exalted as man, has so ridiculous an aspect to common sense, that the boldest scepticism, with perhaps a few exceptions, dare not directly advocate it. It is so obvious that some new and special power must have been concerned in his creation, that unbelief is baffled and confounded — just as it would be now if another being, as much superior to man as he is to other animals, should start into life before our eyes.

But it is said that, after all, man's creation, like every other great event of the universe, must have taken place according to law; for how absurd to suppose God ever to act without law! that is, without a settled principle of action; and if an event is conformed to law, does it not take away the idea of special divine power? In other words, is not a miracle, according to the common understanding of the term, an impossibility?

I fully admit that there is a law of miracles, as well as of common events; but this law may contravene, intensify, or weaken nature's ordinary laws, and therefore it requires God's wisdom and power to introduce and give it effect. It is an alteration of the established course of things; nor does the fact, that God acts according to fixed rules, make such a change any the less special and designed to meet a particular exigency.

Now, of all the events which science shows to have transpired on this globe, none bears upon it so distinctly the marks of special miraculous power as man's introduction. The records of the earth's past history, engraven on its rocky strata, do indeed show us other events, and even economies of life, which miraculous power can alone explain. But as man is confessedly placed at the culminating point of all terrestrial economies, and forms, indeed, the crown of this lower world, his introduction is not only a miracle, but the most glorious of all miracles earth has ever witnessed. Nay, though I cannot fathom creative power in any of its manifestations, I confess that the mystery of producing dead matter out of nothing does not seem greater than to take that matter and mould it into a living man, and then unite with it intellectual and moral powers, such as ally this creature to its Creator, and require an immortal existence for their development. It seems to my mind to be the crowning exercise of infinite wisdom and infinite power, and therefore the most wonderful of all miracles.

Such is the parallelism between the facts of revealed and natural religion, as to the creation of man. It forms a solid and firmly compacted basis, on which we may erect some inferential truths of no small importance.

My first inference from this discussion is a presumptive argument in favor of the Mosaic chronology.

I refer to the chronology of man and contemporary animals; for it is well known that in respect to the chronology of the matter of the globe, many regard the Scriptures as not responsible, because they do not give the date of its origin, but only say that, *In the beginning, God created the heavens and the earth.* And in regard to the date of man's creation, compared with the advent of Christ, as well as of many intervening events, particularly the antediluvian, it has long been known that there is room for a diversity of opinion, amounting to some thousands of years, according as we follow the Hebrew, the Samaritan, or the Septuagint text; so that when I speak of a presumption from my subject in favor of the Mosaic chronology, I mean, in favor of its general accuracy. Whichever system of biblical chronology we follow, the creation of man and existing animals was comparatively recent; and science teaches the same lesson, although geological periods cannot be reckoned definitely by years.

Perhaps it may be thought that a coincidence so general, between the scientific and revealed records, is of small importance. But I judge otherwise. For undesigned coincidences are among the best of collateral proofs of the truth of Scripture; and in this case, the coincidence is as exact as the nature of the case will admit. Had there been discrepancy on this subject, how eagerly would it have been seized upon to throw discredit upon biblical chronology! This is a point against which scepticism aims its deadliest shafts. It is pleasant, therefore, to find our confidence in the accuracy of Scripture history strengthened by the record which we find instamped upon the rocks.

My second inference enters a protest against those materialistic views, widely prevalent at the present day, which sink men, or at least some varieties of men, almost to the level of the brutes.

It is not strange, perhaps, that such views should be adopted, when we look at some of the prevailing systems of anthropology. It is first assumed that the size and shape of the cranium determine the intellectual and moral character;

and since some of the races in this respect approach certain brutes, it is inferred that in character they approximate as nearly as in phrenological development. For the next step is to deny, or at least to doubt, the existence of any thinking principle in man, independent of matter, and of course the mental and moral calibre will depend upon the size, delicacy of organization, and facile action of the brain. The third step is, to take the ground that the different races of men are not mere varieties, but distinct species, with plurality of origin. The Caucasian is always placed at the head of the species, and the negro at the foot. According to the theory, the inferior species are incapable of elevated ideas or religious emotions. "Lofty civilization," says a recent writer of this school, "in all cases has been achieved solely by the Caucasian group. The black African races, inhabiting the south of Egypt, have been in constant intercourse with her, as we prove from the monuments, during four thousand years; and yet they have not made a solitary step towards civilization — neither will they, nor can they, until their physical organization becomes changed. No line can be drawn between men and animals, on the ground of reason. Did space permit, I could produce historical testimonies, by the dozen, to overthrow the postulate which claims for certain inferior types of men any inherent recognition of divine Providence — an idea too exalted for their cerebral organizations, and which is fondly attributed to them by untravelled or unlearned Caucasians, whose kind-hearted simplicity has not realized that diverse lower races of humanity actually exist, uninvested by the Almighty with mental faculties adequate to the perception of religious sentiments or abstract philosophies, that in themselves are exclusively Caucasian." *

* Types of Mankind, pp. 461–463.

How diverse are such views of the human family from those presented in the Bible! *And God said, Let us make man in our image, after our likeness. So God created man in his own image, in the image of God created he him. He hath made of one blood all nations of men to dwell on all the face of the earth;* and Christ commanded his disciples to *go into all the world, and preach the gospel to every creature.* At last, however, physiologists have found out, by an examination of the crania, that "diverse lower races of humanity" have never been invested by their Creator with the mental faculties adequate to the perception of religious sentiments, which belong exclusively to the Caucasian race.

These degrading views of the human family are also contrary to the lessons of experience. For two hundred years, at least, almost countless experiments have been tried by able, conscientious, and persevering men, upon every variety of our race, to see if they were capable of intellectual and moral culture. To this work, thousands upon thousands of devoted missionaries have consecrated their lives; and from every quarter of the globe — from the wigwam of the American Indian, the mud hut of the African negro, and the kraal of the Hottentot, as well as from the burrow of the Greenlander, and the cities of the semi-civilized Mongolian — the same testimony has been sent back. Not only are all these races capable of such culture, but vast multitudes of the young have shown nearly as much intellectual power and susceptibility to religious emotions as the Caucasian race, and have been reclaimed from their savage state, instructed in the arts of civilization, and have lived the life and died the death of the Christian. Yet all this evidence passes for nothing with the anthropologists to whom I have referred. With them a single degree more or less in the facial angle, a half inch added to, or subtracted from, the circumference of the cranium, or a shade lighter or darker in the color, weighs more than the testimony of a thousand missionaries, whom they speak of as unlearned Caucasians, whose "kind-hearted simplicity" renders them incapable of judging of the intellectual and moral ability of those among whom they spend their days.

But finally, these degrading views of man are contrary to self-consciousness. I will admit, if you please, that in bodily organization I am paralleled by the quadrumana. But I am conscious of intellectual and moral powers within me, which, although now intimately linked to matter, and perhaps may be, in some other form, forever, are still distinct from matter, independent of it in nature, and raising me immeasurably above all forms of organization, and every being not possessed of like powers. If, by my physical structure, my animal life and instincts, I am allied to the brutes, by my higher faculties I am assimilated to my Creator; and I glory in the thought that I was made in his image. In such a nature there can be nothing defective, or degrading, but sin. This, I acknowledge, has made dreadful havoc with my nobler powers. But the fair columns erected by an infinite Architect still stand with their entablatures and arches, and I look with confidence to the same divine hand to clear away the rubbish and the defilement, and to make the whole temple more beautiful and glorious than even Eden could boast. For I look forward to an immortal existence, and to a state of sinless perfection — nay, more, to the society of holy angels and communion with the infinite God. In the conscious possession of such powers and aspirations, which ally me to all that is exalted and noble in the universe, how instinctively do I recoil from views which make thought and conscience mere functions of the brain, to perish, of course, with organization!

My third inference derives from this subject a refutation of the most plausible arguments for atheism and pantheism, and presents a new argument for the divine existence.

There are two points which atheists consider their strongholds; the one is the eternity of the world, and the other the eternal succession of processes and races. And so long as they could be met only by abstract metaphysical reasoning, they could not be fairly driven from these coverts. But the fact of man's creation cannot, by the utmost ingenuity, be woven into conformity with these dreamy hypotheses. Had it been made known only by revelation, atheism would have evaded its force by denying the authority. But science, teaching the same fact, cuts off this subterfuge. Or did not both these records give so very recent a date to the human species, unbelief might have hidden itself behind the veil of antiquity. But now the fact is too firmly established to be denied, that the most perfect and exalted of all terrestrial races was introduced, probably, the latest of them all; and thus is demonstrative evidence furnished of a direct and special intervention of wisdom and power such as no being but God possesses. Suppose, then, you admit the eternal existence of matter, and even the eternal succession of the lower animals; still you have in man's creation as imperious a necessity for a Deity, as the origination of matter, or any of its other modifications, would demand. And it must be a personal Deity, not a mere blind force pervading nature, such as pantheism admits; for to create man, infinite wisdom, as well as infinite power, must be brought into exercise.

The argument from the design, every where apparent in nature, for the divine existence, requires an admission that the existing processes and races had a beginning. But this the atheist denies, as we have already seen, and not without some degree of plausibility. Yet in man's creation we have a work demanding an infinite Deity, accomplished within a definite period. It is not, indeed, the original creation of matter, but rather its re-creation, with the bestowment of the higher principles of life and intellect. It may be regarded, therefore, as a new argument for the divine existence, or rather, perhaps, the old argument cleared of every difficulty, and having the freshness and transparency of demonstration.

My fourth inference derives from the subject a refutation of the wide-spread doctrine of creation by law, and of the unmiraculous development of the higher from the lower forms of organic life.

This hypothesis, though old as Democritus, and finding a lodgment occasionally in the brain of here and there a cloistered sceptic, has never till our day assumed a popular dress, and ventured forth to gain the attention of the crowd, and become the theme of discussion in the place of public resort, and even by the fireside of private life. La Place first attempted to show how suns and systems might be formed from eternal matter in a nebulous state without a Deity. Next, the French naturalists, improving upon Democritus, described the process by which inorganic matter became organic, in the lowest and simplest degree; and, finally, with the aid of Anglo-Saxon sceptics, they traced the development of the vital particle called a monad in its upward progress, through higher and higher tribes of animals, till, finally, even man was evolved from the quadrumana, by what was called "a tendency to improvement" and "the force of circumstances." And all these changes depended, not upon miraculous intervention, but upon the operation of laws eternally inherent in nature; so that the hypothesis may properly be denominated *creation by law.*

To sustain these views, appeal has been made to almost every department of nature, especially to those parts over which, through difficulty or defect of investigation, obscurity still hangs. But though unsustained by any department of science, it seems to me that its absurdity is eminently manifest from the creation of man. The mere attempt to state the process by which the orang outang is converted by natural law into the human species can hardly fail to excite the smile of common sense. But if the views presented in this discourse are true, it will excite a sigh, rather than a smile, to find that reasonable and intelligent men have no higher idea of the intellectual and moral nature of the immortal mind than to suppose it capable of derivation by a natural process from the orang outang — nay, from a vitalized, but scarcely organized monad. How strange, how impious even, to talk of the evolution of God's image from a quadrumanous brute! Make out, if you please, a near corporeal relation; but who that is not himself brutalized can try to bridge over the wide gulf between man's higher nature and the most sagacious brute by that abused and ill-understood phrase, a law of nature?

My fifth inference not only removes all presumption against Christianity as a miraculous dispensation, but furnishes a strong presumption in favor of the miracles of revelation.

We have seen that the most remarkable miracle of the Bible, the creation of man, is also a miracle in the history of science, and the most striking, too, of all the miracles in that history. It contains others — such, for instance, as the creation of the inferior animals. But I would fix my eye, at this time, solely on man. From the dust of the ground I see him start into life in the full perfection of his powers, and with a nature so much superior to that of any other terrestrial creature as to preclude the idea of any connection, save that they all belong to the same great system of organization. Philosophy is utterly baffled in attempting to explain by any known laws and processes of nature the derivation of such a being from any preëxisting races. Strive as she does to avoid it, she is forced to the conclusion that special divine wisdom and power must be called in to explain such a phenomenon. So long as revelation alone asserted the recent origin of man, scepticism could imagine his existence in an endless series. But now that the earth itself has opened its mouth to confirm the testimony of revelation on this point, miraculous power alone can solve the great problem of his existence.

And what a host of sceptical doubts and surmises, which have long been fastened as vipers to the hand of Christianity, does that one great miracle of nature paralyze! so that, instead of seeing her fall down dead, as an unbelieving world have long expected she would, they now behold her shaking them off, and feeling no harm. The moment you bring the famous cavil of Hume respecting testimony, or the mystic hypothesis of Strauss, or the shadowy dreams of the anti-supernaturalists, or the fancied inspiration of the infidel spiritualists, into the presence of this one great fact of man's miraculous creation, they fall flat upon their faces, like Dagon before the ark of God. A miracle once admitted in the history of nature, and all presumptions against analogous miracles in Christianity vanish like fog before the sun. Nay, more, we obtain a positive presumption in favor of all which revelation describes. The ponderous metaphysical and rationalistic tomes that have been written to disprove the miraculous character of Christianity, and their equally voluminous replies, now lose their potency, and we may suffer them to pass into the limbo of forgetfulness.

If these things are so, then may I add, as another inference, that we gain from the whole subject a presumptive proof of the truth of revelation.

If science had been discrepant to revelation in relation to the creation and character of man as much as it is now in agreement, it surely would have been seized upon as casting suspicion upon Christianity. Why, then, should not these remarkable coincidences strengthen our conviction of its truth? When the writer of Genesis placed man's creation on the last of the demiurgic days, who told him that when the earth's rocky archives should be deciphered man's registry would be found only near the close of the long roll? When he represented the work as eminently miraculous, who told him that the science of the nineteenth century would teach the same? And when he placed man at the head of creation on earth, who told him that psychology and ethics would make the same classification? Who told him? How natural the conclusion that it was the same infinite Instructor whose hand laid the foundations of the earth, filled it with life and beauty, and who therefore could not be mistaken in its history!

In view of this whole discussion, may I not add, in conclusion, that it furnishes an instructive example of the use that may be made of natural religion by the minister of the gospel?

Imperfectly as the subject has been presented, may I not presume that my hearers feel that the teachings of science, in relation to man's creation and character, do lend a strong confirmation of the biblical account, and that this united testimony throws much light upon several important principles in the theory of religion? I have touched, however, upon only a single point, where natural and revealed theology meet; and doubtless other points, equally prolific of important instruction, lie along the line of junction, waiting only careful investigation. And is not this sort of research what the spirit of the present age demands? Infidelity has long since claimed the testimony of science as on her side; and I fear that too often the expounders of revealed theology have half admitted the claim, and felt that the less they had to do with natural religion the better. But this jealousy of the religious bearings of science is entirely unfounded; and if ever she has seemed to speak against revealed truth, it was ventriloquism, and not her natural language. Let the preachers of the gospel diligently explore the fields of natural religion, and many a rich gem of truth shall reward their search, which, polished by the hand of learned piety, shall sparkle even in the fair crown of Christianity. To preach Christ crucified should be, indeed, their chief aim and effort. But if they would be workmen that need not be ashamed, they should be able to draw the illustration and defence of the truth from the whole field of nature, as well as of revelation. And whether they seek responses at the shrine of God's word, or his works, or his providence, they will find unity, harmony, and mutual corroboration. The rays of truth coming through these different media may, indeed, be of different colors; but they will be found sweetly blending into one unbroken bow of light, painted on the retiring cloud of error and sin, and presaging the glories of earth's latter day.

THE CATALYTIC POWER OF THE GOSPEL.

The kingdom of heaven is like unto leaven, which a woman took, and hid in three measures of meal, till the whole was leavened.

Matthew xiii. 33.

It is not often that the discoveries of modern science elucidate and make more impressive the language of Scripture. The text, however, is one of these rare instances. It describes, indeed, a very familiar process, — that of bread making, — which, as a practical matter, has been known from very early times. But the principles on which some parts of the operation depend are even yet among the most recondite in chemical science. Something is known of them, however; and although the person who is acquainted only with the process of leavening bread must be struck with the peculiar force and appropriateness of this illustration, yet the man acquainted with its rationale cannot but realize it more deeply. I shall feel justified, therefore, in spending a few moments in scientific details, which would be appropriate to the chemical lecture room; nay, I should feel condemned if I did not take this course, because I am confident that I can thus make the beauty and force of this passage more obvious and impressive. And in doing this, and introducing a few technical phrases, I hope my hearers will not charge me with pedantry, till they have heard me through. Gladly would I avoid these scientific details, could I in any other way bring out the full strength and appropriateness of the text.

The phrase *kingdom of heaven*, in this passage, demands a passing exegetical notice. The radical idea contained in it, as well as in the cognate expression *kingdom of God*, is that of dominion or government. Even when it means heaven itself, as it sometimes does, this original idea clings to it; for in heaven, the most prominent manifestation of the Deity will be through his government. In the New Testament, however, this phrase often designates the reign of the gospel dispensation; and hence it very naturally is sometimes put for the principles of the gospel. Such seems to be its precise meaning in the text. Christ evidently meant to say, that the truths of the gospel, when brought into contact with society, operate like the leaven of the bread maker, when mingled with the dough.

And how, precisely, does this operate? Chemistry, to some extent, informs us. It is an example of those changes in bodies, which, for the want of a better name, is called *Catalysis*. This term embraces a great variety of decompositions and recompositions, which are not explained by the common principles of analysis and synthesis. In catalysis, the mere presence of a certain body among the particles of another produces the most extensive changes among those particles; and yet the body thus operating is itself unaffected. Thus a stream of hydrogen poured upon a piece of platinum will take fire — that is, unite with the oxygen of the atmosphere through the influence of the platinum; and yet that metal will remain unaltered.

In cases of catalysis, more analogous to the example referred to in the text, the substance itself, which is the agent of the change, is in a decomposing condition. This is the case with leaven, or, as it is sometimes called, ferment or yeast. One sees, from the commotion among its particles, that a change is going on in its internal condition, and that new compounds are forming out of its elements. Introduced in that state into the meal, it communicates a change to the whole mass, analogous to that which it is itself experiencing. This is called fermentation. In bread, it is not allowed to proceed very far, but is arrested by the heat of the oven.

It is found that the remarkable power of leaven to change the character of compounds depends on a peculiar principle which it contains, called *Diastase*. This substance is so powerful in its action, that one part of it, mixed with two thousand parts of starch, will change the whole into sugar in a few hours.

It had long been a great mystery how so small a quantity of one substance should be able to effect such a change upon so large a mass of another. But the discovery that leaven in its active state contains a fungous plant, which multiplies with prodigious rapidity, and is sustained by the matter into which the leaven is introduced, furnishes an explanation. This *yeast plant*, as it is called, consists of myriads of cells, scarcely more than one three thousandth of an inch in diameter; and it has the power of converting sugar into alcohol and carbonic acid, and finally into vinegar. All the steps of the process by which the starch of flour is changed into these various products may not be fully understood; but it seems settled that the starch affords the nourishment to the plant, at least in all ordinary cases of fermentation.

The history of catalytic changes, then, furnishes us with two principles of importance in elucidating the text. The first is, that it needs but a very small quantity of leaven to produce a complete change in a very large amount of farinaceous matter. The second is, that it is only necessary to start the process of change in one or a few spots in the mass, where the particles of the leaven happen to be, in order to have it permeate the entire heap. It is not necessary that a particle of the leaven should actually come in contact with every particle of the mass. It need only commence a process in one spot, which will spread of itself through the whole, or at least to a great extent.

To return now to my text, — such a power does Christ declare the gospel to possess. *The kingdom of heaven is like unto leaven, which a woman took, and hid in three measures of meal, till the whole was leavened.* Hence I take for my subject on this occasion, *The Catalytic Power of the Gospel.* I wish to show that wherever that is cast into the dead and inert mass of human society, it shows a quickening, expanding, and multiplying power possessed by no other human institution.

In order to avoid misapprehension, let me premise one or two remarks. Because I shall attempt to show that gospel truth has a mighty power over the human heart, let no one imagine me a disbeliever in the necessity of a special divine influence to give that truth success. In that doctrine most cordially do I acquiesce; and when I speak of a peculiar efficacy of the truth, I assume that the conversion of men is *not by might, nor by power, but by the Spirit of the Lord of hosts.* My only object is to show that the truth, in itself, possesses a peculiar adaptedness to win its way and transform society. And surely it will encourage our efforts, as well as make us feel more deeply our obligations, to learn what an admirable instrument God has put into our hands with which to labor.

Let us now look at the evidence of the catalytic power of the gospel.

In the first place, such a power is derived from the adaptedness of the gospel to human wants.

How well adapted it is to promote the temporal welfare and happiness of man, may be seen by comparing the condition of society in Christian lands with that of heathen and Mohammedan countries. So striking is the contrast, that truly and literally we may say of Christianity, it has *the promise of the life that now is, as well as of that which is to come.* But it is mainly of man's spiritual wants that I speak at this time. For though felt more or less by all, and by many with great intensity, they are met and satisfied nowhere save in the gospel. Yet how purblind men are to this panacea! They search for remedies every where else. They run the whole round of sensual gratification in the vain expectation of relief; but they find only a bitter aggravation of their sufferings. They toil for wealth, for honor, for power, and perhaps are eminently successful. But the void in their hearts is only made larger and more painful. They resort to social enjoyments, or to learning, or to splendid worldly enterprises; but all in vain; the terrible craving of their nature continues, and, like the cast-out unclean spirit, they *go through dry places, seeking rest, yet finding none.* They resort finally to deeds of charity, to self-mortifications, and to the rites of a religion of forms; and here they fancy they must find peace. But if they do, it is only a false and a transient peace — the peace of self-delusion, not the peace of God. And when some trying exigency of life overtakes them, the visor drops from their eyes, and the cheated soul within cries out in anguish for something to lean upon in the hour of suffering and of death.

Such are the vain phantoms which most men pursue through all their days, urged on by the deep, restless, unsatisfied wants of their nature. Nor does one in a thousand fancy that he is walking in a vain show, until God's Spirit opens his eyes to see the plague of his own heart. He is amazed and overwhelmed by the view. Such deep and dreadful depravity, pervading his whole nature, he never once suspected. He can live with such a heart no longer. Ah, he sees now what he wants, and, prostrate in the dust, he cries out, *Create in me a clean heart, O God, and renew a right spirit within me.* His prayer prevails. He rises a new creature in Christ Jesus. The aching void in his heart is filled — filled with divine love and divine peace. He is saved by the washing of regeneration and the renewing of the Holy Ghost. He has found, at last, the grand panacea which nature could never discover.

"This remedy did wisdom find
To heal diseases of the mind,
The sovereign balm, whose virtues can
Restore the ruined creature, man."

During the preparatory process that goes before regeneration, as well as in the act, the peculiar adaptedness of another great doctrine of the gospel to human wants is made most manifest. The man is deeply conscious of having broken the law of God; and when he is made to feel how reasonable that law is, and how holy, he does not see how he can be pardoned. The law only condemns him, but discloses not one gleam of hope. He looks around solicitously for some way of escape. He inquires whether he can himself make any offerings to God that will be a ground of pardon. Especially may not the sacrifice of animal life avail? To such sacrifices have men in all ages and countries resorted, either by the promptings of instinct or revelation. And it shows, at least, how general is the conviction of men, that sin cannot be pardoned without some expiation made by a substitute. But a voice from the Scriptures replies, *It is not possible that the blood of bulls and of goats should take away sin.* The sinner sinks down in despair at this announcement. How well prepared, then, to receive another, issuing from the same inspired record! — *The blood of Jesus Christ cleanseth us from all sin. Christ being come, a high priest of good things to come, not by the blood of goats and calves, but by his own blood, he entered in once into the holy place, having obtained eternal redemption for us.* The great central truth of a vicarious atonement gradually opens upon his agitated mind. At first, he sees it only dimly and doubtingly. But, ere long, his heart perceives that here is the divine remedy for its otherwise hopeless case. Here, *mercy and truth meet together; righteousness and peace embrace each other.* Thus *God can be just, while he justifies the believer.* Faith can doubt no longer. It rushes to the cross, and pardon, peace, and holy joy succeed to anguish and despair. The most pressing want man ever experiences — the desire of forgiveness — is thus fully met; and ever after, the pardoned sinner, addressing his Saviour, exclaims, —

"E'er since by faith I saw the stream
  Thy flowing wounds supply,
Redeeming love has been my theme,
  And shall be till I die.

"Then in a nobler, sweeter song,
  I'll sing thy power to save,
When this poor lisping, stammering tongue
  Lies silent in the grave."

The character of the Being who made the atonement is another doctrinal point most wisely adapted to the wants of man. Whatever may be said as to those engaged in intellectual pursuits, and accustomed to abstractions, the great body of men have ever associated some material or human characteristic in their idea of God. And the Old Testament, out of regard to this want of human nature, has made most of its representations of the Deity quite anthropomorphous. But it is in the character of Jesus Christ that this want is most fully met. In that character, the divine and the human are so beautifully blended as to invite confidence without destroying veneration. Had it been said only that the *Word was with God, and was God*, man would feel as if there were an infinite gulf between him and his Saviour. But when it is added, that the *Word was made flesh and dwelt among us*, the idea of a common nature draws us to him, and especially when he calls us his brethren, and declares that he was tempted in all points as we are, for the very purpose of affording succor to them that are tempted, and to stand as our Daysman, our Advocate and Intercessor, our hearts can no longer resist the appeal, and we approach the throne of grace boldly, because we know that we have a sympathizing Friend to plead our cause. And yet he is an almighty Friend; and what more can we ask? No wonder that the heart cleaves to such a Saviour with a supreme and undying love.

"Clothed with our nature still, he knows
The weakness of our frame,
And how to shield us from the foes
Whom he himself o'ercame.

"Nor time, nor distance e'er shall quench
The fervor of his love;
For us he died in kindness here,
For us he lives above."

It is hardly strange that to the acutest minds, unenlightened by revelation, this world should seem to be a hopeless enigma; or that it should be looked upon as a state of retribution, and that the half Christian Manichee should imagine two supreme principles, one of good and the other of evil, holding with each other an everlasting war. But there are two doctrines of revelation that solve the dark riddle, and show to the eye of faith the full-orbed glories of the Divine Benevolence behind the thickest clouds. One of these doctrines is, that the world is in a fallen condition, and because sin has entered it, suffering has followed; so that, in fact, *the whole creation groaneth and travaileth together in pain.* The other is, that God's providence sits watchfully above the whole scene, and so controls every event, that the final result shall be happiness and glory. It is wonderful how these truths resolve the most agitating doubts, and anchor the soul to a rock amid the fiercest tempests of life. Faith does not fear but that infinite power, wisdom, and benevolence will bring order out of confusion, peace out of discord, holiness out of pollution, and everlasting happiness out of temporary misery. She can see how wisely adapted even the evils of life are to the moral discipline essential to a fallen being. And when the tempests howl around, and the billows come pouring over her, it is enough for her to *know that all things work together for good, to them that love God.* She has reached that happiest condition of human existence, unreserved submission to the will of God.

Springing from such a system of doctrines, cordially embraced, there are hopes and consolations such as nothing else can give. All other hopes and consolations fail to satisfy; but these leave nothing to be desired. The man does not cease to be interested in this world, but he is more interested in another. The consciousness that his eternal future is safe makes every blessing the sweeter which he receives on his way thither; and it also lightens every labor, and neutralizes every trial. So near to immortal and unalloyed happiness, of how little consequence to him are the short-lived inconveniences he meets in his brief sojourn below, especially when he knows how necessary his trials and labors are to prepare him for eternal joy! O, if such a man has not within him the elements of happiness, they cannot be found on earth. Daily the manna falls from heaven around him; and even in the thirsty desert, he can smite the rock, and the cool and refreshing waters will gush out. And he knows that, when he comes to the banks of Jordan, the waters, touched by the wand of faith, will divide for his passage.

Such is the wonderful adaptation of the gospel system to human wants. How could it do more to fill and satisfy them? Now, my argument is, that whenever men are made conscious of their spiritual wants, and such a gospel is made known to them, it will be eagerly embraced. And if embraced by a few, they cannot but make it known to others; and thus, if no untoward influences prevent, will the whole mass at length be leavened. It does, indeed, meet with a powerful obstruction in human depravity; and were it unadapted to the necessities of man, it could make no progress; but now it has a catalytic power, which enables it to find its way through the sluggish mass.

In the second place, man's conscience testifies to the truth of the gospel system, and thus prepares the way for its admission to the heart.

Of all the powers of the human soul, conscience has suffered least from the blasting influence of the apostasy of the race. The corrupt heart is able to make every other faculty its pander and slave; but conscience always stands erect and unsubdued, ready to lift her voice in defence of the right, and to rebuke the wrong. Her mouth may, indeed, for a time, be forcibly closed, and her sensibilities blunted, by the hot, searing iron of iniquity; but her internal vitality remains unaffected; and when, at length, her liberty and vigor are restored, her retributions will be terrible.

Now, it is an interesting fact that unperverted conscience is a stern advocate for evangelical religion. Tell an unconverted man that his heart is deceitful above all things and desperately wicked, and his pride and self-sufficiency will resent the charge; but his conscience knows it to be true. Tell him that with such a heart he could not be happy in heaven, and that therefore he must be created anew in Christ Jesus, and his corrupt inclinations will muster a stout defiance against the mortifying truth; yet the faithful inward monitor often compels him to acknowledge its reality. Hence you will often see the strange anomaly of a man confessing his utterly lost condition by nature, and his entire unfitness for heaven without a new heart, and yet so bolstered up by pride and self-sufficiency, that he feels little anxiety, and makes no efficient efforts to change his condition.

Again, in spite of all the struggles of perverted reason, conscience often compels men to acknowledge the justice of the penalty annexed to sin. Sophistry may enable them to make out a very clear demonstration of the inconsistency between divine benevolence and eternal punishment. But conscience compels them to acknowledge that they deserve it. They know that, with such wicked hearts, they could never experience any thing else but punishment; and they are conscious of having done nothing to lay God under obligation to give them a better heart; so that, without his interposition, eternal misery follows as a natural consequence.

But though thus dependent upon God's grace, conscience will not release them from their obligations to love and serve him; for that faithful and keen-eyed observer testifies that their inability arises from a perversion of the powers which God has given them, and not from any natural defect; and therefore they are as much bound to love and obey their Father in heaven as a perverse child is to exercise filial affection, and do service to his earthly father.

In this dilemma, how strenuous an advocate for the doctrine of special grace does conscience become! Instead of pleading the sinner's apology on the ground of inability, and striving to release him from obligation, she charges him with having crippled himself, and therefore as lying under the full weight of responsibility to the divine law. Yet how certain to perish, if the special power of God do not interpose!

In the human conscience, then, we have a powerful instrumentality for the diffusion of the gospel. Once let the leaven of its great principles be brought into close contact with that conscience, and, in spite of the hostile influence of pride, selfishness, and passion, it will rouse and transform the torpid soul, and make it henceforth alive to duty and to God. That soul will, in fact, *become a new creature in Christ Jesus, old things having passed away, and all things become new.* But such a perfect network of sympathies is human society, that you cannot change the feelings and character of one individual, and not send a like influence into the hearts of those around him. Let one man's conscience be roused to do its office, and his neighbor's conscience cannot be wholly quiet. So numerous are the points of contact between men, that no one can remain long wholly ignorant of a moral change in his neighbor, nor unaffected by it when known. Thus through the force of conscience a self-propagating power is imparted to religious reformations. Once start the process in a particular spot, and conscience will become the catalytic agency to transmit it from individual to individual, we cannot tell how widely.

In the third place, the history of Christianity shows it to be possessed of an extraordinary catalytic power.

Recall to mind the circumstances under which the gospel was first introduced. Its Author, a poor, persecuted wanderer, chose twelve illiterate fishermen for his council, his heralds, his body guard, and his successors in propagating his system of truth among men. The whole world, too, stood armed to the teeth to resist its introduction. All its prejudices, its social, political, religious, and even its military power, was ready to be arrayed against the gospel; and, in fact, all these forces were employed to arrest its progress, and to root it out of the world. Ten times within three hundred years did the mighty Emperors of Rome assail Christianity with fire and sword. And they felt sure of a triumph; for how could a few feeble, contemptible fanatics, without wealth, power, or influence, resist an array that had conquered the world? But how little did these worldly-wise rulers know of the inherent vitality, the self-sustaining and self-propagating power of the gospel! So that, in fact, while they supposed they were giving the finishing blow to the system, it was silently and irresistibly working its way into the hearts and affections of all classes of the community, till at length, in the beginning of the fourth century, it became the established religion of the empire.

Perhaps you will say this was the effect of the miraculous agency that was manifested in the church in apostolic times.

This might have had some influence in the first introduction of Christianity; yet far less, even then, I apprehend, than is generally supposed; for it is usually quite easy to get rid of the influence of a miracle by imputing it to imposture, jugglery, and delusion, as we know was done in those days. But it is not settled whether the power of working miracles was possessed by any after the days of the apostles; certainly that power was withdrawn a century or two before the days of Constantine. Nor have we evidence that there was any thing peculiar in the divine influence which was exerted upon the hearts of men in primitive times. It seems to have operated then, as now, according to the established laws of mind, and in proportion to the means employed. Furthermore, we have the testimony of the Bible to the position, that men are no more apt to be convinced by miracles than by the ordinary truths of the gospel; for *if they hear not Moses and the prophets, neither would they be persuaded though one rose from the dead.* We must, therefore, impute the extraordinary success of the gospel in early times, and in the midst of fiery persecution, mainly to its adaptation to human wants and the human conscience.

In subsequent periods of the world's history, this same experiment has been often repeated. And it has ever been true that the kingdom of heaven cometh not with observation. No loud trumpets have sounded its advent; no powerful array of means has ushered it in. A few obscure men, without money or influence, and perhaps with little of worldly wisdom or policy, unarmed saved by the Bible and faith, have gone into the arena of conflict, like David to meet Goliath. And so inadequate have the champions and their weapons seemed, that the world have looked upon them with as much contempt and derision as Philistia's giant did upon

David. And yet the despised pebble has found its way to the giant's forehead, and the Galilean has conquered.

Take Great Britain, for an example. The conquests of that kingdom by Julius Cæsar, by the Saxons, the Danes, and the Normans, are all on record, and constitute distinctly-marked epochs of history. But who can tell us when and how Christianity won its more thorough and enduring conquest, penetrating where the arms of the Roman, the Dane, and the Saxon could not reach, and converting tribes of the rudest heathen into civilized and Christian men? It is, indeed, said that Augustine and a few other monks were once sent as missionaries to Britain; but how feeble an instrumentality to accomplish a work a thousand times more extensive and important than all the conquests to which Britain has ever been subject, or which she has made by her arms since her political existence began. Had there not been an unseen, self-propagating power to carry forward the work, begun only in here and there a spot by humble missionaries, the whole mass could never have been so thoroughly permeated.

The same fact exhibits itself when we compare Christian with pagan or Mohammedan nations. In the latter you meet with much more of the external manifestations of religion than in the former. Temples, images, processions, public prayers, and other rites, are rife every where; but, after all, you perceive that little influence, save an injurious one, is exerted in such countries upon the public morals, manners, or welfare; yet, in Christian lands, it is manifest that an influence has gone deeper into the public heart and conscience; and hence you find more kindness, amenity, and decency, more of civilization, and respect for morality and piety. The rude and ferocious elements of human nature are more tamed and moulded by Christian influences than by pagan or Mohammedan.

I believe this is true of all nominally Christian lands, although we must confess that, in many of them, the gospel has been well nigh deprived of its vitality, and little more than its external covering remains. But even there Christianity exerts a decidedly better influence than the most refined system of human invention. Moreover, we may impute whatever of good moral influence is exerted by Mohammedanism to the principles — and these are not few and unimportant — which it has purloined from the Bible.

Again, you will find that just in proportion as Christianity has been corrupted, and the Bible is withheld from circulation among the people, will the literary, civil, social, and moral condition of a nation be degraded. Suppose you had the power to pass suddenly from such a country as New England, or Old England, or Scotland, into Austria, Russia, Spain, or France. Would you need a geographer to tell you that you were in a land where a withering blight had come over the pure gospel? While you would meet crucifixes, oratories, cathedrals, chapels, and confessionals every where, you would find the Bible nowhere. And while you would hear *Te Deums*, and chanted prayers, and the praises of the virgin and the saints in all places of worship, and on all days and hours, you would listen in vain for unadulterated gospel truth at any time. And while the antiquated walls of monasteries and convents would meet you in every place, the academy and the school house would be wanting in all places. And when you became acquainted with the character of the great body of the population in those lands, you could not doubt that the gospel, which you had seen doing so much in the country from which you came to elevate, enlighten, and bless, was here shorn of the lock of its strength, and had been moulded and trimmed to adapt it to systems of superstition, ignorance, intolerance, and despotism.

The whole history of the missionary enterprise, foreign and domestic, affords decisive proof of the leavening influence of the gospel. To mere worldly wisdom, the most striking feature of that enterprise is the total inadequacy between the means employed and the expected results. When a man, who has been accustomed to estimate the amount of outlay and preparation requisite in any successful undertaking in commerce, manufactures, or agriculture, or who knows the amount of effort necessary in a successful political campaign, — when such a man looks at the very slender instrumentality which the ablest missionary societies employ for the conversion of the world, it seems to him a want of wisdom amounting to infatuation to go forward. Why, men are more tenacious of their false systems of religion than of any thing else; and yet you send one, or two, or half a dozen plain, powerless men among twenty or fifty millions, and are disappointed if, in a few years, you do not hear of numerous conversions.

Alike inefficacious do such feeble instrumentalities appear to the heathen and the Mohammedans themselves! And this is one of the grounds on which missionaries are allowed to pursue their work unmolested in countries most hostile to their plans. Imagine, for instance, that the Emperor of China, or the Shah of Persia, or the Sultan of Turkey should learn that one, or two, or even half a dozen unarmed, inoffensive men had taken up their abode in Canton, or Oroomiah, or Constantinople, with a view to preach the doctrines of Christianity, and to teach the principles of human science and literature to the young. Do you think that either of these despots would have any fears excited that the established religion of the country was in danger? Would he not treat the suggestion with contempt, and look on the missionaries as deluded men, whose efforts to proselyte would be harmless, and whose literary instructions would be valuable to the empire, and therefore their residence might be tolerated? And if a British minister would be gratified by having these teachers protected, how ready would he be to issue the decree which should place them and their followers on a footing with their other Christian subjects. But let these rulers learn something of the catalytic power of the gospel, by seeing multitudes converted, as if by a mysterious influence, and you would see the sword of persecution unsheathed and martyrs multiplied. And it is mainly because such conversions have not been in general extensive enough to arrest the attention of rulers, that persecutions by the government are so infrequent. I fear that they are yet to put the faith and courage of the church severely to the test. For by and by, heathen and Mohammedan nations will learn that the leaven of the gospel, hid in the community by the humble missionary, has, unperceived, sent its transforming power through the whole torpid mass, and that their false systems are crumbling into ruins.

A still more manifest example of this mighty though unnoticed influence is often seen in our own land, when the domestic Missionary Society sends its benevolent agencies into some waste place where iniquity is triumphant. In such a place are found, it may be, a few humble Christians, but the wealth, the fashion, and worldly influence are all hostile to the truth; and when the missionary calls around him the few followers of Christ at the prayer meeting and in the church, it only makes matter for amusement and ridicule among others, who, in view of the apparent feebleness of the instrumentality, exclaim, with Sanballat and Tobiah of old, *What do these feeble Christians? Will they revive the stones out of the heaps of the rubbish which are burned? Even that which they build, if a fox go up, he shall even break down their stone wall.* But the despised leaven silently operates; God's Spirit comes down to urge the movement forward, and the great mountain that seemed so strong crumbles down and becomes a plain. The gospel triumphs; decency and refinement of manners take the place of obscenity and vulgarity; temperance succeeds to drunkenness; peace to discord; thrift and enterprise to decay and poverty; and spiritual religion to errors of every name. Yet so quietly was the change effected through the gospel's catalytic power, that opposition and scepticism stand amazed.

From this principle of the self-propagating power of the gospel, thus established, we may derive inferences of great importance, and eminently adapted to encourage and strengthen those engaged in the missionary enterprise, whether domestic or foreign. Indeed, since the recent rapid expansion of our population across this broad continent, these terms, domestic and foreign, have become nearly synonymous.

In the first place, this subject should inspire us with strong confidence in the power of divine truth.

The current of worldliness often sets so strongly against the truth, and the means appointed for its diffusion seem so simple and inadequate, that we are apt to be disheartened, and to forget the mighty power which the doctrines of the gospel possess to work their way amid obstacles, and become mighty through God to the pulling down of strong holds. But when we recollect what that truth has done in time past, how it has transformed whole nations as if by magic, how at this moment, abused and perverted as we know it to be, it makes Christian nations stand out on the world's panorama so conspicuously, and when we think of its wonderful adaptation to the deepest wants of man, and what a stern advocate it finds in the human conscience, and especially how thorough is the renovation of the individual who gives himself up entirely to its influence, we ought to be ashamed of our distrust of its power, and to feel that we have in our hands an instrument which, by God's blessing, can and will create anew and sanctify our lost world. So that wherever we have an opportunity to bring the gospel in contact with the human conscience and reason, we ought to urge its claims with as undoubted an assurance of its efficacy as a woman exercises when she hides only a modicum of leaven in three measures of meal.

Secondly, the subject is full of encouragement to those who are laboring in weakness with great obstacles and discouragements, in the dissemination of the truths of the gospel.

Let them remember that the leaven, when mixed with the meal, seems to be lost, and little or no visible effect is produced, until at length it is found that the whole loaf is thoroughly leavened. Let them remember, too, that the pure gospel, when brought in contact with men's consciences, is as sure to commence a catalytic process there, as good leaven is in the meal, although without special grace it will not result in conversion. Nor will the laborer, perhaps, perceive any good effect produced for a long time, and possibly not while he lives. But moral reformations usually move very slowly onward. It needs time for the leaven to work. And in many cases the sower is not permitted to gather the sheaves. But if they are finally reaped, *he that soweth and he that reapeth will rejoice together.* Let him who is faithful in doing his duty in some barren field of labor, be assured that the truth has never yet failed to manifest, sooner or later, its transforming power. His field of labor may be narrow, and his discouragements many; but let him bear in mind that he has a mighty instrument to work with, and an almighty God pledged to sustain him.

In the third place, the subject shows the fallacy of the doctrine, that the world is growing worse, and will continue to grow worse, in spite of all efforts to spread the gospel.

The world does indeed abound with wickedness, and often the success of the truth in a place is the occasion of a grosser development of iniquity. But the truth has the advantage, because it meets and satisfies man's highest wants so completely, and enlists in its favor the human conscience. And whence arises this want of confidence in the truth, as an instrument of the world's conversion, among these our brethren, some of whom are missionaries, and yet they do not believe the world can be converted by the gospel, but will continue to grow worse till the Saviour makes a visible display of his power? Have they not felt the power of truth in their own souls? and have they not seen its mighty efficacy upon the souls of others? Do they doubt its ability, when applied by God's Spirit, to convert the world? If the world is growing worse, how happens it that all Christian nations, even where the gospel is dreadfully perverted, are so far superior in character and condition to pagan and Mohammedan nations? Surely these men forget the catalytic power of the gospel, as developed in history. True, the improved physical, social, and intellectual condition of a nation is far from being its conversion to God. But it is an important prerequisite to that conversion. And it does imply that some in that nation are truly converted; and why is not all this an earnest of the final and complete triumph of pure religion, if its comparatively few genuine disciples do their duty? For every accession to their number increases their power; and why may not that leavening influence go on till it has reached the world's entire population?

In the gospel, then, you have an agency abundantly adequate to the work; and why then call in miraculous power? for we know that it is a settled principle of the divine government, not to work a miracle when established agencies are sufficient.

Finally, this subject should greatly encourage and animate the hopes and efforts of those engaged in the work of missions.

They learn from it that they need not be discouraged, though the common principles by which men judge of the probable success of their enterprises, should show their chance to be small. The fact that they are following a divine command, to *go into all the world and preach the gospel to every creature*, may, indeed, be sufficient to give them courage and perseverance amid powerful difficulties. But it is important, also, to know what an extraordinary instrument they possess for carrying on the enterprise; how it works its way into the hearts of men, and silently changes their characters and the whole aspect of society, and sends down an influence, they cannot tell how far, into generations unborn. *It is, indeed, quick and powerful, sharper than a two-edged sword, piercing even to the dividing asunder of soul and spirit, and of the joints and marrow, and is a discerner of the thoughts and intents of the heart.* It takes a stronger hold of society than all other influences, and abides longer. Its secret energy rouses human society into action, and propagates the catalytic change from individual to individual, from family to family, from community to community, and sometimes from kingdom to kingdom. Nor can the missionary tell, when he deposits the leaven of the gospel in one spot, even though scarcely heeded there, but he has started a process which shall go radiating outwards over a whole continent; for thus it has often done.

But though thus adapted to cheer the missionary in every land, this principle affords much more encouragement in some countries than in others; and most of all, on American soil; to the home missionary here. To prove and illustrate this from the analogies of my text, let us recur to certain facts respecting catalytic operations in nature, which I neglected at the commencement of this discourse.

The essential principle to which I mainly refer is this: that in order to make leaven or any other catalytic agent operate, it is necessary that the mass to be leavened should be in a certain state, as to consistency, temperature, and permeability. The baker well knows that it is of no use to hide leaven in a mass of frozen dough, nor unless its temperature is a good deal above the freezing point. So if from any other cause it has become condensed and rigid, the leaven cannot spread itself among the particles, and little or no effect will be produced, even though the leaven be in the best condition.

Apply now these principles to the dissemination of the gospel. Attempt to propagate its truths in a country where heathenism, or Mohammedanism, or corrupt Christianity, is firmly established, is sustained by the learned few, and the ignorant and superstitious many, and by wealth and influence; is linked inseparably to the government, and can show a long list of illustrious defenders. By such causes the false system has been knit firmly together, and is settled down into a hard, impenetrable mass, which resists all change. Without a miracle you would expect that if the truth should make any headway, it would be slow and difficult. Whereas in a nation where a false religious system sits loose upon the people, and has little social or governmental support, and especially where commerce, education, and free principles are breaking up the torpid and indurated mass, the way is prepared for the gospel's catalytic power to show its mighty transforming energy.

Facts now corroborate the truth of these principles. For never has the gospel made rapid progress in any country where a false system of religion has intrenched itself behind the prejudices, the social habits, the pecuniary interests, the splendor of rites and forms, and governmental favor ; and its most signal triumphs have been witnessed where the false system has but a feeble hold upon the public mind, or men have begun to think for themselves. Certain conditions seem necessary, in order that the leaven may work ; nor where these are wanting are we to expect success, any more than that the laws of chemistry will be set aside in the process of bread making. God does sometimes, indeed, give unexpected success by the power of his Spirit, to show that, after all, the efficiency lies with him. But such cases are exceptions, which we cannot calculate upon, and are not our rule of judgment or of duty.

From these principles we should confidently infer, that Mohammedanism, and especially popery, would offer more powerful obstructions to the spread of the gospel than any other systems of error. Hence it is, that while missionary stations are multiplied among the heathen, they are yet so few in the great centres of Mohammedan and Papal influence in Asia and Europe. Nor can we doubt, that long after every heathen pagoda has been converted into a Christian temple, — nay, long after the Bible shall have supplanted the Koran in every mosque and minaret, — will the perverted Christianity of forms, propped up by leagues and bayonets, present its yet unbroken front, to be breached only in the *battle of that great day of God Almighty.*

On the other hand, from these same principles, we infer that nowhere on earth is there such a preparation for the spread of pure Christianity as in our own land. Here we have no inert and indurated mass of dead formalism to break up; no frozen and petrified system of rites and ceremonies to arrest the leavening process; no iron arm of government to check the onward movement. But the genial light and warmth of free institutions and of general education have brought the community into a state most favorable for receiving the gospel and giving it free course. Wherever faithfully planted, it is sure to communicate and spread its vitalizing influence outward and onward; and if Christians will only do their duty, they may be sure that the whole land will be leavened.

And here I ought to mention another chemical principle that has a parallel in the condition of our country. Chemists tell us that elements in their *nascent* state — that is, when first produced — unite far more readily than they do afterwards. Now, the elements of our social condition are as yet, in a great measure, in a nascent state, and therefore more ready to be operated upon and form valuable combinations than in the old world, where every thing has long since become immovably fixed, either by affinities within or pressure without. O, how important that the gospel exert its catalytic power upon our population, before that same binding and paralyzing process pass upon them! The wide world does not furnish another field of missionary labor so promising. I mean not by this, that other countries are not open to the gospel, and that missionary efforts should be limited to our own land.

God bless these efforts and increase them a hundred fold in every land. But I do mean, that our country preëminently invites and demands efforts for its evangelization. I do mean, that it is a more promising and a more important field than any other on the globe, and therefore calls for every heart and every hand to engage in it.

Do I seem to any to be taking too strong ground? Let me propose to them an experiment, which I sincerely wish all my hearers could try, to test this opinion. Let them take the next steamer across the Atlantic, and in one fortnight they would find themselves on ground very favorable for a comparison. They would be traversing lands where state religions exist, with all their pompous and imposing rites and ceremonies, with their exclusive and intolerant spirit, and their hostility to freedom of opinion, and to all that is vital in personal piety. Religion there is sustained by governmental decrees and by bayonets. Throttled in the embraces of the state, its lifeless form is made use of as a speaking trumpet, through which are proclaimed, not the doctrines of God, but of man; such as the divine right of kings, the duty of unreserved submission to the government and the church; the infallibility of the church, not of the Bible. The sweet countenance of gospel charity has been changed into that of a persecuting fiend; and the snaky locks of a Gorgon cover her head, freezing and petrifying all around. All places are full of religious forms, but alas! to find its power you must search long and deep. The very highways are studded with crosses and crucified Christs, with oratories and images of the virgin, while the towns abound with vast and venerable cathedrals and chapels, full of golden images, splendid paintings, and sacred relics; and the magnificent organ peals along the sounding arches and thrills the wondering soul, as the gilded priests chant their *Te Deums*, their *Pater Nosters*, and their *Ave Marias*. You enter the convent at the sound of the vesper bell, and a thousand white-veiled nuns are kneeling around you, and gorgeous music lends enchantment to the vesper hymn. Every where in the streets you meet the cassocked priest, and often the imposing procession, while the multitudes uncover their heads as it passes. In short, to an American, accustomed to the simplicity of our modes of worship, the most prominent feature in European lands, save in the glorious fast-anchored isle, — and even there to great extent, — is, that in spite of the most imposing externals, the whole is little more than heartless formality — a wretched substitute for the bread of life. Yet when he sees how firmly rooted is this system in the pride and prejudice, the worldly interest, the interests of despotic governments, and a swarming priesthood, and how it is woven into the very texture of society, he cannot but feel that little short of a miracle will be required for effecting a revolution. With what deep interest, then, after only a few weeks of such observation in those lands, will the heart of the Christian American turn towards his own country! In the hallowed language of our gubernatorial proclamations, he will exclaim, "God save the Commonwealth of Massachusetts!" Save her religion from the base alloy of formalism, superstition, and intolerance. Save her system of education from the blighting touch of aristocracy and priestcraft. Save her free institutions from the savage ferocity of the ignorant and unprincipled many, and the grinding oppression of the despotic few. Save her, for the sake of the country. And God save that whole country, for her own sake, and the sake of the world. For to save her is to save the world; and to lose her is to lose the world.

It needs only a short pilgrimage through the old world to

excite such sentiments as these in the heart of a Massachusetts American. And his prayer to God will be, that he may live to go back and labor harder than he has ever done, to build up the cause of pure religion, of learning, and of freedom, in that land which he has now learned to be the only one on earth where, for the present, this indissoluble trio of noble institutions has any chance of wide-spread success. And if this man learns only this lesson by his foreign tour, it is worth all the sacrifice and expense of ten thousand miles of voyage and travel.

What a noble work, then, is committed to our hands! What an inviting field has the Home Missionary Society before it! The man who enters it finds society not only in a state more favorable for casting in the leaven of the gospel, but that the influence of his labors is felt almost to the ends of the earth. Let him be laboring to build up some obscure waste place, say in Massachusetts. He may seem to be unnoticed and neglected. But he is doing his part towards sustaining and perpetuating the free and the religious institutions of the country, and therefore, in fact, the eyes of many millions in Europe are watching his labors with deep interest, and with earnest prayers for his fidelity ; for their chief hope of the world's emancipation rests on the success of civil and religious liberty here. And if the true gospel be not preached and received among us, free institutions must for the present fail. In preaching the gospel, therefore, in the obscurest nook of the land, a man may feel that he is working for the whole country, nay, for the whole world. Indeed, Providence is sending representations from the whole world to our doors. By multitudes they pour in upon us from every European land, and swarms of Asiatics are crowding into the valleys of California. So that in fact we may become missionaries to Papists, Mohammedans, Boodhists, and other heathen, without leaving our own shores.

What responsibility, then, attaches to the name and position of an American! When, in foreign lands, I have met kings and queens, dukes and marquises, counts and viscounts, they appeared to be men and women of only the ordinary stature; but when I first set my foot again upon our own shores, and met free-born Christian Americans, it seemed to me that I was looking upon giants, because God has given them the power of giants to bear up the pillars of freedom, of education, and of religion, and to cast down the pillars of ignorance, superstition, and despotism.

If your patience is not quite exhausted, allow me to add one or two further suggestions, growing out of a scientific view of the text.

In order that leaven should operate effectually, or even operate at all, it must itself be in an active condition, and of a proper temperature. In proportion as its thermometric state is too high or too low, or if there be an admixture of inert substances, or its own decomposition be slow or partial, will its catalytic power be diminished. It must be in such a condition that a living plant can flourish within it. For if there be no life in it, no vital power will be communicated to the surrounding mass.

So it is with the moral leaven of the gospel. If its purity be marred by an admixture of error and vain speculation, or if it be cast into the community distorted by ignorance, or disfigured and blackened by the fires of fanaticism, or enveloped in the ice of formalism, feeble will be its influence, if indeed it do not become a nuisance. Instead of proving the wisdom of God and the power of God unto salvation, men will see in it only the weakness of human wisdom and strength, overpowered by the superior might of human depravity.

Now, it is this perverted and deficient gospel, that too often finds its way into our waste places, into our new settlements, and among the floating population of our cities. It has the name of Christianity, and usually contains some truth, but a larger proportion of error; so that while it produces traces of religion, it shows more of fanaticism, or bigotry, or self-righteousness and formalism. How important, then, that into fields thus grown over with briers and weeds, a pure and holy gospel should be carried by pure and holy men! Those engaged in sending this gospel abroad, through our Home Missionary Societies, should have their piety in that living, active condition, without which their prayers, example, and efforts will only deepen the spiritual slumbers of ignorance and sin. And still more important is it, that the direct agents in this work should preach an unadulterated gospel, not only by their voices but by their lives.

Finally, astonishing as is the power of leaven to change the mass into which it is cast, there is a limit to that power. One part may, indeed, transform two thousand parts of the meal; but if the latter be increased much beyond that proportion, not only will all the excess remain unaffected, but it will operate to prevent the leaven from producing its full effect. Nay, it may nearly or quite destroy that effect. Hence, if the leaven and the mass to be leavened be enormously disproportionate, the best leaven may become powerless.

Now, to apply this principle to home missionary efforts, I fear, my brethren, that this is just what we are doing in our country. The mass to be leavened by the gospel is out of all proportion to the means employed. In 1850, we built between four and five thousand miles of railroad, at an average cost of fifty thousand dollars per mile. During that same year, we expended only enough upon domestic missions to construct five miles of railway. And railways are only one branch of American enterprise out of many. How exceedingly small, then, must be the proportion of our pecuniary means devoted to an enterprise which transcends all others in our country in importance! For if that fail, all others will be smitten with a deadly blight. Irreligion cannot triumph without trampling in the dust our systems of general education, of public enterprise and freedom, and crushing the hopes of liberty through the earth. Our hopes, therefore, must centre in the Home Missionary cause. We make enormous outlays, and labor without weariness to advance our worldly schemes, and that, too, where the means employed have little or none of the catalytic power inherent in the gospel, and where the results bear no proportion in importance to the work of Home Missions. God has committed to American Christians the noblest enterprise which he has given to the present generation in any part of the world. And he has put into our hands an instrument with which to accomplish it, a thousand times more efficacious than those employed in commerce, in manufactures, in agriculture, or indeed any ordinary art or pursuit. How dwarfed must be our piety, how low our standard of patriotism, how contemptible our philanthropy, if we do not supply the means necessary to prevent the leaven of the gospel from being overpowered and neutralized by ignorance and depravity! Ought we to be satisfied to expend fifty million dollars annually for railways, and only one thousandth part as much in working out the grandest problem in politics, in education and religion, of this generation? O, if any cause has motives powerful enough to rouse men to action, it is this. If we enter into the work resolutely and cheerfully, with humble reliance on God's help, we are sure of success. And success will bring such a day of brightness and blessing to this wide continent, as never yet has visited any other. Though the deluge of ignorance, despotism, and false religion should ingulf every other land, ours shall stand high above the flood, and beat back its angry waves ; and, ere the close of the present century, one hundred millions of Christian freemen shall here be found richly enjoying those social, political, educational, and religious rights and privileges, which God originally gave, but which man has hitherto unrighteously withheld.

THE ATTRACTIONS OF HEAVEN AND EARTH ASTRONOMICALLY ILLUSTRATED.

For I am in a strait betwixt two, having a desire to depart and to be with Christ, which is far better. Nevertheless, to abide in the flesh is more needful for you. — *Philippians* i. 23, 24.

Attraction and repulsion are the two great principles by which the spiritual, as well as the material, world is controlled. The former tends to unite mind to mind and matter to matter, the latter to drive them asunder. And the struggle that is going on between them originates most of the movements of matter and of mind in the universe. When we speak, however, of mental attractions and repulsions, we use language figuratively. We mean by the first only those mutual affections which unite those who have similar opinions, and feelings, and aims; and by the latter we mean those antipathies which result from dissimilar opinions, feelings, and aims. There is, however, a strong analogy between the literal attractions and repulsions of matter and the affections and antipathies of mind, so that the latter may be illustrated by the former. And to some illustrations of this sort I wish to call your attention at this time.

The text represents Paul as almost balanced between two powerful attractions — those of heaven and those of earth.

So far as his own happiness was concerned, the attractions of the heavenly world were vastly the more powerful; for he says that to depart and be with Christ is *better beyond expression* — using the strongest superlative in the Greek language, and to which we have no phrase exactly corresponding, but which Dr. Doddridge renders by the words *better beyond expression.* When he thought of the glories of the heavenly state, and of being admitted to the immediate society of Christ, his heart was drawn upward by an almost overwhelming force. But when he thought of leaving his Christian friends and converts in a dangerous world, and that by his continuance with them he might help them in their spiritual warfare, and be the means of the conversion of others, he felt the ties that bound him to his friends, and his duty holding him to the world with an equal power; so that, upon the whole, he could not decide in which direction he was more forcibly drawn.

The attractions of heaven and of earth are the two great influences by which men in all ages, and especially Christian men, are governed. Very few indeed are in doubt which is the stronger force; for, alas! most of us know very well that our hearts cleave to this world with almost irresistible impulse, while heaven seems distant and but feebly attractive. Still we shall find, now and at all times, some at almost every point along the scale between the extremes of entire devotion to the world and entire devotion to God; and it may not be unprofitable to spend a few moments in drawing some illustrations of the mode in which these two influences operate from the laws of attraction which control the heavenly bodies, as they are developed by the researches of modern astronomy. Most of these illustrations are derived from the manner in which the earth, moon, and sun operate upon one another

— the sun representing heaven, the moon the Christian, and the earth the central point of all influences which act on man this side eternity.

And here I ought, probably, to apologize for an innovation which I shall venture to make upon the usual mode of sermonizing, by the introduction of a few sensible illustrations, or diagrams, to make my meaning intelligible and impressive. My reasons for this course are the following: First, I do not suppose I could otherwise make my meaning clear even to a highly intelligent audience; secondly, the only object of the diagrams is to make scientific truths understood and remembered, not to indulge in curious scientific speculations; thirdly, I conceive that the religious applications of science are its most important use; and I know not how such a use can be made of science, if we may not employ enough of sensible illustrations to make its truths clearly understood. However, if the novel course which I adopt seem objectionable to any after I shall have finished, let it be condemned. But when I recollect how often science has been used in opposition to religion, I do not anticipate condemnation in this attempt to make it auxiliary to the sacred cause of holiness, although the object of my illustrations is not to prove any point, but merely to elucidate and impress religious truth.

In the first place, in order to cause any body to revolve around a larger one in a circular orbit, so as to be always equidistant from it, it is necessary that a certain amount of force be imparted to the revolving body, and in a certain direction. In the case of the planets, the two forces are so balanced as to produce a nearly circular motion; but in the case of the comets, they are so unequal, — the impulsive or tangential force so predominates over the attractive, — that they move in elliptical orbits. Now, let us imagine the earth

(E, Fig. 1, Frontispiece)* moving in a circular orbit around the sun, (S,) by a proper equilibrium of the two acting forces, and at a certain point of its orbit (say E) to receive a new impulse in the direction of its motion. The consequence would be to change its orbit from a circle to an ellipse. It would, however, return to the place where the additional force was given; and when it reached that point, which would be the perihelion of its orbit, suppose it to receive another new impulse, and at each return another. The effect would be to make it revolve in orbits more and more eccentric, until at length they could not be distinguished from what the mathematicians call a parabola — a curve which never returns into itself. In other words, the earth would at last go off to a returnless distance, or beyond the control of the centre around which it had revolved.

Make another supposition. Imagine the earth, when revolving in a circle, at a certain point of its orbit (E, Fig. 2) to come under the influence of an impulsive force which, like gravity, shall ever afterwards continue to act upon it. The effects will be, that it will receive a constantly increasing velocity, and consequently will be continually receding farther and farther from the centre, describing a sort of helix, which never returns into itself. Thus would the body be carried an infinite or returnless distance from the centre.

These two cases, it appears to me, afford a good illustration of professed Christians who act under the influence of impulses derived neither from the Bible nor the Spirit of God. So long as they are controlled by the divine Spirit, or by motives derived from the Bible, they will move around the

* In all the figures, the body colored yellow represents the sun, the green one the earth, and the red one the moon.

great Centre of light and love in circular paths with uniform motion and steady light. But whenever they give themselves up to other impulses, from whatever quarter, they are sure to be carried farther and farther from God in eccentric paths; and nothing but his interposition can save them from flying off beyond the hope of return.

Take the case of the man who gives himself up to the influence of worldly impulses. Its riches, honors, or pleasures become the powerful controllers of his movements, and urge him forward with a constantly accelerated force. Religion has not lost its hold upon his conscience; and he still fancies that he is revolving around the law of God, as the centre of attraction. But to all others it is obvious he is flying off farther and farther from that centre, and therefore getting more and more out of its control. Like the revolving earth, when, as I have supposed, it receives a new and constantly accelerating impulse, the path of this Christian conforms less and less to the divine law; he feels less and less the power of heavenly things, and they seem more distant. The light of God's countenance becomes fainter and feebler. Meanwhile the impelling power, the love of the world, rapidly gains strength; and in a little time, without being conscious of it himself, and unless special, marvellous, I had almost said miraculous grace bring him back, he will become *a wandering star, to whom is reserved the blackness of darkness forever.*

Or take the case of the Christian controlled and impelled by spiritual pride. Harmoniously and beautifully did he commence his revolutions around divine love, as the centre of attraction, and with a sense of duty to impel him onward. But he chanced to discover his own picture in the glass of vanity, and made it his idol. Spiritual pride came in at once and took the control of his heart; and now, instead of worshipping God, he adores his own exalted piety. Bigoted and censorious towards others, he can see no loveliness in their characters, nor tolerate any thing that does not conform to his own selfish standard. While he boasts of his religious enjoyment, and fancies himself living near to God, he is in fact driven so far from God that it would be strange if he should ever return.

Next comes the case of the fanatic. A frenzied zeal took the place, in his heart, of that charity which suffereth long and is kind, by which he seemed to be controlled in the early days of his religious course. That zeal did, indeed, greatly quicken his race, but it was only to drive him farther from the true source of all knowledge and light; and away he went, with lightning speed, into the region of *ignes fatui*, which he mistook for the Sun of Righteousness; and the wild dreams of fancy which were floating in that limbo he mistook for new revelations; and the sparks of his own kindling he took to be fire from heaven. The word of God he interpreted by impulses, instead of sound learning, which he regarded as a satanic delusion. Impelled by passion himself, he strove to urge others forward by the same blind impulse; and reason in religion he denounced as the enemy of all proper zeal in the cause of God. The divine prophecies he interpreted, too, by impressions, and made up for deficiencies by interlarding his own dreams and fancies. With him, some terrible event — the downfall of an empire, the devastations of an earthquake or a volcano, a wasting sickness, the second coming of Christ, or the destruction of the world — was always near at hand, and for the best of reasons, viz., his own strong impressions. Such a man as this often shows, nevertheless, some valuable fragment of Christian feeling and conduct. But in what an eccentric orbit does he revolve! His eccentricities usually become greater and greater, until at last he flies off in an orbit which carries him entirely out of the regions of common sense and rational religion — never to return.

A case, however, may be quoted from the opposite extreme. A man begins his religious course in a circular orbit — that is, there is a proper balance in his mind between the influences and principles that form a religious character. He bows down to the authority of the Bible, and receives it as a little child. With him, it is evidence enough for any doctrine or precept if he can be assured that God has announced it. But at length his heart begins to be less interested in religious things, and a spirit of speculation and scepticism takes possession of his mind, and becomes a new and mighty impulsive power which carries him rapidly away from the quiet path in which he had been moving. He soon finds religion to be full of difficulties which he cannot solve. Having broken loose from his former principle, that he would implicitly receive whatever statements God had made, and which formed his sheet anchor, he is now adrift on the stormy sea of speculation, with human reasoning only for his compass. One doctrine after another, fairly subjected, as he fancies, to this ordeal, and found wanting, he throws overboard, until his creed has become a mere wreck of old opinions, with nothing in their place. His increasing scepticism calls forth the animadversions of his Christian brethren; and this wakens in him a pride of opinion to defend his new views. He soon finds, however, that the full inspiration of the Scriptures stands in his way; and he clearly perceives that the sacred writers sometimes reason incorrectly, and therefore they sometimes reason without inspiration. Thus is he driven farther and farther away from the controlling influence of the Bible by the new and powerful impulse which speculation and scepticism have given him; and the more the Bible and its doctrines sink in his estimation, the less is the hold of practical religion over his heart. In short, his path is becoming wider and wider from God and heaven, and of course their power over his heart and conscience is less, while the force which urges him away from God is gathering strength; nor can we have any hope but in the all-powerful grace of God that his wanderings will ever cease.

I proceed to a second illustration, which may be derived from the relative situation and mutual attraction of the sun, earth, and moon. When the moon is exactly between the earth and sun, it is obvious that it will be attracted in opposite directions by these bodies; and it is only because it is so much nearer the earth than the sun, that it is not at once drawn away towards the latter so as utterly to forsake the former. It is easy, now, to conceive that it might be removed so near to the sun, (say to A, Fig. 5,) that it should henceforth cease to be governed in its movements by the earth, and obey only the attractive influence of the sun. On the other hand, it might be brought so near the earth,— certainly, if brought in contact with it, (say to B,) — as to be governed entirely by it, and no longer be affected by the sun's attraction, except as constituting a part of the earth.

This last supposition reminds us of the individual who has suffered the love of the world to gain so strong a hold upon him that he is beyond the reach of the influence of religion. He cleaves to the world as firmly as the moon would, should she fall from her orbit. Heaven, with all its glories, exerts upon him apparently no power. It matters not that all in the universe which is pure, and noble, and truly worthy is there assembled. They have no charms for him. There are unfolded in infinite splendor the glories of the eternal God; and there the Lamb that was slain is enthroned the chiefest among ten thousands, and altogether lovely. There is gathered in sweet communion and everlasting love the countless throng of the angels of light; and as they take up their golden harps, the whole company of the redeemed from earth join in the sweet song of Moses and the Lamb. It is the New Jerusalem, whose foundations are precious stones, whose gates are pearls, and whose pavements are gold; the city through which flows the river of the water of life, with the tree of life on its banks; the city whence all that is sinful and all that is mortal is forever excluded; the city where every thing grand, and beautiful, and attractive to a pure mind meets together. And yet this man can look with stupid unconcern upon the picture, and feel not one desire to be of the number who are admitted to its joys. Nay, he turns away with loathing from the sight, and says to the vanities of the world, These be my portion — these the objects to which my heart cleaves with fond desire, and which I prefer to heaven. O, is it not a contemptible choice for an immortal soul, made in the image of God? And yet it is a most common choice. All around us we see multitudes deliberately preferring earth to heaven — a world of change, of ignorance, sin, sickness, and death, to a world where all is permanent, and holy, and happy.

But, blessed be the power of God's grace, there are some who have given up their hearts to the full influence of that glorious world, and feel from day to day its mighty attractions. Though not insensible to the affairs of this world, they are more alive to that which is unseen and eternal. They have learned to relish the employments, as well as the enjoyments, of heaven. Often, in the retirement of the soul, and away from the sight of their fellow-men, do they hold communion with that pure world. Not with their mortal eyes, but with the eye of faith, do they gaze and gaze upon its unspeakable glories; and the ear of faith listens to the songs of the redeemed, until their hearts heave with strong emotion, and *pant after God as the hart panteth after the water brooks.* As they muse the fire burns, and their souls are borne away by a strong impulse towards the celestial city. In short, they do sometimes approach so near it, and drink so deeply into its glories, that their souls become deeply imbued with its spirit. Now, such men live so near to heaven that their conversation is there, and the attractions of earth are comparatively feeble. They are aptly represented by the first supposition which I made, wherein the moon was imagined to be removed so far from the earth, and so near to the sun, that the attraction of the earth had become almost null upon it, and that of the sun almost the only controlling force. It is the same with eminently holy men, who have long been disciplined in the school of Christ. They have in a great measure got the victory over the world, and heaven seems to them not a distant place, but near at hand. They seem to stand so near its confines, that when the clouds of doubt and unbelief clear away, as they often do, and the Sun of Righteousness pours down his bright beams, they can look across the dark valley between the two worlds, and see the sweet flowers of the world beyond, its noble rivers and plains, its magnificent mountains, and its sunny vales; and this world shrinks into insignificance in the comparison; and, like Paul, they cannot but *feel a desire to depart and be with Christ.* And around their Saviour they see the bright throng which he has redeemed by his blood, and made them kings and priests unto God. And how can they but long to go and join that happy circle ! — a circle which sin can never pollute, nor death ever break. O, what a happy state is it, thus to live under the full influence of the heavenly world, thus to feel its strong attractions, thus to have its spirit breathed into our souls, and thus, as it were, to begin its songs and its joys while yet on earth !

I derive my third illustration from the manner in which the earth and moon perform their journey together around the sun, and around each other. This is not generally understood. We know that the moon accompanies the earth around the sun, and we see it every month complete its revolution around the earth. We are hence apt to infer that its actual path must be an exceedingly irregular curve. But it is not so. Excepting some very slight disturbances of its motion, which need not here be taken into the account, its actual path in the heavens differs very slightly from that which the earth makes in its annual revolution; that is, it differs very little from a circle. Indeed, were the moon's path to be drawn thirty feet in diameter, it would require a practised eye to distinguish the curve from a true circle. (Fig. 4 shows the paths of the earth and moon for one month ; the black line representing the earth's orbit, and the red one the moon's path.)

Thus it appears that the moon, as well as the earth, obeys the influence of the sun in its annual revolution ; and yet it does actually move round the earth, and perform important service for its inhabitants every month. And it is to these two facts in connection that I wish to call your particular attention.

It is a well-known fact, that the most eminently holy Christians frequently exhibit a very strong and tender affection for their families, if they have any, or for their friends and neighbors, and manifest a deep interest in secular pursuits, and in the welfare of the community and country in which they live. And it has often been inquired how such deep interest in worldly things was consistent with supreme love and devotion to God. Indeed, this inquiry has often distressed the Christian himself, and he has feared that his strong attachment to friends and neighbors, and his lively interest in worthy objects of a worldly kind, were unfavorable indications in respect to his character for piety. But in the moon's motion behold a solution of these doubts and difficulties! While she most faithfully performs her duty to the earth, (if I may be allowed such a personification,) she is not for a moment unmindful of her relation to the great centre of the solar system. Looking to her fidelity to the earth, we should suppose her unmindful of any other influence; whereas, in fact, she is every moment obedient to a higher attraction. And so long as she obeys that higher influence, there can be no interference between the two movements. Just so with the Christian. So long as the will of God forms the great controlling central power by which all his affections and conduct are regulated, — so long as every minor influence which the world exerts upon him is kept completely within the control of that higher influence which emanates from the eternal world, — he need not fear any interference between his affection to his family, his friends, and his country, and his affection for God. It is just as consistent for him to yield to the impulse of nature, which prompts him to love and serve his friends and his country, while at the same time he loves and serves God supremely, as it is for the moon to obey the influence of the earth, and constantly to revolve around it; while at the same time she moves in a still wider circle around the sun, and is perfectly controlled by that great centre. Nay, to yield up the heart to divine influence, — to give God a supreme place in the affections, — brings into the heart a livelier affection for mankind than nature gives. For nature would limit that affection by friends and by country: but supreme love to God rebukes such selfishness, and bids us love our neighbor as ourselves; and then informs us that all mankind are our neighbors.

We learn, then, that the Christian need not fear that his attachment to friends and to other worldly objects is improper, or injurious, so long as it does not interfere with his love and duty to God. If he suffers them to draw off his affections from God, or from heaven, as his final home, so that he is turned aside from the path of duty, then indeed they become a dangerous, and may become a fatal influence. If the interest which he takes in his friends or favorite worldly pursuits diminishes his interest in the things which are unseen and eternal, — if their society draws him away from communion with God and heavenly things, — then, indeed, have they become the controlling power of his heart and his life; and if the charm be not broken, he will be driven from God beyond recovery. But no man need fear, when he finds his attachment to his friends, or country, or secular pursuits, increase, provided he finds a correspondent increase of interest in God and eternal things.

To introduce my fourth illustration, let us suppose the moon placed directly between the earth and the sun, while between the moon (A) and the sun is a fourth body, (R, Fig. 3,) which repels instead of attracting the moon. The consequence would be, that the latter would be drawn nearer to the earth, and therefore be more attracted by that body; hence it would be driven farther from the sun, and be less attracted by it, until that fourth repellent body be taken away.

It is true, that among the heavenly bodies we know of none that repels the others. They all mutually attract. But we know that on earth repulsion is one of the great regulating powers of nature, as in electricity and magnetism. It cannot be objectionable, therefore, to suppose, for the sake of illustrating religious truth, a repelling body situated between the moon and the sun.*

Between the Christian and heaven there is also an object from which nature shrinks back with dread and aversion. At one time his imagination pictures it as a dark valley, where no ray of light enters, where no friendly voice is heard by the lonely passenger, but where hideous and menacing forms ambush his path. At another time his fancy paints it as a deep and dismal defile, where he must go alone, and where a hideous monster stands in panoply complete, to dispute his passage, and to awaken in the disembodied spirit indescribable terrors. In short, it is what men universally call death, and from which nature, almost without exception, recoils in dismay. But from earth to heaven there is no passage save through that region of terror. Many a Christian would gladly leave the earth and go to possess his inheritance in the skies, did he not dread a boisterous passage through that untrodden valley. Nature approaches the brink of the precipice, and strains her eye to penetrate the gloom ; but she can discern only the swift and dark waters of Jordan rolling by, and the unrelenting countenance of the King of Terrors, with his menacing dart, while ever and anon the dying agonies of one and another victim assail her ear. She shudders at the prospect.

> "The pains, the groans, the dying strife,
> Fright our approaching souls away;
> Still shrink we back again to life,
> Fond of our prison and our clay."

* I might have taken stronger ground. Says Professor Loomis, "The phenomena exhibited by Halley's comet at its return to the sun in 1835, require us to admit the existence of repulsive as well as attractive forces."—*Recent Progress of Astronomy*, 3d edition, p. 147.

Some, indeed, through fear of death, are all their lifetime subject to bondage. Their weak and disordered nerves, their morbid and excitable fancies, start at the rustling of a leaf. No wonder, then, if their souls are overcome when they think of taking a last look upon this fair world, of grasping the hand of friendship for the last time, and of taking the fearful plunge, which throws them at once into the hands of that unsparing conqueror, whose heart never yet relented. No wonder that they cling to the world with a desperate grasp, and almost cease to feel the attractions of heaven. But let faith now put into nature's hand her magic wand, and it will be the traveller's passport through the dark valley, and the smitten waters of Jordan shall divide, and a ray from heaven come in to trace out his pathway. Let the Christian endeavor, while faith is in lively exercise, to render death familiar by frequent meditation, and he will find, that —

> "Death and his image, rising in the brain,
> Bear faint resemblance — never are alike;
> Fear shakes the pencil, fancy loves excess,
> Dark ignorance is lavish of her shades,
> And these the formidable picture draw."

He will find that the physical pains of death he has overrated, and that often, instead of an unknown dreaded agony, it is the sweet and quiet termination of all mortal suffering. If he must close his eyes on all the loved objects of time and sense, it is only to open them upon the infinite glories of heaven. If beloved earthly friends can accompany him no farther than the brink of the dark passage, yet friends still more beloved — his God, his Saviour, his Sanctifier — stand on the other side with arms outstretched to receive him. Ah, yes, it is the same Saviour who has himself, in the nature and with the feelings of a man, passed alone through that gulf, and across that turbid stream, and to his fearful followers he cries, *O Israel, fear not; for I have redeemed thee; I have called thee by my name. When thou passeth through the waters, I will be with thee; and through the rivers, they shall not overflow thee: when thou walkest through the fire, thou shall not be burnt. Death shall be swallowed up in victory. Jesus Christ hath*, indeed, *abolished death, and brought life and immortality to light.* He has taken away the sting of death, that is, unpardoned sin. The monster's spectre indeed still haunts the dark valley through which the believer must pass, and brandishes his broken and harmless dart. But faith can sing the conqueror's song, even within the grasp of this once terrific, but now powerless and vanquished foe.

It is by meditations like these that the repulsive power of death is gradually overcome, and the timid believer begins again to feel the strong attractions of the heavenly world. Nature, indeed, will never feel a complacency in death, considered by itself; but its terrors diminish as they are more closely examined, while the glories that lie beyond loom up higher and brighter, so that, to use the language of an eminent saint, "the river of death appears as an insignificant rill, that can be crossed at a single step, whenever God gives permission." As it muses, the soul waxes strong in the Lord and the power of his might, and with holy confidence exclaims,—

One hour, and the dark storm goes by;
One step, and on the heavenly shore,
I stand beneath a cloudless sky,
And drink in joy forevermore.

My fifth and last illustration supposes the moon placed, as before, between the earth and the sun. But in addition to this, it supposes a number of other bodies in contact with the earth, (as Fig. 6,) which exercise a very powerful attraction upon the moon, and of course draw it more or less away from the sun, giving to the earth more, and to the sun less, influence over its motions.

Imagine now that these bodies, thus surrounding the earth, should quit it one after another, and pass over to the sun, (as shown on Fig. 7,) attaching themselves in like manner to his surface. It is easy to see how such a transference would diminish the moon's attraction towards the earth, and increase its attraction towards the sun; so that it might easily be made to break loose entirely from the former, and pass towards, if not directly into, the latter.

The objects that attract the Christian to this world are often numerous and powerfully attractive. We have seen that he may cherish a strong attachment to worldly and worthy objects, if the love of God so reign in his heart as to bring every thing else into subordination. We have seen that love to God sanctifies and ennobles every inferior affection. And the fact is, that no class of men exhibit a stronger affection for every worthy object than devoted Christians.

They ardently love their friends. And in this they do but follow their great Exemplar. Even the young man, who turned away sorrowful from the exhortations of Jesus, was still loved by him for his interesting traits of character, and by the tomb of Lazarus the Saviour wept; so that the Jews exclaimed, *Behold how he loved him.* He did not love any thing in his friends that was sinful: neither does the Christian. But for all those amiable qualities which make them good members of society he does love them; and still stronger is that affection, if he witnesses in them the graces of true religion. For he regards such friendships as germs which will expand and ripen in heaven.

The Christian also loves the intercourse of his fellow-men.

His religion has not made him a misanthrope, nor eradicated that love of society which nature has implanted in every bosom. He only strives to correct what is wrong, and elevate what is low, in social intercourse; and no man takes a deeper interest than he in whatever promotes the general welfare of the community.

The Christian also loves his country. To promote her welfare, to defend her institutions, to preserve her liberties, and to eradicate whatever is unjust, cruel, and debasing, he is ready to make any sacrifices consistent with his duty to God.

He loves science and literature. To cultivate them himself he knows to be the only sure way of giving him enlarged views of truth and duty, and he knows, too, that many of the principles of science will survive the ruin of this world, and become a part of the science of heaven. And to promote knowledge in others he knows to be one of the most important means of the promotion of religion, and of saving piety from degenerating into frigid scepticism or wild fanaticism.

The Christian loves nature. He loves it most because it is the great temple of Jehovah, whose lofty columns and arches show divine wisdom and love in their construction. Wherever he wanders through its vast galleries and labyrinths, he hears God's voice and sees his hand at work. Indeed, all nature is but one vast sounding gallery, echoing and reëchoing with Jehovah's name and Jehovah's praise. He loves nature, too, because he was cradled in her arms and nursed on her bosom, and her sweet voice ever touches a sympathetic chord in his soul, and brings out the sweetest melody to which earth ever listens. Every thing which man's harpy fingers have touched bears the defilement of sin; but nature is untarnished, and her virgin robe reminds us of that which she wore in the bowers of Eden. And therefore does the Christian love nature.

Such are the objects that draw the Christian's soul to this world with strong attraction, and tend, therefore, to weaken, or to make less sensible, the attractions of heaven. But as time advances, and changes come over him, and adversity shrouds his prospects in clouds and storms, and death's ruthless hand tears one and another fond object away, these earthly ties grow weaker, and one after another are sundered; leaving the soul to be more easily drawn upward towards the world of cloudless skies, of permanent repose — the great attracting centre of the universe.

It is more especially, then, to the case of the advanced Christian — advanced in years and in piety — that my illustration under my last head applies. He may have commenced his religious course early, and have become convinced even then of the vanity of the world. But after all, the world then appeared to him in a far more fascinating aspect than it now does, after a few decades of years have taught him many impressive lessons of its emptiness. It then lay before him an untrodden field, glowing with the charms of novelty, and as seen through the prism of youthful fancy, decked with a thousand rainbow hues. As he pressed eagerly on, and plucked from time to time the golden fruit that hung temptingly over his path, he did not know how much of it would prove like the apples of Sodom.

> "This more delusive, not the touch, but taste,
> Deceived: he, fondly thinking to allay
> His thirst with gust, instead of fruit,
> Chewed bitter ashes; which the offended taste,
> With sputtering noise, rejected."

So long as the delusion lasted, the young Christian felt himself strongly drawn towards the earth. But in advanced life he has been so often deceived by its fair fruit, and drank so often of its bitter waters, that he no longer anticipates a fulfilment of its fair promises; and though he has enjoyed enough to make him very thankful, he has enjoyed too little to make him desire to tread the same path over again. He has learned that this world was never intended to afford a pleasant and permanent home, but only comfortable accommodations for a journey. He has ceased, therefore, to feel the strong attraction to earth, which health, and hope, and novelty, and youth, threw around him in early life. Faith, and hope, and desire, now reach forward towards that world

> Whose fruits and streams
> Are life and joy; where day eternal shines;
> Where love, ineffable, immortal, reigns.

One of the objects of lawful pursuit by the Christian is the acquisition of wealth, with the intention of using it for worthy objects. And this is an object that often presents a fascinating aspect to the youthful mind, and becomes one of the strong cords that bind him to the world, if he is successful in the pursuit. When he first begins to recline upon the downy couch of affluence, and fawning friends multiply, and the fashionable world condescends to smile upon him, how distant and uninviting appears his home in heaven, and how terrible the passage thither! He can enter fully into the meaning of the Son of Sirach, when he says, *O death, how bitter is the remembrance of thee to a man that is at ease in his possessions; unto the man that hath prosperity in all things, and hath nothing to vex him.* But it will not be long before this man will find, that as he sinks deeper and deeper into his bed of down, it is underlaid by a bed of thorns. He will find that the apostle spoke true words when he said, *They that will be rich fall into temptation and a snare, and into many foolish and hurtful lusts, which drown men in destruction and perdition. For the love of money is the root of all evil; which while some coveted after, they have erred from the faith, and pierced themselves through with many sorrows.* If God means to save this man, the effect of his experience will be to teach him the truth of these things in season to rescue him from utter ruin, and he will learn henceforth not to *trust in uncertain riches.* The strong hold which they have had upon his heart is broken, and he pants after the riches of paradise. It may be, too, that his riches take to themselves wings and fly away, and want succeeds to abundance. Then, when the friends of his sunny days forsake him, and the world leaves him alone to bear the iron rule of poverty, O, how sweet it is to look forward to his treasure in heaven, *where moth and rust do not corrupt, and where thieves do not break through and steal!*

Here let me add, that want and destitution, whether they have succeeded to competence and wealth, or have been the Christian's companions through life, are among the most powerful means which God uses to make heaven sweet and attractive. And it is in advanced life, especially, that poverty's cold skeleton hand seems most heavy and rigid. The Christian may have toiled on through many a wearisome year, unable to secure even a competence; and now that age and infirmity palsy his efforts, still must he labor on and struggle harder in the unequal conflict. With what a strong impulse will his heart reach out after *an inheritance incorruptible, undefiled, and that fadeth not away, reserved for him in heaven!* How often has the widowed mother, toiling at the midnight hour over her unfinished task, and unable to provide for her numerous offspring, felt the talismanic power of that reserved legacy in the skies! How often has the father's heart, fainting under his vain labors to satisfy his children's hunger, wept tears of gratitude to that Saviour who has purchased for him so precious a boon!

Another worldly good, which may have been with the Christian an object of strong desire and effort, is a reputation for learning and wisdom. And he may have been in a measure successful. But God usually so orders events, that his honors shall sit uneasily upon him, and prove a crown of thorns rather than of flowers. When he commenced his career of learning, those who had already climbed up the steep and difficult way cheered him with encouraging words, and held up the dazzling crowns which they had won, sparkling with jewels, to stimulate his zeal. But no sooner had he reached the eminence on which they stood, than he found them equally ready to pluck off his laurels, and to crowd him back again into a humbler sphere. So long as he was beneath them, they were overflowing with benevolence and patronage. But to have the ignorant boy, whom they had helped out of the mire of poverty and ignorance, become their peer, — nay, rise above them, and seize a richer crown than theirs, — was more than human pride could brook. So that the Christian scholar found that reputation had only brought him into a battle field with powerful and implacable enemies. In his path, too, he often found coiled up the viper envy, charged with venom; and the scorpion hatred often crept under his pillow, to sting him in an unconscious hour. In his own heart, also, he found the pride of science choking the growth of the Christian graces, and poisoning the springs of religious joy. In short, a few years of such experience taught him that to be elevated in society is to be a mark for the arrows of ignorance and sin; and often, too, the intelligent and the virtuous will interpose no shield of defence, so that you are left alone, with little power to do good.

"Truths would you teach to save a sinking land,
All fear, none aid you, and few understand.
Painful preëminence! yourself to view
Above life's follies, and its comforts, too."

Progress in knowledge will also give a man many a forcible lesson of the narrowness and imperfection of human science, so that the wisest are compelled to see through a glass darkly. Not only must they look through a glass which refracts the rays and colors and distorts objects, but they must see them darkly or obscurely.

These various disheartening circumstances, with which the Christian scholar almost always meets, more or less, as he advances in life, do not, indeed, wean him from the love of science; for he finds in its pursuit enjoyment as pure and ennobling as any thing earthly can give. But they do tend to rob learning and distinction among men of much of the charm with which they are invested in the eyes of the inexperienced. They do weaken science and reputation in their power to chain the Christian's affections to this world; and they lead him to look with strong desire and lively hope to that sweet world of light and love where the grossness of sense will be gone, where no unholy passions will mar and pervert the truth, and where its rays will come pure, with no intervening prism to distort them from their original source.

Vigorous health is one of the strongest bands by which we are fastened to this world; for it is that which gives its full relish to every other blessing, and without which they would all become tasteless or disgusting. The man who enjoys this health has only an indistinct apprehension of his liability to death, although he may be an eminently holy man. But advancing age brings its infirmities and pains to almost every one; and to many it brings occasional assaults of sickness or constant feeble health. In the failing appetite, the faltering step, the trembling hand, the aching head, the feverish pulse, and the irritable nerve, they have constant premonitions of the approach of dissolution. They perceive within them a constant struggle between life and death — the latter becoming stronger and stronger, and the former weaker and weaker; and, like Job, they often feel as if they were a burden to themselves. Life loses its charms because it cannot be enjoyed; and the sombre hue of melancholy is cast over all its scenes. But they know that there is a world where the inhabitants shall not say, *I am sick;* and they trust it will be their inheritance. O, with what earnest desire do their thoughts stretch forward, and anticipate the time when they shall enter *the building of God — the house not made with hands, eternal in the heavens!* Once, in the buoyancy of health and youth, this world put on enchanting smiles. But now the dream has passed by, and heaven only is clothed with beauty.

But even though the constitution may long hold out, and health continue, yet advancing years bring with them infirmity and decay, which point in no doubtful manner to the close of life. The flattened eye, requiring the optician's aid; the ear failing in its sensibility to sound; the palate losing its keen relish of savory viands, and the olfactories of sweet odors; the blood coursing sluggishly along the veins; the brain torpid and heavy in its movements; and the shrunk muscle, easily tired, and moving heavily the failing limb, — all, all tell the traveller that he has almost reached the end of his journey.

> "Eheu, fugaces, Posthume, Posthume,
> Labuntur anni; nec pietas moram
> Rugis et instanti senectæ
> Afferret indomitæque morti."

Nor do the bodily powers alone give way. The mind, too, dependent on bodily organization by unalterable laws for its free exercise, sympathizes in the decline of the physical powers. The proud heights which she once scaled can no longer be reached; the heavy blows which she once dealt out can no longer be given. She may, indeed, say, like Samson, *I will go out, as at other times, and shake myself;* but she will find that the lock of her strength has been shorn.

> "Sic fatus senior, telumque imbelle sine ictu,
> Conjecit."

First of all the memory feels the change, and reels, and staggers, and sinks under her charge. Next the judgment begins to waver; and, last of all, the imagination comes fluttering to the earth. O, who could bear thus to see his immortal mind falling into ruins, were he not able to look forward to her resurrection in a spiritual body — a body as incorruptible and immortal as the soul itself? But in view of that renovation, with what cheerfulness can the Christian see this earthly house of his tabernacle dissolve, and the powers of his mind give way, because it shows him how soon they will be delivered from their prison house of flesh and sense, and henceforth expatiate and exult in the unshackled freedom of heaven!

But there is a weight more heavy than flesh and blood which drags down to the earth the Christian's soul. It is the burden of a sinful heart; and the longer he lives, the more oppressive does it become, and the more deep his convictions that he shall never throw it off till his spirit escapes from its material tenement. But the oath and promise of God assure him that he shall drop this body of death when he passes over Jordan into the heavenly Canaan. That deliverance is the strongest desire of his heart. Even though he may fear to die, he pants for that emancipation; and the more, as longer experience makes sin more hateful, and his own sinfulness more manifest and burdensome. It helps reconcile him to death. It is one of the strongest attractions of heaven that no sin will be there.

In like manner does the wickedness and wretchedness of this alienated world weigh more and more heavily upon the Christian's spirit, and make heaven's holiness and happiness seem doubly sweet. He sympathizes with the feelings of Cowper: —

"My ear
Is pained, my heart is sick, with every day's report
Of wrong and outrage with which earth is filled.
There is no flesh in man's obdurate heart;
It doth not feel for man."

Gladly indeed would the Christian labor as long as God wills to bring man back to holiness and happiness; but how slight an impression do his efforts make, and the efforts of the whole Christian church, upon the mass of human wickedness! And how can he but feel a strong desire to reach that happy shore, and that glorious community, which sin has never polluted!

After all, the strongest ties that bind us to this world are friendship and natural affection. How many tender and fond associations cluster around the names of father and mother, wife and children, brother and sister, friend and companion! Point me to the man who has had all these tender relations sundered, and who stands on earth as an isolated being, and I will point you to one who has lost all sympathy with human kind, and would gladly depart from a desolate world. Now, mark the wisdom and benevolence of God in respect to this subject. In the first place, new attachments are rarely formed by us, of much strength, in advanced life, because the laws of our nature forbid it. In the second place, God removes the Christian's friends, one after another, as he can bear it; so that, if he be spared to advanced life, he finds himself almost alone on earth, with but few ties to be sundered when his turn comes to depart. How full of benevolence is such a dispensation! Could we form strong attachments in riper years, we might, even at the last, find ourselves so fastened to the world that the final separation would be full of anguish. But now he cuts one earthly tie after another; so that, when the time of our own separation comes, this world has almost lost its power over us, and the few remaining cords that bind us to it are easily sundered. On the other hand, all our departed friends have gone to that same world whither we must go; and there they form a centre of attraction of strong power. We know that those of them who have entered the celestial city will issue from its portals, and, clothed in immortal beauty, and with the warm and holy affection of glorified spirits, will welcome us to our everlasting home. O, what mercy is here! Come, thou disconsolate mourner, whose heart has been made so often to bleed by the departure of beloved friends, see how God is preparing to make your own departure easy, by sundering beforehand the ties that bind you to the world, and gathering your friends together in the great centre of holiness and happiness, to draw you thither with irresistible force. With such a power to draw you away, and with so feeble a force to retain you, how slight will be the final pang! how triumphant your passage through the dominions of death!

But the details that have now been given will justify a more general inference. We may regard the astronomical illustration which I last gave (Fig. 6 and 7) as describing a general principle of the divine administration, viz., that a leading object of God's treatment of men is to weaken their attachment to this world, and to concentrate in heaven an attractive influence of overwhelming power. And, really, when we consider how much he does to weaken our hold upon the world, and to draw us towards heaven, instead of wondering that a few Christians are willing to die, we ought to wonder that any of them are willing to live. This was, indeed, the state of feeling with ancient saints. Their grand difficulty seemed to be how to be reconciled to life, not to death. This was the feeling of Job when he said, *All the days of my appointed time will I wait till my change come* — as if he had been anxiously looking for that time. This was the feeling of Jacob when he exclaimed, *I have waited for thy salvation, O Lord.* And such eminently was the feeling of Paul when he said, *I have a desire to depart and be with Christ, which is better beyond expression.* O, what a mighty impulse towards heaven reigned in the apostle's soul! He longed to leap out from his bondage to matter, and become a disinthralled spirit before the throne. Whenever he alludes to the subject, his soul is all on fire, and he exclaims, *I am now ready to be offered, and the time of my departure is at hand. I have fought a good fight, I have finished my course, I have kept the faith. Henceforth there is laid up for me a crown of righteousness, which the Lord, the righteous Judge, shall give me at that day.* He had reached that lofty point of Christian experience when only a single tie bound him to the world, and that was a sense of duty to his brethren; and this he might not sunder till God should give permission. But all the other objects of his hope and desire had been transferred to heaven, and there formed a mighty centre of attraction. (See the representation in Fig. 7.)

And do our hearts, my brethren, vibrate in sympathy with that of the apostle, or is the thought of departure chilling and agonizing? It is not strange that he who is young in years and in Christian experience, to whose unpractised eye the world spreads out so many fascinating scenes, should find his heart shrinking at the thought of death; nor that he who is in the midst of business and usefulness, basking in the sunshine of public favor, and linked to the world at a thousand points, should find the wrench terrible that separates him at once from so many cherished objects. But if we are advanced in Christian experience and in years; if a large part of the objects that once interested us have either ceased to fascinate or have been transferred to the eternal world; if increasing infirmities admonish us how soon the soul's material tenement must be taken down, surely we ought no longer to view death as an enemy, but as a friend come to deliver us from sin and sorrow, to unbar our prison doors, knock off our fetters, and to let the soul go out to breathe henceforth the vital air of heaven. No Christian, whatever his age or condition, ought to be wholly destitute of these feelings. But they especially become him who has long been in the school of Christ. He is in the condition represented by my last illustration; and his soul ought to swell with strong emotion whenever he turns his eyes towards the heavenly world. There are collected many of his earthly friends, and all his heavenly friends, beckoning to him to come to their sinless and unchanging home. O, what a group of beloved objects are congregated there, and how ought we to look upon the day of death as the time of coronation and victory!

"When life in opening buds is sweet,
And golden hopes the spirit greet,
And youth prepares his joys to meet,
Alas, how hard it is to die!

"When scarce is seized some borrowed prize,
And duties press, and tender ties
Forbid the soul from earth to rise,
How awful then it is to die!

"When, one by one, those ties are torn,
And friend from friend is snatched forlorn,
And man is left alone to mourn,
Ah, then, how easy 'tis to die!

"When trembling limbs refuse their weight,
And films, slow gathering, dim the sight,
And clouds obscure the mental light,
'Tis nature's precious boon to die.

"When faith is strong, and conscience clear,
And words of peace the spirit cheer,
And visioned glories half appear,
'Tis joy, 'tis triumph, then to die."

MINERALOGICAL ILLUSTRATIONS OF CHARACTER.

Behold an Israelite indeed, in whom is no guile. — *John* i. 47.

DECEIT and duplicity, cunning, craft, and artifice, are the characteristics which we attach to guile. The man under its influence does not exhibit his real character, but assumes a false one, to accomplish some sinister end.

An Israelite indeed — such as Nathanael was, who is alluded to in the text — is a man of great simplicity and purity of character; one who fears God, and endeavors to conform his life in all respects to the precepts of the gospel. That trait, which is here described as a freedom from guile, I would denominate *transparency of Christian character.* Its opposite we might call *opacity of character.* And these terms may represent the extremes of good and bad in character.

Those conversant with the science of mineralogy will perceive that I have borrowed these terms from thence. I have conceived the idea of attempting to illustrate the subject of character by the facts of that science; not, indeed, because there is any connection between mineralogy and Christian character, excepting that what is true literally of certain minerals is true figuratively of certain characters. Hence the minerals, which are objects of sense, may be employed to fix important moral principles in the memory. I know that this mode of exhibiting religious truth has no little quaintness about it. But if it convey no error, and makes the truth more impressive, perhaps I may be pardoned for employing it; since the highest use to which we can put science is to make it subservient to religion. Nor, if we avoid the extremes of the earlier writers, in their attempts to spiritualize natural objects, can quaintness, which is in fact often only a high degree of originality, be considered a great fault.

Between perfect transparency and perfect opacity of minerals, as well as of character, there is an endless variety of intermediate conditions. There are, however, certain well-marked stages in this gradation in minerals, which well symbolize certain corresponding grades of character. I propose to describe several of these by terms derived from mineralogy; but I shall confine myself, at this time, to what are called the optical characters of minerals, that is, their relations to light.

1. *I shall first describe the wholly transparent character.*

The most perfect example of a transparent mineral is, one through which the outlines of objects may be seen, and not be colored, nor their position changed. We have fine examples in quartz and selenite.

I wish I could say that the entirely transparent character were as common as such crystals. But it appears, now and then, pure enough at least to be entitled to the commendation contained in the proverb — "An honest man's the noblest work of God." He is emphatically the work of God; not simply as to the creation of his physical nature, but more especially as to the new creation of the soul. The highest specimens of moral purity which we meet among men, whom divine grace has not transformed, will not come up to the standard of Nathanael, in whom was no guile. Many unrenewed men there are whose characters are of a noble stamp, but the simplicity and godly sincerity of elevated piety are wanting.

As to the truly transparent Christian character, the world stand in no doubt, though guile and malevolence, thereby severely reproved, sometimes try to make out consummate hypocrisy, where, to unjaundiced eyes, all is clear. They know what such a man's principles are, for he avows them; and they know he will not flinch from maintaining them, even though all others desert him:

> "Among the faithless, faithful only he."

The public are not afraid to trust such a man with their most important interests. They have no fears of chicanery and trickery, because his integrity has been so often proved.

All this does not imply that the man of perfect transparency of character should disclose all his plans and purposes to the world. A pure homogeneous crystal does not show every thing that it contains. Let the chemist subject it to the power of reagents, and he will show that it is composed of several elements, whose harmonious and perfect combination, to the exclusion of foreign impurities, give it a beautiful transparency. So there may be plans and purposes in the mind of the Christian which he does not disclose to the world, because often that would be sure to defeat them. Indeed, every man who means to be useful must have the power of keeping out of sight his yet unattempted plans of usefulness; for if known beforehand, there is malignity enough in a wicked world to thwart them, and their disclosure would do nobody any good. But no man, who means to keep a conscience void of offence, should ever form any plans or purposes which he is not willing to have laid open to the universe at any moment; and the only reason why he does not expose them should be, that he may thereby accomplish more for the good of the world. Concealed for such a reason, and they do not disturb the clearness and beauty of his character; but kept out of sight for any other reason, and they mar his transparency.

I remark, also, that objects seen through the most perfectly transparent crystal do not appear as distinct as when viewed through a vacuum, or the air. This well illustrates the imperfection of the best of human characters. Divine grace does not choose to make them absolutely perfect in this world. Perhaps it is no more possible that a descendant of Adam should exhibit perfection, than that a crystal, formed out of mineral matter, should transmit light without intercepting some of its rays. It remains for a higher state of existence to bring out the Christian character in its full glory. In that city whose foundations are formed of the choicest gems, a correspondent beauty and perfection will be developed in the Christian's soul.

Thus far I have spoken of transparent crystals, that transmit only white light; and these I have made the emblem of the most perfect character. But the light is sometimes colored; it may be deeply so; and though the essential transparency remains, objects seen through the crystal will be also colored. Examples may be seen in amethyst, rose mica, and red rock salt.

This fact symbolizes another variety of character, less perfect than the first, yet more frequent. It is not very uncommon to meet with a man whose character in the main belongs to the transparent class, yet he suffers himself to be swayed by strong prejudices, and these color every object at which he looks. He is sincere in desiring to view every object in its true light, and is not aware that his eye always looks upon colored objects. But an eagle-eyed world perceive it, and though they do not perhaps doubt his honesty, they lose their confidence in his judgment.

Another Christian, of the same general honesty and transparency of character, fixes his eyes so exclusively upon some particular doctrines or duties, that they give a coloring to all his views. He over-estimates their importance, and they injure the symmetry of his religious character, producing as much deviation from perfect transparency as color does in the crystal.

The same effect is sometimes produced upon character by long-continued poor health. Some diseases do actually give an unnatural color to objects seen through the eye. And there are jaundiced minds, as well as jaundiced eyes. Nor can the man avoid viewing the world with a morbid and melancholy hue thrown over it, when the nervous system is deranged, any more than a yellow tinge can be removed from external objects, when the eye is suffused with bile. He whose health is firm, and whose mental eye is clear, smiles at the delusions of the invalid, and takes pride in his superior philosophy and religion. But let a slight shock be given to his nervous system, and the same sombre cloud will overshadow him, and his boasted philosophy and religion will succumb to a deranged sensorium.

2. *I shall in the second place describe the hydrophanous character.*

Hydrophanous minerals are such as are not transparent till they are immersed in water, when they become so; as the hydrophane, a variety of opal.

So it is with many a Christian. Till the floods of adversity have been poured over him, his character appears marred and clouded by selfish and worldly influences. But trials clear away the obscurity, and give distinctness and beauty to his piety. It is necessary often that the waves should roll over him again and again, before his soul becomes thoroughly permeated, and his character wholly transparent. But if God means to make him an instrument of eminent usefulness on earth, or eminent in glory in heaven, he will not lift him out of the waters till the work has been thoroughly accomplished.

3. *The third character I would symbolically describe is the semi-transparent.*

Through a semi-transparent or sub-transparent mineral objects may be seen, but there is no distinctness of outline, as in gypsum, selenite, and quartz.

The semi-transparent character is no uncommon one, even among professed Christians. Light enough is transmitted from such, and through them, to lead us, in the exercise of charity, to place them among the really pious; yet every thing about them is indistinct and cloudy. They have no clear and definite ideas of the doctrines of the Christian system, and there is a correspondent looseness in respect to Christian duties. Their religious experience, both at its commencement and subsequently, has no strongly marked features. There is no clear line of demarcation in their minds between worldly morality and Christian ethics. Hence they conform very much to worldly maxims and practices; so much so as to raise doubts of their piety in the minds of many; and yet they will cordially unite in every good work, and thus often do they clear their characters from suspicion. There is so much of flexibility in their principles and character, that you cannot tell where you will find them in times when decision and independence are needed. In short, it seems as if such persons were aiming to secure both this world and the next, and you fear that they may lose both.

Semi-transparency may symbolize a character still more unlovely and repulsive. The very mineral I have taken to illustrate it — gypsum — was used under the name of *phengites*, by some of the most hateful of the Roman emperors — Nero, for example — for the windows of their palaces. So nearly transparent was it, that these tyrants could look out and see what the people were doing, while the latter could not look in and see what was going on there. And this is just what jealous and cruel despots, and others of like disposition, desire. Others they wish to scrutinize with eagles' eyes, while they themselves keep in the dark, and from thence give the assassin's stab.

4. *I pass, fourthly, to describe the translucent character.*

Minerals are translucent when light is transmitted through them, but objects are not seen.

There are two varieties of translucency. In the first, light seems to penetrate the entire mass, but not enough to produce even semi-transparency. The difficulty seems to have been, that the particles, when the mineral was in the process of formation, were not thoroughly dissolved, and therefore could not be so arranged by the laws of crystallography as to allow the light to pass freely through. And yet it seems as if the work had been nearly accomplished. Examples may be seen in fibrous gypsum and rose quartz.

This mineral aptly represents the man who seems to stand about upon the line between the world and the Christian. There is so much that is good, both in his principles and his practice, that you are disposed at times to class him with the latter. But you cannot see through him, and there is too much room left for guile and artifice to hide themselves, and unexpectedly to develop unlovely traits of character, so that you stand in doubt of him. You greatly wish that divine grace had thoroughly dissolved native selfishness and worldliness, so that they should not so mar and mystify the whole character. The man probably considers himself a Christian, and possibly he is so, but of a very low grade of piety. More likely he has only been convicted, but not converted; and great is the danger, if that be the case, that he never will be.

Another variety of mineral exhibits translucency only on its edges. The central mass is dark; but holding the specimen to the light, and light is transmitted dimly through the thin edges. Marble and flint, or hornstone, are examples.

In these specimens, we have a good symbolization of the man, who has been brought so much under the influence of Christianity, that it has modified his external conduct, produced some regard for true piety, led to some outward reformations, and caused him to adopt some of the forms of religion. Yet the darkness of unregeneracy reigns within. The central mass of character has never been permeated by the subduing and remodelling power of divine grace, and therefore no heavenly light can pass through. Friends, and possibly the man himself, mistake the rays that struggle through the edges of his character for genuine Christian experience. But until the light can reach the soul's centre, if guile still reigns there, along with selfishness, pride, and worldliness, external translucency can avail nothing in the sight of God. Nothing but divine alchemy can rearrange and transmute the elements of character, so as to give it the transparency of true religion.

5. *My fifth symbolization embraces the doubly refracting character.*

A doubly-refracting crystal is transparent; but it gives two images of objects seen through it. Ordinary refraction produces one, and extraordinary refraction another, by splitting the ray. A good example is Iceland spar, or calcite.

Just so some Christian men, apparently without guile, and found in the main on the right side, do sometimes so split the rays of truth as to give a false image of things. They so speculate and philosophize about doctrines, that the formularies they present have the aspect of heresy, although it is in fact nothing but idiosyncrasy. So, in regard to Christian duties, there is often some extraordinary refraction which gives those duties an aspect different from the common one. The moral reformations and Christian enterprises of the present age, also, seen through their optics, put on features which no other eyes can see. In short, there are peculiarities in their mental or moral constitution that make it difficult for others to act or think in concert with them. The truth is, the leaven of self-esteem and love of distinction is working within them, and so bends the ray of truth that a false image is formed, which these men honestly believe to be the true one.

6. *The sixth character which I shall describe is the phosphorescent.*

Certain minerals, when rubbed against each other, or exposed to a considerable degree of heat or to the light of the sun, and then are removed to a dark place, will emit light for some time, and sometimes beautifully, although previously opaque. This is called phosphorescence. Examples are quartz, fluor spar, and the diamond.

You have probably anticipated me in the character I would symbolize by these examples. For how common is it to meet with men who never seem to feel any interest in any good cause till they are brought under the influence of others!

They have an excitable temperament; and if others go before them, and call after them to follow, they begin to throw off phosphorescent sparks; or when warmed by the tongue of eloquence or the mesmeric power of sympathy, their souls seem to be permeated by a phosphoric glow that promises much. But as the light of the phosphorescent mineral fades, and soon disappears, when the extrinsic heat is taken away, and daylight is let in upon it, so do the ardor and zeal of these men depart when foreign stimulants are withdrawn, and they are left to their own resources. Their benevolence, being the fruit of external excitement, and having nothing to feed it within, soon dies away, and leaves the man as unfeeling, as narrow-minded, and as selfish as ever.

7. *My seventh symbolization describes the dichroic character.*

Dichroism consists in a mineral's exhibiting different colors on different faces. Thus dichroite, or iolite, is often deep blue along its vertical axis; but on a side perpendicular to this axis it is brownish yellow. The phenomenon results from the manner in which the particles are arranged for reflecting and transmitting light. The whole internal structure must be changed before the same color shall be presented on all the faces.

Moral dichroism consists in a man's being Janus-faced — that is, double-faced both in his principle and his practice, in order to secure popular favor and avoid odium. The chameleon is said to have the power of assuming the color of the object on which it fastens; so this man means to conform his creed and his practice to those which are most popular in the community where he happens to live or sojourn. In one place, he is orthodox; in another, heterodox; — in one, an advocate for temperance; in another, loose in this matter, both in theory and practice; — in one place, proslavery; in another, antislavery. His moral and religious principles are not settled, or rather he makes them bend to his worldly interest; and you have no way of determining where to find him in any circumstances, except to inquire what aspect self-interest will require him to put on. Nor will it ever be essentially better until divine grace shall have transformed and rearranged the elements of his character.

8. *My eighth symbol will illustrate a chatoyant character.*

A chatoyant mineral exhibits a beautiful play of prismatic colors as it is turned around. It is not a mere surface phenomenon, but proceeds from the internal arrangement of the particles. The diamond affords, perhaps, the most perfect example, unless it be the precious opal.

Mineralogists make some distinction between a play of colors and a change of colors in crystals. But the difference is unimportant in the point of view in which I am looking at the subject; and I include both those varieties under the term chatoyant. Hence I should quote, as a third example, Labrador feldspar, or labradorite, which, though less brilliant than the diamond, has the advantage of presenting a much larger surface, glowing with prismatic hues.

I regard brilliancy of character as the trait most aptly represented by the chatoyant property of minerals. I mean chiefly brilliancy of intellect. This may be conjoined with humble piety, without destroying its transparency; and the character thus formed becomes eminently attractive, and is well symbolized by the diamond, the most precious and perfect of all minerals. But brilliancy of parts is quite apt to derogate from the purity and simplicity of Christian character, so that its transparency is marred, just as is the case with the opal and the labradorite. We are delighted with their splendor, but regret that we cannot see through them.

9. *The irised or pavonine character is symbolized by my ninth example.*

Irised minerals often give a splendid exhibition of most of the colors of the spectrum; but it is produced by a mere superficial film, while all beneath is opaque, as in a specimen of anthracite coal.

The pavonine character, so called from its resemblance to the feathers of the peacock, is so common as hardly to need a particular description. It is the man who has a strong passion for outside display, but has no corresponding sterling qualities within. He may be gaudy as the peacock without; but just penetrate beneath the thin film of external character, and all will be found either hollow or opaque within. Frequently the interior will be found a hiding place for artifice, cunning, and duplicity, and always for vanity and self-conceit. Such a character is frequently a rather harmless one — not so much from a want of disposition as from a want of ability to do much mischief.

There are some minerals — mica, for instance — that are essentially transparent, but show the prismatic colors in their interior. This is called iridescence; but it differs little from the irised character, which is limited to the surface. For the interior iridescence proceeds from a metallic film introduced into some crack or fissure, producing a brilliant tarnish there of the same nature as that upon the irised surface. Example, iridescent mica or quartz.

The iridescent mineral has its counterpart among men; for we meet with not a few excellent Christian men who show an inordinate fondness for external display. Costly and elegant dwellings and furniture, elegant horses and carriages, and rich, if not gaudy, clothing, they do not regard as inconsistent with their obligations to conform to the precepts and self-denial of their Master. But this passion for show can be regarded only as a flaw in their character, marring its transparency as iridescence does the pure crystal.

10. *My tenth and last example describes the opaque character.*

We find at least two varieties in this respect among minerals. Some crystals, such as mica, are transparent in one direction and opaque in another.

It is so with some men. In a Christian land, it is not unusual to meet with those who have very clear views of the theory of religion, both doctrinal and practical, and you expect to find their hearts and lives conformed to their belief. But the moment you make the subject personal, you perceive that the opaque side of their character is turned towards you, and all is repulsive and dark. Christ met such a man in the youth whom he loved, and who had kept all the commandments from his earliest days. How clear did his creed and his character seem! But no sooner was the demand made for the sacrifice of his money for the good of others, than the crystal was turned, so as to be impervious to light. Selfishness had too firm a hold upon the heart to be cast out even by the persuasive voice of the Son of God. And so it has ever been, and is now, in the hearts of multitudes.

Another striking exemplification of the character under consideration is seen in the manner in which many men treat some of the important moral reformations now in progress — say that of temperance. Converse with them, and they seem to be strenuous advocates of the cause; but ask them to co-operate with you in plans for its advancement, and you develop a secret and unexpected hostility to the work in every form. Public opinion has forced them to profess friendship for it in general terms; but when they are driven to the wall, and compelled to act one way or the other, you find out that the cause has no more bitter enemies. Their seeming transparency has given place to blank opacity, where guile, and duplicity, and self-indulgence lie coiled up together in the darkness in snaky brotherhood.

The completely opaque mineral, such as coal, transmits not one ray of light, and all within is of course entirely concealed. It fitly represents a character thoroughly bad within and without. The only thing we like about it is, that there is no attempt to assume a borrowed dress in order to conceal the deformity within. The principles are bad, and the conduct is bad; and nothing but divine grace can transform the dark and shapeless mass into order, transparency, and beauty.

I might go on to multiply symbolizations of character from the scientific history of the mineral kingdom, especially were I to derive my illustrations from other features of minerals bsides the optical. But I have probably said enough. Yet a few closing practical remarks will not be inappropriate.

1. *These illustrations may suggest to us some salutary cautions in judging of character.*

Recollect that the transparent character is the standard. Hence, if there be mystery about a man; if he is jealous of others, yet careful to hide himself; if his virtues are cloudy and indistinct; if his opinions are colored by prejudice and passion; if he is trying to accomplish certain darling worldly schemes, which depend mainly on popular favor; if there is more about him of cunning plans than of simple, straightforward integrity; if he assumes different aspects in different positions; and, especially, if he attempts to conceal his principles, and refuses to take a stand on the side of virtue and right, and truckles and panders to error and sin in high places, — then I would say, Be careful how you trust such a man. In short, we have reason to fear for our own and others' characters just in proportion to our departure from the true, transparent model of an Israelite indeed.

2. *The subject affords us an illustration of complete Christian sanctification.*

The grace of God, when it first visited the Christian, found his character, if not absolutely opaque, yet so much so that even the light that was in him was darkness. That grace sent the power of eternal truth into the chaos, and rearranged the purposes and the affections, and made the soul capable of transmitting more or less of uncolored light, so that ever since the false colors of the world, the flesh, and the adversary have been disappearing. But it is not till perfect transparency shall be produced, and guile, with its train of unholy passions, shall have disappeared, that the believer can enter heaven. O, how great a change must still pass upon most of us who profess religion, if we ever reach that holy place!

3. *Finally, how important for our success and usefulness in this life is a perfectly guileless character!*

Jesus Christ is described as one who *did no sin*, *nor was guile found in his mouth* — as if that was the crowning excellence of his character. Indeed, an honest man *is* the noblest work of God. And there have been many such — Israelites indeed, in whom was no guile, though not absolutely free from sin, as Christ was. Hours would be requisite merely to mention the names of such, whose memory the church holds dear; and volumes would be needed to describe their characters. I will refer to only two examples, and that briefly.

It is probable that the world has never seen such an extraordinary instance of moral influence as was acquired among all classes of men by the missionary Swartz, who for fifty years preached the gospel in India. He lived in the midst of Englishmen, Hindoos, and Mohammedans, and was exceedingly plain and faithful to them all in his preaching and exhortations. Yet such was the respect for him manifested by them all, that even in the bloody wars waged among them, all parties regarded him as a friend, and even pagan rajahs gave orders to their soldiers not to interrupt his labors. And often was property intrusted to his hands, as well as the business of pacificator; and the Rajah of Tanjore committed the education of his son, who was to succeed him, to Swartz. "Combined with humility," says his biographer, "was that singular and transparent simplicity, which so powerfully recommended him to men of every rank and every religion, and which was the grand secret of his unparalleled influence and success. Can we wonder that one so pious, humble, upright, and sincere should excite the veneration and conciliate the confidence of all around him; that Hindoo princes, observant and acute, should cultivate his friendship, invite his counsel, and invoke his protection; that Mohammedan tyrants, subtle and suspicious, should respect his integrity and accept his mediation; that European governors and officers, civil and military, should intrust to him the most important concerns, and coöperate with him in all his plans; that by the great body of the people, of every class, he should be revered, idolized, and obeyed?"

Another example, of analogous character, was the confidence reposed in the American missionaries on Mount Lebanon, during a sanguinary civil war between the Druzes and Maronites in that mountain, in 1845. Though the parties were bigotedly attached to their own corrupt religions, and felt no sympathy with the object of the missionaries, and though under the influence of the most ferocious hatred towards each other, they all assured the missionaries that their lives and property would be safe in the midst of carnage, conflagration, and death. And so it proved. Nay, in the very heat of the conflict, when blood flowed like water, they requested the missionaries to act as mediators. "By the blessing of God," say the missionaries, "we secured the confidence of both parties in the region where we reside, and were assured on all hands that we had nothing to fear, whoever should prove victorious. And when the wild whirlwind of war actually swept over Abeih, we not only remained in entire safety, but were able to afford shelter to multitudes of the unfortunate ; nor was the sanctity of our asylum violated in a single instance." O, what a mighty power there is in Christian simplicity and integrity!

Should it not, then, be an object of the highest ambition for every young man, especially, to establish a reputation for a guileless character, which can be done only by actually possessing it? Let the community once get the impression that such is not his character; that, instead of being artless and of unswerving integrity, he condescends to duplicity and artifice, and to partisan jugglery, to carry his points, and long will it be before he can disabuse the public mind of that impression, and recover their confidence. Let him, then, take care, in the first place, early to acquire this brightest jewel in the Christian's crown, and then secure it by a guileless life; and he will find that he has a passport to usefulness and honor which nothing else can give. Guile may sometimes, indeed, carry a point, and gain an ephemeral reputation ; but dreadful will be the reaction when the truth comes out — so that in the end it will appear that honesty is always the best policy. God grant that all of us may so live, that when we depart, an admiring world may write on each of our monuments the inscription, *In simplicity and godly sincerity, not with fleshly wisdom, but by the grace of God, he had his conversation in the world.*

THE INSEPARABLE TRIO.

Blessed is the nation whose God is the Lord, (Jehovah.) — *Psalm* xxxiii. 12.

Therefore my people are gone into captivity, because they have no knowledge. — *Isaiah* v. 13.

If therefore the Son shall make you free, ye shall be free indeed. — *John* viii. 36.

An important reciprocal influence has ever been admitted to exist between religion, education, and freedom; but their inseparable connection and mutual dependence have rarely been maintained or demonstrated. If that can be done, the present is surely an appropriate occasion for attempting it. Such, therefore, is the theme which I shall present to this highly respected audience.

The position taken on this subject is this: —

Religion, Education, and Freedom, are inseparable, and mutually dependent.

It will give, perhaps, a clearer idea of this general proposition, if it be divided and illustrated.

First, then, true religion, an enlightened system of education, and genuine freedom, form the three great vital centres of the social system; just as the brain, the heart, and the lungs are the centres of life in the animal system. Nor can you separate these centres from one another in the one case, any more than in the other, without destroying them all. Without a brain to give sensibility and motion, there would be no beating heart or heaving lungs. Without a heart to propel the blood through the brain and the lungs, the latter would collapse, and the former would be paralyzed. And did not the lungs oxygenate and purify the blood, it would prove a deadly poison to the brain and the heart; and no vital warmth would be imparted to the frame. So in the social system, were there no religion to give sensibility to our relations to God and our fellow-men, and to lead us to act from higher motives than atheism or pantheism could inspire, education, in its legitimate and liberal meaning, would never exist; nor could freedom be enjoyed; since, without the purifying and elevating influence of religion, the strong would oppress the weak, and keep them in hopeless servitude. So, if education were stricken from the social system, religion would degenerate into formalism, or fanaticism; and freedom would soon be drowned in licentiousness, or crushed by an iron despotism. And if freedom were to be smothered, religion would lose its vitality, and become a mere tool of ambition; and education would be ostracized as a dangerous agent, at least in the hands of the people at large.

Secondly, no one of these vital centres of the social system can be in health and vigorous action, if the rest are diseased or palsied. For such is their mutual sympathy, that just so far as one is defective, or its vitality lowered, by an admixture of erroneous principles, will the others be crippled and benumbed. In the animal system, if disease has attacked the brain, we expect, not only that the mind will be oppressed, or act irregularly and wildly, but that the lungs and the heart will partake of the disordered movement. In like manner, if disease or poison be operating upon the heart, or the lungs, we cannot depend upon the healthy action of the brain and the mind. And the degree of irregularity existing in one of these vital organs is the index of the derangement in the others. Just so, if in any country a false or defective system of religion prevails, we may be sure to find corresponding deficiencies and errors in its system of education and its principles of liberty. In like manner, if we find its inhabitants ignorant, we can safely infer that its religion is proportionably erroneous, and its freedom defective. And if the liberties of a country have been usurped by the despotism of the many, or of the few, we may be sure that in the same ratio, its religion will be corrupt and its plans of education imperfect.

Such is my explication and elucidation of the general principle advanced. I may seem to have taken strong ground; but I trust it can be maintained by an appeal to REASON, to the BIBLE, and to EXPERIENCE. I proceed, therefore, to defend my position by evidence drawn from these three sources.

Preliminary to this argument, however, let me say, lest my positions should be misunderstood, that in maintaining the inseparable connection and mutual dependence of these three pillars of a nation's glory and strength, I do not contend that they are equally important. It will be universally admitted that the brain, the lungs, and the heart are inseparably connected and mutually dependent. But who does not know that the brain occupies a place, and executes functions in the system, of preëminent importance? The influence that emanates from it, along the conducting nerves, causes the heart to beat and the lungs to heave: in fact, all the phenomena of vitality depend upon it; and so, in the present world, do the far more wonderful phenomena of intellect. But it is nevertheless true, that disordered action in the heart, or the lungs, will impair the functions of the brain; so that we infer a mutual dependence; while at the same time we assign the highest place, and by far the most commanding influence, to the brain.

In like manner, in the social system, no observing and reasonable man will hesitate to place religion at the head of all those influences by which the public good is promoted, the national character formed, and its destinies shaped. Moral obligation is the only power that can give genuine life and regulated action to a nation's energies; and if that do not send its galvanic shocks into the whole system, not only will education and freedom fail of vitalization, but paralysis will seize upon the whole body politic; — except that occasionally a convulsive agony, the symptom of approaching dissolution, may rack its frame and distort its features. Highest and foremost, therefore, we place religion among the influences that determine a nation's character; although an important reflex influence upon religion, from education and freedom, must be admitted.

It may be desirable to state another preliminary explanation. In maintaining the mutual dependence of these three great institutions of the social economy, so that when one fails or is crippled, the others suffer the same fate, it should be remembered that we speak of the community as a whole, and not of individual exceptions. For such exceptions may exist, of a striking character. The prevalent system of religion may be very corrupt, and yet there may be found bright and beautiful examples of individual piety. So there may exist many splendid examples of scholarship, where the masses are profoundly ignorant. And even under the gloomy sway of despotism, individuals may be found enjoying a high degree of personal independence. But single exceptions of this sort cannot invalidate conclusions based upon tendencies and results, which are generally the same, and whose failure is only as one to a thousand.

But what do we mean by the term religion? Simply, I answer, the unadulterated system taught in the Bible, and illustrated perfectly in the life of the Founder of Christianity, and imperfectly, yet often beautifully, in the lives of those followers of Christ who have been eminent for their self-denying labors and vigorous faith.

And what do we mean by education? Not a system that provides for the gigantic scholarship of a favored few, while the many are left under the cloud of ignorance; but a system that carries the torch of science through every portion of the community, offering it to all as freely as the daylight, and opening the path for the poorest and the humblest genius to find his way to the summit of Parnassus.

And what do we mean by freedom? Not liberty for a few, or even a majority, while a large portion of the community are cut off from its blessings; not liberty for the whole without restraint; not that reckless liberty, which abolishes all the salutary distinctions of society, founded on talents, character, and office, and levels every thing downwards, till all are sunk to the lowest grade; but we mean such a degree of chastened liberty, as experience has shown most conducive to individual happiness and the public good.

From these explanations I turn now to the evidence of the general position, that religion, education, and freedom, are inseparable and mutually dependent. I make my first appeal to REASON; in other words, to the NATURE OF THE CASE. The problem is this: knowing the character of man, and the nature of religion, education, and freedom, does reason alone, irrespective of Scripture and experience, afford a presumption in favor of the proposition, or against it? Reasoning *a priori*, should we conclude these three leading institutions of the social system to be mutually dependent, and so connected that diseased action in one shall be communicated to all the rest?

In order to obtain a satisfactory answer to these inquiries, let us make a series of suppositions.

Let us, in the first place, imagine that religion is stricken from this trio. Can education and freedom long survive?

To live without religion, is to be destitute of all sense of moral obligation to God or our fellow-men, and to be free from all influences and sanctions drawn from a future state of retribution. In such circumstances we need not resort to any theological dogma to show that supreme selfishness would be the controlling law of life, and consequently, that every man would strive to gain as much power, and distinction, and property as possible. But the more talented and discerning few would soon discover, that in proportion as the mass of men were enlightened and free, would be the difficulty of gratifying their selfish desires. While, therefore, they might encourage education and freedom among a favored few, they would try to keep the many ignorant and in servitude. This is, in fact, the very process that has been acted over a thousand times in the history of our globe. The masses must be kept ignorant and degraded, or the few cannot monopolize the power, wealth, and influence, which selfish nature urges them to seek after with irresistible impulse. To root out religion, then, is to aim a death blow at education and freedom.

Let us next suppose a nation to be blessed with religion and freedom, but without education. Can she long retain the former?

Although the great principles and precepts of religion are simple, they are liable to be misunderstood and misapplied, if the intellect be uncultivated. Individuals quite ignorant may become devotedly pious, in a community where there are intelligent men to instruct them. But if the vast majority are unlettered, religion will almost inevitably lose its power beneath a multitude of external ceremonies, or run wild with fanaticism. For these extremes are more fascinating to the ignorant mind than the unostentatious piety of the heart, because accompanied by more external glitter and noise. Besides, it is much easier for a heart in love with sin to practise pompous rites and ceremonies, or to cry out with Jehu, *Come and see my zeal for the Lord*, than to carry on a daily warfare with sin within and without, and to set an example of charity, humility, and self-sacrifice. Hence it is, that in an ignorant community, religion never fails to degenerate into formalism or fanaticism; and not unfrequently the two have been united.

No less essential is intellectual cultivation to the support of genuine freedom. Men must understand its principles, or they will either become the dupes, and ere long the slaves, of unprincipled ambition, or they will mistake licentiousness for liberty, and soon be glad to take refuge in the despotism of one from the despotism of many.

Imagine next, that a nation is blessed with religion and education, but has lost its freedom. Can the former flourish under an arbitrary government?

Tyrants are usually eagle-eyed to discover any influences that are hostile to their usurped prerogatives. Now, the whole system of the Bible aims a fatal blow against all unrighteous authority, both because it brings all men on a level before God, and because it shows such authority to be hateful in his sight. Hence despotic power will not be satisfied till it has robbed Christianity of its vitality; and, alas! it has usually found a venal priesthood, ready to perform the mummifying process.

An enlightened system of public education is almost equally hostile to arbitrary power as is Christianity. In fact, you cannot enlighten the people, generally, without teaching them their true character, and showing them that God made them to be free. Either, therefore, the power of the tyrant or education must fall; and the same agency which he has employed to embowel Christianity will be ready to obliterate the primary school, and petrify the college and the university.

These suppositions sustain, I trust, the first part of the general proposition, that religion, education, and freedom are inseparable. But the second part maintains that there is such a connection and sympathy between them, that to mar and deteriorate one is to impart what the chemist would call a *catalytic* influence to all the rest, whereby they shall be degraded and become impure. To show this will require a parallel series of suppositions; and yet by an appeal to history, we might convert these assumptions into facts. But that belongs to my third argument.

We will suppose the religion of a nation to become corrupt, either by the introduction of false doctrines, or the substitution of external forms for the piety of the heart, or by an amalgamation with the world. Now, unadulterated Christianity is a stern advocate for the most liberal system of education; both because it courts the most rigid scrutiny, and because, without intelligence in the community, its plain and honest features would soon be buried, and its vitality smothered, beneath the meretricious ornaments of formalism, or burned over and blackened by the fires of fanaticism. But a corrupt system of religion dreads a pure system of education, lest its hypocrisy should be detected. It knows very well that education must be so modified as not to admit of freedom of discussion or freedom of opinion; and that the great body of the people must be kept in comparative ignorance, or they will not submit to the trammels of a perverted Christianity. And, therefore, it will be hostile to any system of education that is not clipped and moulded to conform to its own degraded standard.

Equally jealous of freedom you will find every false system of Christianity. Religious liberty, especially, cannot be tolerated; for, in such a case, the perversions of the truth, made by an unholy priesthood, or designing politicians, would soon be exposed, and then resisted. Uncomplaining conformity to the prevailing system is the imperious demand of every corrupt religion. And since nearly every such system links itself with the state, it can enforce conformity; if not, at this day, by swords and fagots, yet by the almost equally powerful engines of governmental favors and disabilities. Hence, to pervert Christianity is to put a muzzle upon the mouth of freedom.

Suppose a defective system of education to prevail in a country; one, for example, where the majority of the people are uninstructed, and only the wealthy and aristocratic have access to the fountains of knowledge. The most inevitable result would be, that the educated few would encroach upon the rights of the ignorant many; while the cunning priest would easily *exalt himself above all that is called God, or that is worshipped; so that, as God, he should sit in the temple of God, showing himself that he is God*, and thus persuade the multitude that they must go to him for pardon and life eternal, instead of Jehovah.

Or suppose arbitrary power to have gained the ascendency, where the people are well instructed, and pure religion prevails. In such a case, we may calculate upon one of two results. Either religion and education would teach the people rebellion, — for there can be no doubt but both of them are decidedly hostile to arbitrary power, — or the usurpers would contrive to infuse a narcotic influence into the pulpit, to close the primary school, and to render the press venal.

From the known selfish and ambitious character of man, therefore, and the admitted sympathetic influence between religion, education, and freedom, does not reason decide that to obliterate one is to destroy the rest? and to corrupt one is to sink the others to the same condition? In support of these positions, I make my second appeal to the Bible.

It should not be forgotten, however, that the grand object of the Bible is to instruct us in religion; and no other subjects are mentioned, except as incidentally connected with this. We ought not to expect, therefore, that we shall find the general proposition which we are discussing, stated in so many words. Its leading features, however, I think we can find asserted and defended, directly or indirectly.

The Bible shows us, for instance, how indispensable to a nation's happiness and glory is true religion. The passage first named at the head of this discourse — *Happy is the nation whose God is the Lord* — is an example. It does not say that such would be the effect of acknowledging and serving any other God except Jehovah, the God of the Jews; for so he is called in the original. The poet would make no difference between

"Jehovah, Jove, and Lord."

But the Bible declares, that "though there be that are called gods, whether in heaven or in earth, to us there is but one

God, of whom are all things, and we in him, and one Lord Jesus Christ, by whom are all things, and we by him." It is the service and love of that one God only, through that one Lord Jesus Christ, that can render a nation happy. That God declares that "he is a great king over all the earth; a governor among the nations;" and he challenges their love and service. "Let all the earth fear the Lord; let all the inhabitants of the world stand in awe of him." He goes farther, and declares the consequence of disobedience. "At what instant I shall speak concerning a nation, and concerning a kingdom, to build and to plant it; if it do evil in my sight, that it obey not my voice, then I will repent of the good wherewith I said I would benefit them. If they will not obey, I will utterly pluck up and destroy that nation," saith the Lord.

Thus does the Bible represent true religion as preëminently important to a nation's happiness. It also declares knowledge to be essential to the preservation of freedom and religion. The second text named at the head of this discourse teaches this, at least in part: *Therefore my people are gone into captivity, because they have no knowledge.* Here the loss of liberty is ascribed to ignorance; and this, as we have seen, corresponds with reason, and, as we shall see, with experience also. In another place, it is said, "For the transgressions of a land, many are the princes thereof," — that is, frequent changes and revolutions occur, — "but by a man of understanding and knowledge, the state thereof shall be prolonged;" that is, its prosperity shall be lengthened out. Again, it is said, "My people are destroyed for lack of knowledge: because thou hast rejected knowledge, I will also reject thee." Again, "Wisdom and knowledge shall be the stability of thy times, and strength of salvation."

If it be objected that the term knowledge, in the Scriptures, usually means religious knowledge, and therefore does not embrace modern science and literature, whose acquisition is the chief thing in what we call education, it may be answered, first, that the term knowledge, in such texts as have just been quoted, did embrace every kind of intellectual acquisition that entered into the Jewish system of education; of which, however, religion constituted nearly the whole. Again, who will deny that the religious applications of modern science and literature constitute their most important use? Nay, what principle of science (and of literature we may say nearly the same) does not afford some illustration of the divine character or government, or of man's moral relations, and may not, therefore, be properly called a religious truth? Furthermore, it will be confessed, that the moral and religious teachings and applications of modern education are precisely the principles that are the most important to the preservation of a nation's freedom and happiness. So that what the Bible says of the bearings of knowledge and of ignorance upon a nation's destinies, may be applied to the most valuable and perfect system of modern education.

But the Bible proceeds a step farther, and shows us what is the character of the man who is most perfectly fitted to the exercise and enjoyment of freedom. This is pointed out in the third passage prefixed to this discourse: "If, therefore, the Son shall make you free, ye shall be free indeed." That is, if the transforming power of the gospel has been exerted upon a man, so that he has become free from the power of sin, he is every whit free, — a freeman of the Lord, — fitted rightly to appreciate and become a champion of civil liberty. The Jews resented the imputation of Christ that they were not free, and said, "We be Abraham's seed, and were never in bondage to any man: how sayest thou, Ye shall be made free?" Jesus answered them, "Verily, verily, I say unto you, Whosoever committeth sin is the servant of sin." Till that chain be broken, he cannot be truly free; as the poet has finely expressed it —

> "He is the freeman whom the truth makes free,
> And all are slaves besides."

Finally, in the organization of the Christian church, as exhibited in the Bible, we have a divine testimony to the intimate connection between Christianity, freedom, and education. It seems difficult to read the inspired history of the establishment of the church impartially, without coming to the conclusion that it was a pure democracy — or, rather, its government seems to be what may be called a *theocratic democracy;* by which I mean a government of the people; and yet they are governed by the law of God, and their administration consists mainly in carrying out the divine law. Each church consisted of brethren, with equal rights. They elected their own pastor and deacons, disciplined their own members, settled their own difficulties, and were independent of other churches, except so far as they asked for advice. The pastors, too, were all equal, save so far as age, talents, or superior piety, gave any the precedence. I do not say that all Christian churches, in all circumstances, are required to be organized on such a republican model. The Jewish church — synonymous with the Jewish nation — was a theocracy; and I sincerely respect the opinion of eminent men, who have thought the diocesan and metropolitan forms of church government the best for men in other circumstances. I sincerely respect that opinion, I say, so long as they base it upon expediency, and not upon the Bible. That book certainly describes the primitive church, established by Christ and his apostles, as an institution thoroughly democratic; and is not this a strong testimony in favor of free civil governments? especially when they, and they alone, harmonize with the whole spirit of Christianity, which regards all men as brethren of a common Father. Indeed, though the Bible directs Christians to obey whatever rulers Providence may have placed over them, so long as they are tolerable, yet where has it given a testimony in favor of any other except a free government?

In the characteristics both of the members and the ministers of the church, which the Bible has given, we find also a testimony in favor of education, as essential to the purity of religion and freedom. It demands, first of all, an intelligent and rational submission of intellect and heart to the authority and will of God; and then it directs believers to "prove all things, and to hold fast that which is good" — a requisition impossible to a mind entirely uneducated. Then, too, if we read Paul's descriptions of the ministerial character, especially in his Epistles to Timothy, we shall see a demand for a very thorough mental discipline. Even under the old dispensation, it was said that "the priests' lips should keep knowledge." We are not, then, surprised to hear Paul exhorting Timothy "to give attendance to reading," as well as to "exhortation and doctrine;" also, to "meditate on these things, and give himself wholly to them, that his profiting might appear to all, and that he might make full proof of his ministry." Surely, nothing but thorough literary discipline could qualify a man for such a work. Theology, the noblest of all sciences, is but the quintessence of them all; and he only who has studied them can extract and condense it.

Is it not clear, then, that the Bible, while it places religion immeasurably above every thing else, does yet, directly, or by fair implication, strongly advocate the most enlarged system of education, and the purest form of national freedom? And does it not represent the absence, or defects, of the two latter to be fatal or injurious to the former?

But I make my third appeal, in support of this position, to experience — by which I mean history. And here the difficulty is not to find appropriate examples, but to make selections.

Let us first look at some examples where attempts have been made to sustain one or more of the institutions under consideration, while the rest were wanting.

The ancient Jewish state was an example, where the religious system, so far as it was developed, was pure, but the education was defective. Excepting a knowledge of their own history and religion, there was almost nothing that could be called literature or science; and the views of the body of the people were very narrow and bigoted. Mark, now, some of the effects. One was, that in spite of the awakening power of a miraculous dispensation, and the repeated warnings of Jehovah himself, and their strong national pride, they were almost constantly falling into the idolatry of the surrounding nations. Another was, that Jehovah found it desirable, out of regard to what the Scriptures call the "hardness of their hearts," to allow certain practices among them, which most enlightened nations shrink from; such as polygamy, slavery, and bloody wars. Another effect was, that instead of allowing them freedom, it was necessary often for Jehovah not only to suffer them to have kings, but such kings "as would chastise them with whips and scorpions." And notwithstanding all the wisdom of Jehovah in managing their national affairs, and his mercies, judgments, and warnings, at the time of Christ they had become a province of the Roman empire, and their religion had degenerated into the whited sepulchre of phariseeism, or the yet more repulsive carcass of sadduceeism.

Look now at an opposite example, in the effort made in France, near the close of the last century, to establish freedom and education without religion. It was like an attempt to erect a noble edifice without any foundation. It was worse; it was like placing such an edifice upon ground that was already rocking and heaving by the stifled fires of a terrific volcano. The fires of ferocious passions, fanned into a sevenfold heat by the sirocco breath of atheism, did soon break forth beneath that temple of liberty, and it was blown to atoms; while streams of scorching lava were belched forth over every European nation, and the gloom of a military despotism settled down upon the fairest portion of the globe, the whole forming a memento of the terrible retribution that follows an effort to dethrone God and deify human reason.

Another fact which history furnishes, illustrative of this subject, is the intimate connection that has ever existed between despotism, ignorance, and false or perverted religion — *par nobile fratrum.* I am not aware of a single exception, in the whole annals of our world; and where the tyranny has been the most grinding, the religion has been the most corrupt, and the ignorance the most profound. As illustrations of this statement, in ancient times, memory shows, imprinted on her tablet, Assyria and Media, Persia and Egypt; in the middle ages, almost the whole of Europe; and in modern times, nearly all of Asia; over whom the triple-headed monster above named is seen enthroned in gloomy sovereignty — a snaky Gorgon, converting every thing fair and lovely to stone by his hideous aspect. On such a soil, true religion, or popular education, or true freedom, could no more flourish than the palm tree on the glaciers of Spitzbergen.

It will doubtless be objected, that despotic governments have often been liberal patrons of learning and of art, and that countries thus governed have produced many splendid examples of genius and scholarship. And why has this patronage been extended? Because such governments have learned that knowledge is power, and so long as it is confined to comparatively few, they can monopolize it, and make it instrumental in upholding their authority. But they would not dare to extend its blessings to the community at large, because their power would be apt to change hands. Accordingly, we do not find that despotic governments encourage or permit the great body of their subjects to seek the blessings of an enlightened system of education; or if, in a few instances, they have made education somewhat popular, they have found themselves compelled, ere long, to allow more liberty to their subjects.

All the ancient republics, and most of the modern, furnish us with examples of the blighting influence of false religion upon popular education and freedom. It will not be doubted that, in the ancient republics, much freedom of thought and action was enjoyed by certain classes; and we know that literature and speculative philosophy were carried to a high degree of perfection, and that the fine arts, also, were most successfully cultivated. We are apt, however, to be dazzled and deceived by the splendor of those literary and artistic productions that have escaped the ravages of time, and are yet the models of style and taste. We need to ascertain what was the character of the freedom enjoyed in those republics, and what the condition of the mass of the people. Accordingly, history informs us that, in the Athenian and Lacedæmonian states, a large majority were slaves, over whom their masters exercised the power of life and death, and whom they treated with the most inhuman rigor. Nay, since the debtor became, *ipso facto*, the slave of the creditor, a large part of those nominally free were in fact bondmen. Those, then, who were really free, constituted, in truth, only a numerous nobility, or aristocracy; so that the government was really an oligarchy. The military spirit, also, controlled and moulded every thing else; and we know how, in Sparta, it obliterated the domestic relations, justified theft and deception, and substituted an iron-hearted martial law for the tender charities of life. If the fine arts were cultivated in the Grecian states, yet agriculture and commerce were neglected and despised.

In Rome the state of things was no better. There you find the same horrid system of slavery; the same right of life and death in the hands of the father and the master over the child and the slave, — resulting in the practice of infanticide, murder, and gladiatorial combats. There, too, the patricians were engaged in endless contests for power with the plebeians; yet all united in submitting to the severest military discipline, and, while professedly free themselves, in subjecting all other nations to an iron yoke. In short, while you find a small part of the people — a numerous aristocracy — boasting of freedom, and well educated for the times, the great mass are left ignorant and in servitude, and the whole community is moulded by a martial code, inflexible and bloody, which, indeed, nourished some of the sterner virtues, but stifled the tender charities of life, and, while it guarded with jealous care the honor and liberties of the state, kept a large multitude in hopeless servitude at home, and with insatiable ambition preyed upon surrounding nations, till the world and the Roman empire became synonymous terms.

Suppose, now, any one of the systems of government that were adopted by these ancient republics, with its military spirit, its slavery, and its religion, were to be introduced into New England. What a contrast to the systems of government, religion, education, and social life, which now exist among us! Who of us would not rather choose any of the monarchical, nay, even of the despotic, systems of civilized Europe?

After all, however, there were many noble hearts in those ancient republics, in whom the true spirit of freedom glowed, and who did all they could to impart true liberty and knowledge to their fellow-men. What, then, were the causes that counteracted their efforts, and rendered it impossible for a true system of freedom, or of education, to succeed; which in fact marred and blackened the fair countenance of liberty and civilization with some of the most hideous features of despotism and barbarism? The philosophical historian and politician have long attempted to answer these inquiries; and doubtless some of the causes they have assigned were powerfully instrumental of such results: but they seem to have overlooked one great source of influence, and that is, religion. They speak, indeed, of the necessity of public virtue to the purity and preservation of freedom; but they seem not to realize that virtue which springs not from religion is spurious and ephemeral, and that consequently, if the religion be false or corrupt, the virtue, the freedom, and education will be proportionably defective. True, the polytheism of Greece and Rome was the least offensive heathenism, modified as it was by philosophy and poetry, which the world ever saw. Still it was false enough, and pernicious enough, to permit opinions and practices inconsistent with genuine freedom and popular education.

Were there time, it would be easy to point out similar corrupting and paralyzing influences, emanating from perverted systems of religion, upon most modern republics. But this would require too much of detail for the present occasion.

The history of the efforts made to establish free governments in South America, and in Mexico, strikingly illustrates and confirms the position taken in this discourse. The people there doubtless wonder why their exertions to build up free institutions have produced only a succession of civil wars, with short intervals of military despotism. But when we learn the intolerant character of their religion, we wonder not at the ignorance and superstition of the people, nor that they cannot be governed by any thing save despotic power. To expect freedom with such a religion, and such ignorance, is like looking for grapes upon thorns, and figs upon thistles.

Another historic fact, illustrative of this argument, is, that a state religion has always exerted an unfavorable influence upon popular education and civil and religious liberty. The mere existence of a state religion, indeed, puts an end to religious freedom, by the bestowment of governmental patronage upon one denomination, and thus leaving the others, at the best, to exist by mere sufferance. Despotism has always found religion a most convenient instrument for riveting its chains upon the people. The state first embraces religion, as if for protection, but soon throttles it, and then uses its lifeless form as a speaking trumpet, through which is proclaimed the divine right of kings, the duty of unreserved submission to their authority, and other anti-republican dogmas. Witness Turkey, Italy, Russia, and Austria; and, I might add, almost every Asiatic kingdom. There you see the perfected fruit of a union of church and state, in the almost total ignorance, degradation, and servitude, of the people. In some milder governments, however, as Great Britain, and Prussia, and other German states, the attempt has been made to combine state religion with the education of the people at large; and Prussia especially presents us with a model system, so far as the mode of instruction is concerned. But the government directs what shall be taught the people, and takes special care that monarchical principles and war doctrines shall be instilled. And since every educated man depends upon the government for a place, either in the state, the army, or the church, very little of true freedom of opinion can be enjoyed. Nor will a New England man think very highly of the system of popular education in Great Britain — Scotland excepted — when he learns that of the sixteen millions of England and Wales, nearly half cannot write their names, and nearly one third cannot read their mother tongue. Surely there must be some powerful obstacle to the diffusion of knowledge in such a country; but a state religion and a system of aristocracy explain it all. Of all monarchical countries, however, Great Britain possesses the most freedom, the most intelligence, and the most true religion; and would she divorce church and state, almost the last incubus would be removed from her prosperity and happiness.

But arbitrary governments, especially on the continent of Europe, are beginning to learn that to instruct the people at large is a hazardous experiment, even though the system of instruction be carefully adapted to the support of their power and the state religion. For if you once put the human mind upon thinking, it will not always stop where you would have it. And in the countries referred to the people are demanding at least the right of popular representation in the government; and though cannon and bayonets may for a time stifle this demand, it will soon gather explosive force enough, if not regarded, to rend the throne to atoms. The rocking thrones of continental Europe clearly evince that education is in advance of liberty and religion. But the reciprocal influence that exists between them will ere long bring them upon a level — by elevating the two latter, as we may hope, and not by sinking the former.

History furnishes another support to this argument in the fact that the countries most distinguished for freedom and general education are those where the Bible is most widely circulated. For examples we may refer to the United States, Scotland, and Iceland. The latter country, separated from all the world, with arctic snows upon and volcanic fires beneath its surface, and too poor to be an object of cupidity, though nominally subject to the Danish government, is in reality a free state, and is blessed with a most effective, though peculiar system of education, and with primitive simplicity of piety. Scotland, too, is nominally a part of a monarchical empire. But it were to be wished that all republics enjoyed as much liberty, and their people were as well educated, and their virtue and piety as pure and elevated. With the exceptions above referred to, we might say the same of England, where the Bible has a wide distribution. The republics of Switzerland, too, may be quoted as a striking illustration of this argument. For here we have professedly free states, lying side by side, in some of which the Bible is restrained in its circulation, and in others it is widely diffused; and it is said that the traveller needs no map to inform him when he has passed from one description of these provinces into the other.

Now, it needs no time spent to show that, if education and liberty follow in the track of the Bible, and, with a few unimportant exceptions, are cramped and sickly where that book is not diffused, — it requires, I say, no labored argument to show that that book is eminently favorable to free institutions and popular instruction. But if further evidence on this point be required, we have it in the history of the Scotch Covenanters and the English Puritans.

Little did these men, who for two hundred years suffered an unrelenting persecution from despots and hierarchs, imagine that they were working out and giving to the world the great principles of civil and religious liberty. Driven from their native land by the persecutions of Mary, Providence sent them to Geneva, where, in the church founded by such men as Farel and Calvin, they found freedom of opinion and the rights of conscience asserted. Having caught the spirit of that church, when permitted to return to England and Scotland, they could not resist the impulse to establish religious freedom there. But, in this attempt, they found that they could not secure freedom of conscience without securing also civil liberty. Hence they threw themselves manfully into the contest; and the result was the independence of Scotland, and the establishment of the commonwealth in England. A later, but still more important, result was the settlement of this country by men who drew their religious principles directly from the Bible, and who carried their lofty ideas of religious freedom into the civil constitution and into all their plans of education. To these men, therefore, was the world indebted for the first clear development of the true principles of civil and religious liberty. To them, says Hume, the English people owe the whole freedom of their constitution; and, as a more recent and eloquent writer observes, "then were first proclaimed those mighty principles which have since worked their way into the depths of the American forest, which have roused Greece from the slavery and degradation of two thousand years, and which, from one end of Europe to the other, have kindled an unquenchable fire in the hearts of the oppressed, and loosed the knees of the oppressors with unwonted fear." *

Such is what may be called the inseparable trio — religion, education, and freedom. And such are the arguments by which it is proved how strongly linked together they are by a chain of influence that conveys with electric speed the strength and purity, or the weakness and corruption, of one to all the rest.

The subject suggests a multitude of important inferences; and with a brief notice of a few I will relieve your exhausted patience.

1. *It shows us the reason why arbitrary governments and corrupt religions have been so much afraid of the circulation of the Bible.*

Their supporters have usually been sagacious enough to discover that the Bible is a stern advocate for civil and religious freedom, and uncompromising towards all corruptions of its spirit. They know that the man who submits himself fully and sincerely to its principles and spirit becomes thoroughly republican, and hostile to false doctrine. Hence they sympathize with the priest of a perverted Christianity in England, soon after the art of printing had begun to multiply copies of the Scriptures: "We must root out printing," said he in his sermon, "or printing will root us out." This was a true prediction; and in these times we are witnessing its fulfilment.

2. *The subject shows us that the religious element is fundamental, in order to the support of free institutions.*

Nor is it a false religion, or a perverted Christianity, that

* Macaulay.

will do this; but there must be genuine piety in the community, or liberty will ere long degenerate, if it does not utterly expire. And it was the lot of Puritanism, for the first time in this world's history, to discover, and by its sufferings and struggles and triumphs to demonstrate, this most important of all principles in the science of government. Even yet the world is purblind to this truth; and men are every where struggling for liberty, and expecting to sustain it when acquired, though religion have but a feeble hold upon the community. And when they are disappointed, as they always are where pure religion does not prevail, enlightened statesmen seem in general to overlook this fundamental defect, and attempt to account for the failure upon other principles. But the Puritan has ever been distinguished, — and in almost every country but our own has been hated and persecuted, — not more for the uncompromising features of his theology than for his stern independence of character. Yet that independence is founded in his religion; and not till his views prevail, and his example be imitated, will men come into the full realization of their dreams of freedom.

3. *The subject shows us that the prevalence of true religion will insure the prevalence of education and liberty.*

Christianity is as stern an advocate of education among all classes as for the freedom of all. Nor can it conceal features so strongly marked; so that wherever it prevails in its purity it will insist upon enlightening men's minds, and in breaking from their necks every yoke. And here, too, Puritanism has set the example. Wherever she has planted her foot, her first care has been to rear a temple to Jehovah, then to found the college, the academy, and the primary school.

4. *We see how important to the defence and purity of*

true religion are education and freedom among all classes of the community.

Though an ignorant man and a slave may exercise pious feelings, he can neither defend Christianity against sceptical objections, nor accurately expound its doctrines, nor guard its spirit against the frosts of formalism or the wildfire of fanaticism. When the metaphysician by subtle arguments attempts to show that the external world has no existence, and consequently no argument can thence be deduced for the being of a God; when the phrenologist makes virtue and vice dependent rather upon cranial conformation than upon moral causes; when the physiologist maintains that mental phenomena are a mere function of the brain, and that organic beings, as well as all natural operations, may be the result of law, without a Deity; when the astronomer demonstrates that the earth is not fixed, nor does the sun literally rise and set, as it was formerly supposed the Bible taught; when the geologist describes a preadamite earth of indefinite duration, and the chemist declares that the world has already been burned, and therefore can undergo no future conflagration; and when the philologist throws doubts over the obvious meaning of Scripture, and converts its plainest truths into enigmas; and when baptized philosophy makes divine and poetic inspiration synonymous, — O, what but ripe learning can harmonize all these apparently discordant elements, and vindicate and enucleate the pure truths of the Bible? And what but general intelligence can secure the mass of the community, amid such angry waves, from making shipwreck of the faith?

5. *The subject shows us when it may be safe and expedient to unite church and state.*

Let no one be startled when we maintain that church and state should be united at the proper time. The only difficulty is, that men have attempted it too early. We have endeavored to show that the government of the church, as described in the New Testament, is a democracy, where the members are governed by supreme love to God and equal love to all mankind. Now, suppose the church to be enlarged till it embraces all the world, and all its members conform strictly to these great principles. Suppose, moreover, that all civil governments become strictly republican, and the rulers take the law of God as the basis of all political action. How much, in such a case, would the church differ from the state? Unless there are political measures that have no moral character, the two institutions would be nearly, perhaps precisely, synonymous. Both of them would be what I have called a theocratic democracy; and there would be but one government and one church in all the earth. That would indeed be the perfect state of society so much talked of and so little understood. When such a state of the world arrives, — alas, how long will it be delayed! — then let church and state be united. Indeed, you cannot keep them apart. But till then, their union will be as incongruous and incoherent as the parts of Nebuchadnezzar's image of gold, brass, iron, and clay.

6. *We see in this subject the reason why so many efforts to secure freedom have failed of success.*

Men under despotic rulers suppose that the grand point is to obtain their freedom; whereas a much greater difficulty is to secure it. Knowing the character of the religion and the state of education in France before the revolution in 1789, and in South America more recently, we might have predicted the anarchy and the despotism that followed the efforts in those countries to establish independence. As republicans, it was indeed natural for us to entertain hopes that the recent convulsive efforts in continental Europe to establish free institutions would not be wholly blasted. But we were too forgetful of the state of religion and of general education in those countries. If a people who scruple not to hold their political elections, their inductions to office, their public festivals, and their military reviews on the Sabbath can long maintain a pure republicanism, then the history of the world hitherto must go for nothing as a means of judging of the future. The same may be said essentially of that nation where the popular mind is left uninstructed. And when we recollect, moreover, what millions are ready, at the beck of despots and hierarchs, to smother every cry for freedom, we ought to have been prepared to hear the dying shriek of liberty which reached us before the last year's close from every one of these countries but France, and for those rapid developments even there which show her citizens yet unprepared for free institutions. These nations, it may be hoped, will not sink back into as deep a political night as before; yet we may be sure they will sink to the level of the religion and the education among the people.

7. *This subject shows us that nations, as well as individuals, should make the principles of the Bible the basis of their policy and their treatment of one another.*

Strange that any other doctrine should have been promulgated, and that the same men who acknowledged their individual obligation to love their neighbor as themselves, to do unto others as they would that others should do unto them, and to bless them by whom they are persecuted, and even to love their enemies, should maintain that principles of expediency and policy should take the place of moral principles in managing the affairs of nations. For what reason can be urged to bind individuals to conform to the rules of the Bible which will not apply to nations? And if pure religion be, as we have endeavored to show, the most important of all the foundations on which a nation's liberty and true glory rest, can that people expect prosperity if its government substitute something else as the guide of their measures? And yet, had governments conducted towards one another according to gospel principles, what an amount of blood and treasure would have been spared, and what an amount of happiness secured!

8. *In the eighth place, if these three great interests of the community are thus inseparable, then should the different classes appointed for their protection and advancement be united also.*

He whose special business it is to watch over and defend the interests of religion should be in sympathy and harmony with those whose lives are devoted to the cause of education, and with those who are appointed to manage our political concerns. And so should these latter classes reciprocate that sympathy towards the guardians of religion. They all should mutually realize that, if the interests of any one of the trio are not properly and efficiently provided for, the interests of the others will suffer also. Instead of indulging illiberal prejudices towards one another, all should feel as if they had a common cause to sustain, and as if a wound could not be inflicted upon one without reaching the whole. Thus would they form a threefold cord, which both Scripture and experience testify is not quickly broken.

Finally, the subject defines the great outlines of that policy which the rulers of Massachusetts should ever pursue.

Far be it from me to allude to particular political measures in the presence of the constituted authorities of this commonwealth. But my office and my subject force me to speak of the great principles on which a government founded by the

Pilgrims should be conducted. Their first and constant aim was to establish and foster the institutions of religion, education, and freedom. To sustain religion, they found it only necessary to allow perfect freedom of opinion, and to protect all in the peaceful exercise of those forms of worship which conscience dictates to be right. They had learned by bitter experience that to take religion into the embrace of the state was only to cramp its vital powers, and convert it into a furious, persecuting demon. Education, too, they did not attempt to bring under governmental control; but only by liberal benefactions to stimulate individual efforts. And with such a religion, and such means of education, they did not doubt that the people would select those men to manage their political affairs who would defend their liberties and wisely administer the government. It is a matter of just gratulation that all who have filled the places of honor and trust once occupied by the Pilgrims in these respects have followed essentially their system of policy. On questions of political expediency they have had different opinions; but on these fundamental principles they have all been united. Indeed, no Massachusetts statesman could outlive the storm which a desertion of these principles would bring upon him. To honor and sustain religion, diffuse knowledge among the people, and preserve true liberty, — this is a policy as settled in Massachusetts as the laws of the Medes and Persians. She cannot hope for superiority by her numbers, extent of territory, or any natural advantages. But by the fostering care of a free government over her religious and literary institutions, she can qualify and send forth, as she already has done, strong men into every part of the earth to place a lever beneath the abodes of ignorance, sin, and despotism, and lift them up into the sunshine of Christianity, civilization, and freedom.

To give Massachusetts such a character is the noble work committed to the constituted authorities of the state now before me. We congratulate them upon the honor of occupying seats made sacred by so long a line of illustrious men, with so illustrious a beginning. It is indeed a distinction to be coveted to take the place of such men, and to have confided to your management interests so momentous. And it is a delightful evidence that the spirit of our fathers still lingers here to find his excellency the Governor, his honor the Lieutenant Governor, the honorable Council, the honorable Senate, and the House of Representatives, instead of converting the Sabbath into a holiday or a business day, converting a business day into a Sabbath, and calling to their aid the ministers of the gospel, that, at the commencement of their responsible duties, they may recognize their dependence upon an overruling Providence, and baptize their legislation with the spirit of religion.

It is gratifying also to know that the long and eminent public services of the beloved statesmen who for six successive years have filled the two highest places in the executive department of the government have been a practical exemplification of the principles which I have advocated in this discourse; and therefore, although I have given them no instruction, I feel almost sure that I have had their sympathy. Their oft-repeated reëlection affords evidence that the people of Massachusetts are not tired of hearing their rulers called "the just." Nor can I doubt that all the other gentlemen composing the government, and elected by the same people, are imbued with the like spirit, and that their legislation, the present session, will show that they regard religion, education, and freedom as inseparable. God give them success in a career so noble and important! And God inspire all their successors with the like spirit! Then, though, by the expansion of our national territory, Massachusetts should become relatively almost a point, yet shall it be a point radiant with the light of piety, of learning, and of liberty. And as the stars in the heavens above us, that revolve within the circle of perpetual apparition, never sink below the horizon, so shall this commonwealth ever shine bright in the political hemisphere — a morning star to usher in the full daylight of civilization, of freedom, and of happiness, to the benighted and oppressed in all the earth.

A CHAPTER IN THE BOOK OF PROVIDENCE.

Amid all the darkness and confusion of this world, there is one precious volume, to which the Bible furnishes the key, and which, if carefully studied, shows us how to trace out the relation of events apparently casual or discrepant, and clears up most of the enigmas by which we are surrounded. It is the book of divine providence. There is one chapter of that volume which seems to me peculiarly appropriate to the present occasion. Its leading object is to show that when God has an important object to accomplish, he raises up, and prepares by the most appropriate discipline, the individuals or the communities best adapted to the work. If I can succeed in giving you the contents of this chapter, and thus establish and illustrate this most important position, I shall feel as if I had fulfilled the commission with which I have been honored to-day.

In the divine administration of the affairs of this world, it becomes necessary to raise up instruments, sometimes to punish, and sometimes to bless, individuals and communities. Hence we can often see as much of providential design in the history of the wicked scourges of the world, as of its choicest benefactors.

In looking over the page of history for examples illustrative of this subject, the difficulty is, not to find them, but, among so many, to make an appropriate selection.

The Bible is eminently a book of divine providence; or rather, such is its object, that the events detailed in it are seen to be more distinctly related to one another, and to a specific object, than the details of profane history. Hence we must not omit to appeal to that volume on the present occasion.

We may go back even to the antediluvian world. The extreme wickedness of the race made it necessary that God should specially interpose for its destruction by a flood of waters. But he needed at least one eminently holy man, who might be saved, and prevent the extinction of the race. Such a man was Noah. He had the firmness to persevere for one hundred and twenty years in building an ark, amid the scoffs and jeers of all around him, who depended on nature's constancy, and laughed at God's threatenings. A man of ordinary piety, and of feeble mind, never could have sustained such a trial, and therefore God raised up one, even in those times of deep degeneracy, of extraordinary energy and piety; and thus was the object accomplished, and the race preserved.

The effect, however, of this terrible penal infliction was soon lost, and idolatry and wickedness again triumphed. God therefore determined to select a particular family as the progenitors of a race to be kept distinct from all the rest of the world, and over whom he would exercise a special and even miraculous providence. It was important that the father of this nation should be a man of extraordinary mental and moral worth. No other man could lay broad and deep the foundations of a new and peculiar nation. Abraham therefore appeared at the proper time, and was made to pass through such discipline as would have crushed an ordinary man. The first startling command which he received was, to leave his father's house, his kindred and his country, and go out, *not knowing whither he went.* In the exercise of unconquerable faith he obeyed, and wandered long ere he reached the promised land of Palestine. There, after various discipline, he was called to a trial of his faith, probably the most severe which God ever imposed on man — I mean the command to offer up his only son as a burnt offering. Yet, having obeyed, he became well entitled to be called the father of the faithful.

But although descended from such a progenitor, it was necessary that the Hebrew nation should pass through a long and bitter experience to make them worthy of being called the chosen people of God. Four hundred and thirty years of hard bondage could alone train them for the work God had assigned them; and appropriate instruments must be prepared to bring about this result. Joseph was appointed to lead the way in bringing the whole of the descendants of Abraham into servitude. Mildness and quiet submission to whatever God laid upon him seem to have been the predominant traits in his character. Such a man could bear to be made governor over all Egypt without losing his humility and fraternal sympathies, even though sold as a slave by his brethren. Thus were the Israelites decoyed, as it were, into servitude. They found one of their own number to protect them, and place them in the richest part of the country, so that they multiplied exceedingly. Ere long, however, they began to feel the rigors of their bondage, and sighed for a rescue. The appointed time at length came. But now a different set of instruments must be prepared for the work; and God knew how to provide them. On the one hand, it was necessary that a leader of great energy and wisdom should be ready to undertake the gigantic labor. And such a man was

Moses. He needed the best education that could be given him in Egypt, and Providence took care that he should, in his infancy, become the protégé of Pharaoh's daughter. Yet he must not lose his attachment to his own kindred, and therefore he was permitted to witness such oppression of a Hebrew as roused the man and the patriot within him, and led him to take the sword of avenging justice into his own hand. Thus was he compelled to flee from Egypt, and by a forty years' discipline in a humble and obscure station, he became eminently fitted for the great work that was before him; from which, however, he now shrunk, because he had learned its magnitude, and his own weakness. But when the harness was fairly buckled on, and he felt God's arm underneath him, he bore up manfully, and acquitted himself nobly, because God had disciplined him for the work.

In order, however, that the power and justice of Jehovah should be signally displayed, and the Egyptians severely punished for their cruelties towards the Hebrews, it became necessary that a savage and unfeeling tyrant should be placed on the throne. And the Pharaoh who then occupied it was eminently fitted to become the scourge of God. Even miracles could not subdue him for a long time, and there was abundant opportunity for the display of God's power. If the wonderful miracles that preceded and accompanied their exodus did not make an indelible impression on the Hebrew mind and heart, nothing could do it. But they have ever since been appealed to by that people as certain evidence of God's special favor towards their race, and have served to keep them distinct to this day from all other nations.

If we follow down the path of Jewish history, from the earliest to the latest times, we shall be met continually with illustrations of this subject. When God thought proper to rescue the Hebrews from the twenty years' cruel oppression of Jabin, the Canaanite, he educated two women, Deborah, a judge and a prophetess, and Jael, the wife of Heber, and inspired them with a heroism that seems to have been wanting in the men of that age, and led the first to the battle field, and the last to drive a nail through the head of Sisera, and thus deliver the land from bondage. How eminently fitted by nature and by discipline for the trying work assigned them were Elijah and Elisha! And by what a series of hardships, privations, and dangers, was David, the shepherd boy, gradually conducted to the throne, and even made a type of the Saviour! How different the education of his son Solomon! but as wisely adapted to the peaceful yet magnificent scenes through which he was to pass.

An unrighteous decree for the destruction of the Jews scattered through the one hundred and twenty-seven provinces of Persia and Medea, had been surreptitiously obtained from Ahasuerus, and their fate seemed inevitable. But God had long ago provided for their rescue, and prepared the appropriate instruments. Mordecai and Esther were educated and sent into the palace of the king for this very purpose; the first, a stern old man, inflexible in his religious character; and the last an amiable woman, of great personal beauty, who had obtained a strong influence over the king, and yet had not lost her attachment to her own people, nor become insensible to the moral obligations that came upon her from her exalted position. She therefore resolutely put her life in jeopardy, and thus saved herself and her people, and brought the avenging sword upon their persecutors.

When the captivity of the Jews in Babylon had continued long enough to answer the divine purposes, Cyrus was placed on the throne of Persia and Medea, with a heart prepared to promote their return to Palestine. This was accomplished under Zerubbabel; and when, after many years of trial, it became important to have the walls of Jerusalem rebuilt, and the population reformed from their idolatries and immoralities, then appeared Ezra and Nehemiah, whom God had been secretly educating for the difficult work; and they carried it through only as men disciplined in such a school could do it.

It will be unnecessary, before this audience, to show how perfectly adapted to his work was the Saviour of the world, although in truth it be the most striking illustration of my subject which the world has ever witnessed. But the facts are already in your memories; and were they not, volumes, rather than a few paragraphs, would be requisite to elucidate the subject.

For the same reasons, I need not dwell upon the history of the apostles; and yet gladly would I linger here, especially upon that of Paul. Had you seen him, a proud, talented young man, in the school of Gamaliel, intolerant in the extreme towards every thing connected with Christianity, standing by when Stephen was stoned, and encouraging his murderers, and afterwards rushing like a tiger towards Damascus, to seize the unoffending followers of Christ, who, all this time, could have imagined that such a school was the one best adapted to prepare him for the great work before him? Yet it was just the experience he needed. His future work required talents of the first order, a boldness and perseverance amounting almost to rashness, and such a conviction of the great truths of religion as could result only from personal experience of their power. He who was to combat Jewish prejudices must know from experience what they were, and be familiar with the whole Jewish economy. He who was to teach and illustrate the doctrines of grace, in the midst of fiery opposition, must have been converted miraculously. His convictions of his own wickedness and the deceitfulness of his heart must have been intensely pungent, and his sense of deliverance by a crucified Saviour intensely vivid, or he never could set forth those truths justly and impressively. In short, now that we know the whole history of Paul, we see that his entire course, previous to conversion, was just the one best fitted to train him for the part God had assigned him. And yet, before his conversion, we should have wondered why God permitted such a furious persecutor to live and make havoc in the church.

If we follow down the history of the church for three hundred years after Christ, we shall find evidence of the wonder-working providence of God in the ten terrible persecutions which were then experienced. By these onsets, two important objects were accomplished, which probably could have been secured in no other way. The first was the purification of the church, and the second the speedy publication of the gospel in almost every land. For those who were persecuted without mercy at home were scattered abroad every where, and they *could not but speak the things which they had seen and heard.* Living thus in jeopardy of life, and hunted from place to place, they grew rapidly in piety, and, by their holy lives, won over many to embrace the true faith. Nor were the instruments wanting to carry on these persecutions. God had only to take away his restraining influences from the emperors of Rome, and to worry and devour the virtuous and the holy was only acting out the desires of hearts naturally ferocious and cruel, and rendered doubly malignant and vile by long indulgence. Hence it was, that after these despots had been used to accomplish these important objects for the church, God turned upon them, and punished them terribly for their fiendish assaults upon the followers of Christ.

After these protracted onsets upon the church came the hour of her prosperity, and Constantine proclaimed Christianity to be the religion of the empire. But though Religion could flourish and spread when the powers of earth were arrayed against her, she could not endure success, and she sank into the embraces of the world, and an almost total eclipse came over her glories. For many a long century did the darkness deepen, until at last, when the punishment of apostasy and worldliness had been long and severe enough, God prepared other instruments for the revival of true religion. He chose, as a leading agent in this work, an Augustinian monk; or rather, he so ordered matters that this man, after receiving a thorough education, should choose a monastic life, and become a zealous advocate of Papacy, and a strict observer of its forms, in order that he might learn its corruptions, and how to expose its perversions. It was providential, also, that Luther should come in contact with an infamous vender of indulgences, that he might be roused to put his shoulder to the great work of the reformation. Around him there also sprang up other eminent men, admirably fitted for the various posts which must be occupied and sustained in such a long-drawn and bitter conflict. That contest is not indeed yet ended. But many a splendid triumph has been already witnessed over bigotry, intolerance, ignorance, and clerical corruption; enough to insure final and glorious success.

If we turn our attention away for a moment from affairs more strictly religious, we shall find in uninspired secular history illustrations of my subject of no doubtful character. In ancient times, and before the introduction of the gospel, it seemed important that human wisdom and philosophy should have a fair opportunity to see how much they could do to reform and elevate society without Christianity. Hence God laid the foundation of the Grecian states, and gave to Solon and Lycurgus a fair field for trying the experiment. It was tried most thoroughly; and if severe discipline, elegant literature, sagacious philosophy, and refinement of manners could have secured freedom and virtue in connection with polytheism, the work would have been accomplished in Greece. But her vaunted liberty was, after all, only the freedom of an aristocratic few, while the majority were the most abject slaves. And so it was with her literature and her arts. Though she has left many monuments of refinement and learning, yet the great mass of her inhabitants were brutalized, trampled under foot by the few, degraded by immorality and superstition, and ignorant of the true God. And even the wisest of her philosophers has left us a fine comment on his theoretical theism, by directing, in his dying moments, a sacrifice to be made to Æsculapius. He has left us, too, his despairing and impressive conviction, that if God did not vouchsafe to give a revelation, vain would be every effort to reform and elevate the mass of men. In short, so well had God's providence adapted the agents and the circumstances, that the experiment never need be repeated, to show how utterly impossible it is for man to rise to an elevated condition of true liberty or virtue under the dominion of polytheism and of philosophy alone.

We may not be able to understand all the reasons why God permitted so disastrous an eclipse to come over the world in what are called the dark ages; but we can often see how wonderfully adapted were the agencies which he employed to relieve religion of its incubus, and open a new career for science and civilization. I have already referred to the leading agents in the reformation from Popery. But there were other reformations and improvements that demanded and secured appropriate instruments. It is interesting to observe how the art of printing sprang up just at the right moment — at a time when the human mind was waking up from its long slumber. But its advancement must have been arrested soon, had not some one discovered — what it is said was known much earlier in China, viz. — how to print upon wooden blocks. Who the individual was that first brought out this happy thought, or rather applied it experimentally, it may not be possible to decide. But it was so rapidly improved that the original inventor was forgotten, and at least three German cities contend for the honor. The main point, however, which I wish now to present before you is the fact that these discoveries were made just at that juncture in human affairs when they were indispensable to bring on a high state of civilization.

In order to advance the same object, and others collateral with it, the time had now arrived when it was desirable that a new continent should be brought to light. But the great mass of men, even the highly enlightened, were ready to regard the suggestion that such a continent existed as a mere quixotic dream. To breast this strong current of popular opinion and feeling, it needed most extraordinary qualifications. But they appeared in Columbus. So strong was the principle of faith in his mental constitution, that he trusted even in a false theory — I mean his notion that there must be a western continent to counterbalance the eastern. He believed in this so firmly that he was borne through almost insuperable difficulties and dangers to an ultimate triumph — just as, in some parts of mathematics, an erroneous supposition leads to the truth. In vain did the courts of Genoa, Lisbon, and London reject his proposals. Ferdinand and Isabella gave him at last the desired aid. But in the superstitious fears and discouragement of the sailors he had a still more formidable difficulty. Yet his forty years' nautical experience enabled him to triumph even here. The results of his success have even yet only begun to be developed. But the uses to which Providence has already put this western continent are an earnest of the yet more important part it is destined to fulfil in working out the destinies of the race.

The manner in which progress in civilization, learning, morality, and religion has usually been made is by developments made, first in one field and then in another, by individuals or communities fitted for the work. When, for instance, the period had arrived in which it was desirable that civilization should be carried into the inhospitable regions of Russia, Peter the Great appeared, possessed of the requisite qualifications. Had he not been a fierce and unyielding tyrant, he never could have controlled the ferocity or overcome the prejudices of an ignorant people. But he must also be willing to take the place of a humble learner, or he never could have gone into the ship yards of Holland and England as a common carpenter and blacksmith, and even at home to make his own generals and admirals take precedence of himself, while he was learning military and naval tactics. To expect, however, that such opposite qualities should be long exhibited by any man, and especially by one who was at the head of forty millions of people, with unlimited power, was absurd, unless some peculiar controlling influence was brought to bear upon him. Therefore it was that God gave such a power to the foundling girl Catharine, who could control the fiercest paroxysms of the tyrant. In this singular manner did Providence do more for the civilization of Northern Europe in that one reign than centuries have accomplished in other lands.

Through many a dark century the Christian church had forgotten the injunction of her risen Saviour, to "go into all the world and preach the gospel to every creature." But the eclaircissement of the truth by the reformation in the fourteenth century prepared the way for the revival of the missionary spirit. It showed itself, indeed, at the first, in the Romish church; but it seemed rather a zeal for conversions to Papacy than to Christianity. Yet the example roused the Protestant world to engage in the work. And though it was too much for any one man to have the honor of being the prominent leader in such an enterprise, yet God prepared and brought forward at the right time a large number, who went forth, shoulder to shoulder, to this mighty conflict; and as they have fallen successively, others have always been found fitted by nature and by grace to catch their mantles and urge forward the world's conversion. The work is indeed most arduous and difficult; but Providence has found men eminently fitted for its successful prosecution.

As the precepts of the Bible became more and better understood, benevolent men were led to search out the various forms of human suffering, to lift up the dark curtain which self-interest, or arbitrary power, or bigotry and intolerance had covered over many a den of cruelty and wickedness, and show to the world how man had brutalized his fellow, and how he had,

> "Clothed in a little brief authority,
> Played such fantastic tricks before high Heaven
> As made the angels weep."

With a martyr spirit, Howard went down into the infected

dungeons of the prisoner, and carried there, what never before had visited him, the light of hope and Christian sympathy, along with such physical amelioration of his condition as was consistent with the proper objects of imprisonment and punishment. Buchanan went among the suttees and idol temples of India, and sketched so vividly their horrid rites as to arouse the Christian world to interpose the shield of protection over the helpless victims, and to pour the light of the gospel into the hearts of their oppressors. Nay, he penetrated even the charnel house of the Romish Inquisition, and showed the world how much worse than heathenism a perverted Christianity may become.

Long had the abominations of the slave trade been unheeded, and the groans of the victims of oppression smothered by the thick folds of cupidity and a perverted public opinion. But God's justice could not sleep forever; and the time at length came when he raised up the fit instruments for enlightening the public mind and arousing the public conscience. A leader among them was Wilberforce, who stood in the British Parliament, like a rock from which the angry waves of prejudice and passion were thrown back broken and dissipated. Defeated ten times, in that body, in his attempts to bring the arm of the government to crush this horrid traffic, he lived to see the eleventh effort, by his friend Pitt, successful. And since that day, the same Providence has provided other instruments, not less adapted to advance the cause of human liberty; and it is easy to see that the days of this unrighteous system of oppression are numbered, and well nigh finished.

Equally well adapted was Wilberforce for another important enterprise; and that was, to vindicate the truths of evangelical religion before the higher classes of Great Britain, and to show their practical influence upon the life. In his own character, of beautiful simplicity and consistency, his contemporaries saw a refutation of the vile calumnies with which a flippant scepticism had assailed vital religion; and, since his death, his Practical View of Religion, already translated into most of the languages of Europe, and having passed through more than fifty editions in the English language, still renders experimental religion respectable among the higher classes of society, and doubtless proves the means of salvation to many.

But no less important was it that the lower classes of society, in professedly Christian countries, should be enlightened and brought under the influence of the gospel. Hence God, by a very simple instrumentality, started a system which has already done much, and is destined to do much more, for the rising generation in all lands, especially for the poor and destitute. I refer to Sabbath schools, and to their humble founder, Robert Raikes. The thought that led him to collect the poor and the vicious for instruction on the Sabbath seemed probably to him an accidental circumstance; nor could he have dreamed that that thought would prove a germ from which would spring and spread a tree whose fruit should be for the healing of all nations. But in God's plan the whole system lay spread out in far wider ramifications than have yet been developed to mortal vision. And yet how appropriate the instrumentality by which it was commenced!

In order that civilization should make much progress, it was necessary that all branches of learning should be developed. And the bright names that shine, as stars of the first magnitude, along the path of literature and science, show how admirably fitted, by nature and by discipline, were the distinguished founders of the different branches of knowledge, and the great discoverers of nature's laws. Take, for an example, such a man as Sir Isaac Newton, of whom it was hardly exaggeration for the poet to say, —

> "Nature and nature's laws lay hid in night;
> God said, 'Let Newton be,' and all was light."

With equal propriety might we say the same of Linnæus in natural history, and of Cuvier in comparative anatomy. In the same category might we place the name of Jonathan Edwards as the Coryphæus of metaphysical theology. In his case, how interesting to observe the course of divine Providence! In the science to which he devoted himself, it was not necessary, as in physical science, that there should be a costly array of instruments to work with. By having the Bible for his theology, and his own mental constitution as the basis of his metaphysics, it was as easy, perhaps easier, for Edwards to work out the difficult problems of liberty and necessity, the freedom of the will, free agency, and divine efficiency in the solitudes of a missionary life among the American Indians as in the universities of Europe. At any rate, those problems were so handled by the American divine as to lead such a man as Dr. Chalmers to say, "There is no European divine to whom I make such frequent appeals in my class room as I do to Edwards; no book of human composition which I more strenuously recommend than his Treatise on the Will, read by me, forty-seven years ago, with a conviction that has never since faltered, and which has helped me, more than any other uninspired work, to find my way through all that might otherwise have proved baffling, and transcendental, and mysterious in the peculiarities of Calvinism.

But society can never attain to a very advanced condition

unless means are provided for the thorough education of the female mind. Yet it was not till a comparatively late period that this truth began to be admitted and appreciated. Nay, through many a dark century did the opinion prevail — would I could say it has even now entirely disappeared — that woman was not capable of that discipline, enlargement, and vigor of mind which man has exhibited, and therefore her education was comparatively of little consequence. Man first monopolized all the means of intellectual culture to himself; and then, because the neglected female mind did not manifest equal mental power and development as his own, he very sagaciously inferred its inferiority. To show the absurdity of such an unphilosophical inference, God has suffered, from time to time, such a woman to appear as Mary Somerville, the author of the Connection of the Physical Sciences; and to give to the sex generally an opportunity to show what are their mental characteristics, he has, in recent times, raised up such women as the five Misses More, to open seminaries for the education of their sex, and to give to Hannah, the youngest, a power with the pen rarely equalled as a means of doing good among all classes and both sexes. Gladly would I linger to show how finely adapted she was by nature and by discipline for her important mission. But time will not permit.

We may observe the same principles of divine Providence in bringing out discoveries in the arts as in the sciences. Neither the men who have made these discoveries nor their contemporaries have been fully aware of the part they were acting, or of the wide ultimate influence of their dimly-seen and imperfectly-developed conceptions; nor did they imagine that Providence had any thing to do in the business. It seemed a small matter when the Marquis of Worcester, in

1655, described his "admirable and most forcible way to drive up water by fire;" yet it was the germ of the steam engine, which has so much changed almost the whole aspect of society. And when Savary threw his wine flask into the fire, how apparently accidental was it that he was led thereby to discover the mode of creating a vacuum by the condensation of steam! So, too, when the multitude on the wharf at New York were laughing at the first unsuccessful effort of Robert Fulton to work a steamboat, how much more easily might they have been led to believe that he was given up of Providence to infatuation than that he was a chosen agent to work out one of the greatest improvements of the age! The discovery that takes precedence of all others in anatomy, that of the circulation of the blood, brought so much obloquy upon Harvey, and so diminished his practice as a physician, that he was prevented afterwards from publishing other discoveries. The physician who first tied an artery was hooted at. He who first used cantharides was imprisoned by the London College of Physicians. The more recent and highly important discovery of etherization, by one of our countrymen, was made while its author was trying to perfect his favorite art of dentistry. Yet in all these cases there was an unseen Providence who gave these discoverers the right sort of abilities, and placed them in the appropriate circumstances for enucleating the happy thought. Nor does that Providence allow any discovery to come out before the right time, or to be delayed a moment too long.

But, after all, the history of the English Puritans and Scotch Covenanters furnishes the most appropriate illustration of my subject which I can offer. Ever since man's existence on the globe, he has had indefinite yearnings after civil and religious liberty; and many a time has he attempted to realize these blessings by the most profuse sacrifices. But every where, both in ancient and modern times, had he failed of his object; at least, the great mass of the community had always been in servitude. The time, however, was now come when this great problem might be solved — but not without great suffering and effort. God knew, though man did not, that the germ of civil liberty lay coiled up in the constitution of the Christian church. He therefore suffered many of his true worshippers in England and Scotland to experience a persecution from kings and hierarchies of two hundred years' duration — from the days of Wickliffe to those of Robinson. This awakened an intense desire for religious freedom in the bosoms of the persecuted. But it was necessary, to bring about the result, that they should be compelled to flee from their native country, and take refuge in Geneva. There, in the church of Farel and Calvin, they saw the salutary influence of a democratic form of government; and when they returned to Great Britain, they could not but endeavor to establish a church on the same foundation. They had not aimed or thought of a republican civil government. But they soon found that, if they would secure a church without a bishop, they must have a state without a king. The result was freedom in Scotland and the commonwealth in England. But when monarchy and hierarchy again triumphed, these men were driven once more into exile. They did not know the reason; but the subsequent developments of Providence have shown that the object was to people this country with men of deep-toned piety, whose attachment to religious liberty would lead them to be stern advocates for civil freedom. They had already been the means of securing to the people of England all the liberty which their civil constitution contains at this day; and now they were to accomplish a mightier work, by laying the foundations of a wide empire which should prove a refuge for the oppressed of every land. True, at first that people must be tributary to the mother country. But after a time, the arm of Providence showed them a way to independence, and called into their service an extraordinary leader, as distinctly pointed out for their guide to freedom as Moses was to conduct the Hebrews to the promised land. O, could these Puritans and Pilgrims have seen the glorious results of their sacrifices and sufferings, how would the prospect have cheered them in the darkest hour! But they have seen it all long ere this; and it has often swelled into rapture their song in heaven.

But why should I go back into history, or abroad to other lands, for illustrations of my subject, when the place and the occasion furnish me with an example quite as striking as any that history can present, and to us of much deeper interest? To pass by all others, whose presence we miss, but whose lives might well illustrate our subject, every thing around us to-day — the subdued greetings of friends, the starting tear, this vacant seat, these badges of mourning, ay, and yonder marble, too — reminds us that one is absent whose life has filled a large page in the book of Providence. Is absent, do I say? Where can we turn our eyes without seeing her? Is she not present in every one's thoughts — in every one's heart? Nay, may she not be virtually present? Do the blessed cease to be interested in the welfare of the human family because their home is in heaven? Can it be that, wherever she is, she should not desire to be present? And would not the God who gave her strength to do so much in this place for his glory gratify this desire also?

But if Miss Lyon be not here to-day, her works are; and they show us impressively for what purpose Providence raised her up, and how well he adapted her for her work. Chronological dates and biographical details I leave to others; but the great lessons of providential wisdom, and design, and goodness taught by her history I must not pass by.

What, then, was the chief object or objects for which our lamented friend seemed specially adapted by nature and education? Every one will doubtless answer, It was the promotion of female education. But this statement is too general; for to a great extent her labors were specific. She was, indeed, an eminent teacher of the young, and this seems to me the first great object for which Providence fitted her. But there were some marked peculiarities in her teaching; the most important of which was the predominance she gave to the truths of religion in all her instructions. The second great object of her life was the founding and management of a new and somewhat peculiar seminary. Let us now see what there was in her nature, and in the preparatory discipline through which she passed, that adapted her for the eminent success which she attained.

And here I ought to acknowledge my indebtedness for many facts and suggestions to those ladies, well known themselves as distinguished teachers, who still live, and were long associated with Miss Lyon as teachers and companions.

But I may be allowed to add that it is no second-hand representation which I make, but one founded upon a personal and intimate acquaintance of more than thirty years, during which my house was frequently made her home.

We will first consider Miss Lyon's physical adaptation to the work assigned her.

God gave her a vigorous and well-balanced physical constitution. Her stature was at a medium; the muscular powers were displayed in great strength and vigor; the vital apparatus was very strong, so as to give a full development to the whole system, and impart great tenacity of life. The brain was largely developed, and in proper proportion to produce a symmetrical character. The nervous system was full, yet free from that morbid condition which in so many produces irritation, dejection, or unhealthy buoyancy of the spirits and irregular action of the mind. In short, all the essential corporeal powers were developed in harmonious proportion. You could not say that any of the marked temperaments were exhibited, but there was rather a blending of them all.

Now, just such a physical system seemed essential to the part in life for which this lady was destined. Many, indeed, have been distinguished as instructors of youth whose constitutions were frail, and whose shattered nerves thrilled and vibrated in every exigency. But Miss Lyon had another office besides teaching to execute, which demanded unshrinking nerves and great power of endurance. In building up a new seminary, not conformed in many respects to the prevailing opinions, she could not but meet many things most trying to persons of extreme sensibility, and needing an iron constitution to breast and overcome.

We will consider, secondly, Miss Lyon's intellectual adaptation to the work assigned her.

And it gives a just view of the character of her mind to say that it corresponded to that of her body; that is, there was a full development of all the powers, with no undue predominance to any one of them. It were easy to find individuals more distinguished by particular characteristics, but not easy to find one where the powers were more harmoniously balanced, and where, as a whole, the mind would operate with more energy and efficiency. She did, however, exhibit some mental characteristics, either original or acquired, more or less peculiar. It was, for example, the great features of a subject which her mind always seized upon first. And when she had got a clear conception of these, she took less interest in minute details; or, rather, her mind seemed better adapted to master fundamental principles than to trace out minute differences. Just as the conqueror of a country does not think it necessary, after he has mastered all its strongholds, to enter every habitation to see if some private door is not barred against him, so she felt confident of victory when she had been able to grasp and understand the principles on which a subject rested. Her mind would work like a giant when tracing out the history of redemption with Edwards, or the analogies of nature to religion with Butler, or the great truths of theism with Chalmers; but it would nod over the pages of the metaphysical quibbler, as if conscious that it had a higher destiny. And yet this did not result from an inability to descend to the details of a science, when necessary. Else how could she have so long and so successfully conducted in her school the manipulations of a chemical laboratory, or have kept her eye so keenly open to all the details of the new seminary, or even of ordinary instruction, for so many years?

The inventive faculties were also very fully developed in our friend. It was not the creations of fancy merely, such as form the poet, but the power of finding means to accomplish important ends. Nor was it invention unbalanced by judgment, such as leads many to attempt schemes impracticable and quixotic. For rarely did she attempt any thing in which she did not succeed; nor did she undertake it till her clear judgment told her that it would succeed. Then it mattered little who or what opposed. At first she hesitated, especially when any plan was under consideration that would not be generally approved; but when, upon careful examination, she saw clearly its practicability and importance, she nailed the colors to the mast; and though the enemy's fire might be terrific, she stood calmly at her post, and usually saw her opposers lower their flag. She possessed in an eminent degree that most striking of all the characteristics of a great mind, viz., perseverance under difficulties. When thoroughly convinced that she had truth on her side, she did not fear to stand alone and act alone — patiently waiting for the hour when others would see the subject as she did. This was firmness, not obstinacy; for no one was more open to conviction than she; but her conversion must result from stronger arguments, not from fear or the authority of names. Had she not possessed this feature of character, Mount Holyoke Seminary never would have existed, at least not on its present plan. The peculiarity of its domestic arrangements, especially, was pronounced injudicious and impracticable by a large part even of the friends of female education, and made a subject of ridicule by the enemies of the institution. I once asked a judicious friend, who was opposed to this feature, how long the experiment must be successfully tried before he would believe it practicable. Five years, said he. Before his death the plan had been in successful operation nearly twice that time; and yet he was not convinced. It has now gone on prosperously for twelve years; and never were the prospects of its continued success brighter than now. Like every thing human, it may be changed — as it could be without endangering the prosperity of the seminary. But its triumphant success for one third of a generation is a striking illustration of the far-reaching sagacity and accurate judgment of its originator.

Besides this seminary, the most striking example of the inventive powers of our friend is that only volume which she has left us, — I mean the Missionary Offering, — called forth by an exigency in a cause which she dearly loved, and whose most striking characteristic is its missionary spirit. Yet it is, in fact, a well-sustained allegory, demanding for its composition no mean powers of invention and imagination.

Miss Lyon possessed also the power of concentrating the attention and enduring long-continued mental labor in an extraordinary degree. When once fairly engaged in any important subject, — literary, scientific, theological, or economical, — there seemed to be no irritated nerves or truant thoughts to intrude; nor could the external world break up her almost mesmeric abstraction.

This almost total absorption in a favorite subject did, indeed, operate sometimes to render her conversation less inviting, and even tedious, to others, because she dwelt upon a subject too long and too minutely for those who were less interested. I think this was one of her defects as a teacher; for the best instruction consists in saying just enough about a subject to make it clear and impressive, while there is danger of saying so much as to confuse and mystify. But it must not be forgotten that teaching was only one of the great objects of our friend's life. And this power of concentration and absorption was essential to accomplish the other grand objects of her existence.

It has been also complained, and probably with reason, by those in feeble health, that her great power of physical and mental endurance led her to expect too much of her pupils. She tried, I know, to guard against this tendency, being well aware how natural it is to estimate the capabilities of others by our own. And it should also be known that it was not her design to attempt to educate those of feeble constitution and delicate health, though she did not object to others making the most possible of such greenhouse plants. But she aimed rather to provide for those who might be able to stand in the front rank in the great battle which learning and religion have to sustain with ignorance and wickedness.

Another mental characteristic of our friend was her great power to control the minds of others. And it was done, too, without their suspecting it — nay, in opposition often to strong prejudice. Before you were aware, her well-woven net of argument was over you, and so soft were its silken meshes that you did not feel them. One reason was, that you soon learned that the fingers of love and knowledge had unitedly formed the web and woof of that net. You saw that she knew more than you did about the subject; that she had thrown her whole soul into it; that in urging it upon you, she was actuated by benevolent motives, and was anxious for your good; and that it was hazardous for you to resist so much light and love. And thus it was that many a refractory pupil was subdued, and many an individual brought to aid a cause to which he was before indifferent or opposed.

Finally, I must not omit to mention her great mental energy and invincible perseverance. That energy was a quiet power, but you saw that it had giant strength. It might fail of success to-day; but in that case, it calmly waited till to-morrow. Nay, a score of failures seemed only to rouse the inventive faculty to devise new modes of operation; nor would the story of the ant that fell backward sixty-nine times in attempting to climb a wall, and succeeded only upon the seventieth trial, be an exaggerated representation of her perseverance. Had she lacked this energy and perseverance, she might have been distinguished in something else, but she never would have been the founder of Mount Holyoke Female Seminary.

But I hasten, thirdly, to speak of her religious adaptation to the work assigned her.

And it is in her religious character, and there alone, that we shall find the secret and the powerful spring of all the efforts of her life which she would wish to have remembered. But I approach this part of her character with a kind of awe, as if I were on holy ground, and were attempting to lay open that which she would wish never revealed. In her ordinary intercourse, so full was she of suggestions and plans on the subject of education, and of her new seminary, that you would not suspect how deep and pure was the fountain of piety in her heart, nor that from thence the waters flowed in which all her plans and efforts were baptized and devoted to God. But as, accidentally, for the last thirty years, the motives of her actions have been brought to light, I have been every year more deeply impressed with their Christian disinterestedness, and with the entireness of her consecration to God. Without a knowledge of this fact, a stranger would mistake for selfishness the earnestness and exclusiveness with which she often urged the interests of this seminary. But in the light of this knowledge, the apparent selfishness is transmuted into sacred Christian love. Her whole life, indeed, for many years past, has seemed to me to be only a bright example of missionary devotedness and missionary labor. I have never met with the individual who seemed to me more ready to sacrifice even life in a good cause than she was; and had that sacrifice been necessary for securing the establishment of her favorite seminary, cheerfully and without a moment's hesitation, do I believe, she would have laid down her life. I would, indeed, by no means represent her as an example of Christian perfection. I could not do so great injustice to her own convictions. But since her death, I have looked back over the whole of my long acquaintance with her, in almost every variety of circumstance, to see if I could recollect an instance in which she spoke of any individual in such a way as to indicate feelings not perfectly Christian, or if I could discover any lurkings of inordinate worldly ambition, or traces of sinful pride, or envy, or undue excitement, or disposition to shrink from duty, or of unwillingness to make any sacrifices which God demanded; and I confess that the tablet of memory furnishes not a single example. What I considered errors of judgment I can indeed remember, but not any moral obliquity in feeling or action. They doubtless existed; but it needed nicer moral vision than I possess to discover them.

I ought to add, that this eminence of Christian character was founded upon a clear apprehension of biblical principles. She thoroughly understood and cordially embraced the doctrines of the Puritans, just as they lie in their massive strength in the Bible — not as they often come forth, alloyed and weakened, from the moulds of a self-confident philosophy. To study these truths was her delight. To explain them to her pupils was one of her most successful efforts as a teacher. Would that I could present on canvas the picture of Miss Lyon, as it lies in my memory, when she was engaged on the Sabbath in the study of Christian truth. I have frequently seen individuals in the somnambulic and mesmeric state, but none of them apparently more unconscious to external scenes that she was when thus absorbed in the contemplation of divine truth. Would that she had left us some delineation of her views and feelings in these biblical trances, and still more of those exercises of soul in her nearer approaches to God, when away from every eye but the divine. But she had a strong aversion to religious diaries, and was probably unconscious of any thing in her experience that would benefit the world, if left on record.

There were two religious principles which exerted an overmastering influence upon Miss Lyon's character. One was a sense of personal responsibility; the other, trust in an overruling Providence. As the Saviour, when he went up to Jerusalem for the last time, with all his sufferings full in view, advanced before his disciples, as if in haste to suffer, so did she, when duty called, never wait for others, but was ever ready to precede them, and measure the amount of her sacrifices, donations, and efforts by her sense of duty, rather than by the example of others. And it was this sense of personal responsibility which she urged always upon her pupils, and with great success. So strong, too, was her faith in a special Providence, that delay and discomfiture in the execution of her favorite plans produced little or no discouragement, but led her merely to inquire more carefully whether there was not something wrong in her or her plans which occasioned the delay; and having done all she could, she would wait long and cheerfully for the divine manifestation. And so often had she witnessed interpositions in her behalf almost miraculous, that her faith might often be seen steady and buoyant when that of others had yielded to appalling difficulties and dangers.

As the result of such principles and such piety, the standard of Miss Lyon's personal efforts and sacrifices in every good cause was so high as to put to shame the measure of duty which most Christians adopt. I am assured, on the best authority, that the amount of money which she devoted to the cause of benevolence was more than double all which she expended for herself, excepting her board. What a bright example for imitation! and what blessed results should we witness if one in ten among Christians were to come up to such a standard! Some have sneered at her rigid economy as if it were parsimonious and unbecoming. But in the fact just stated we see the motive of her economy. And let those who would censure wait till their standard of beneficence is as high as hers before they condemn the only means by which she reached such a standard.

Another blessed result of her elevated piety was the almost constant presence, in the schools which she taught, of that special divine influence which brings about the conversion of souls. She lived, it is said, to witness nearly thirty special revivals of religion in all her life, and not less than eleven in the twelve years' life of her new seminary — many of them surpassing, in the comparative number of converts, almost any revivals which I have ever heard of in any other community. Indeed, it was almost an uninterrupted display of divine converting power. And yet so busy and enthusiastic in literary instruction were Miss Lyon and the admirable band of teachers which she knew how to gather around her, that you would hardly have thought of the existence of that deep under current of piety, which seemed to flow from the river of God, and to refresh the whole landscape. But the current was always there, deep and strong; and thence came the power that kept the windows of heaven always open.

We will inquire, finally, into the adaptation of the discipline through which Miss Lyon passed to fit her for her work.

And by discipline I mean all the circumstances of her birth and education. We have seen that God gave her a sound mind in a sound body. But without cultivation, they would have been only as metal in the ore, or marble in the quarry. Therefore God placed her in circumstances appropriate to the desired discipline. He brought her into existence in the alpine regions of Massachusetts, where the pure water from the rock, and the atmosphere uncontaminated by pestilential miasms, send health bounding through the veins; where the deep ravines, the broad mountain slopes, and the vast prospects that stretch away almost illimitably over a sea of mountains elevate and expand the soul, and fit it for large and ennobling plans and purposes. There, too, away from the vices of a dense population, a religious influence predominates, and the manners, habits, and piety are in an unsophisticated state. In those plain and humble dwellings which city opulence might suppose the abodes of poverty, you will, for the most part, find the answer to Agar's prayer, *Give me neither poverty nor riches.* The parents of Miss Lyon were just in that state of moderate competence (not of deep poverty, as has been represented) which enabled them to make their daughter comfortable and happy at home with industry and economy, but which could not provide for her education abroad. But they possessed one thing of far higher value, and that was devoted piety; and their prayers and labors for their daughter were rewarded by her conversion. That happy home she has vividly described in her Missionary Offering — the dying scene of the beloved father, and "the extraordinary prayers of the sorrowing mother" during "that first cold winter of widowhood." Ah, it may be that the father was taken away in order to excite those prayers, and that they were necessary in God's plans to the future eminent usefulness of the daughter; and that, on the heavenly Mount Zion, they are now rejoicing in the retrospect of God's providence.

The marked preëminence of the young Mary soon raised

up for her benefactors who aided her, though she had to depend mainly upon her own exertions. After a time she joined the school of the Rev. Joseph Emerson, at Byfield. That gentleman's views and plans of female education seem to have been a good deal in advance of his times, and doubtless his instructions contributed largely to give the right direction to Mary's mind. But at that school, twenty-eight years ago, she came under the influence of an individual — an assistant teacher then, and afterwards through life an intimate friend — who probably had more to do in the formation of her character, and especially in fitting her to become the founder of a new institution, than any other person — I had almost said, than all others. That lady was Miss Z. O. Grant; concerning whom, as she is still living, propriety forbids me to say all that I could wish. But I may say that under no influence could Miss Lyon have come better adapted to prepare her for her work than that of one so fitted by nature, by education, and by grace to be a pioneer and a guide in improving and elevating the system of female education. It was during their connection at Byfield two years, at Derry, New Hampshire, five years, and an equal period at Ipswich, that the leading principles on which the Mount Holyoke Seminary was founded were suggested, discussed, and prayed over, and, what is more important, were experimentally tested — so far, at least, as the mode of instruction was concerned.

Thus it appears that the whole course of Miss Lyon's life, and all the circumstances in which she was placed, were only a continued school of discipline for the work assigned her. She could not have seen the bearing of events at the time they happened; but, from the standpoint which we occupy, we can see how almost every minute and often seemingly casual circumstance in her history was important to the final and full development. The guiding hand of God's providence is almost as distinct as when it went before the Israelites in their journeyings in a cloud by day and a pillar of fire by night. This will be the more obvious if we contemplate for a moment the manner in which the two grand leading objects of her life were accomplished.

Upon her character as a teacher I need not dwell, because it is so generally known and appreciated. Not less than three thousand pupils have passed under the moulding influence of her mind; and it was not an influence to be easily forgotten or shaken off. It came from the depths of the soul, and went into the depths of the soul, unless resisted by a perverseness rarely found among respectable young ladies. It has been objected, indeed, to her discipline, that it was too stern and uncompromising; and that many of the minor graces and elegant accomplishments, which give a charm to female loveliness, were too much neglected. She may have erred in this respect; for she had become disgusted with the too frequent substitution, in female education, of artificial for unsophisticated manners, and of superficial and showy accomplishments for substantial and practically useful acquisitions. She never felt called to study or to teach the technicalities and formalities of fashionable life; and she placed in nearly the same category some accomplishments which are generally regarded with much favor — such as painting, embroidery, music, and the like; or, rather, she transferred these subjects from the first rank, which they had long occupied, to the last in importance. Whether the system of manners which she taught and exhibited would be popular in the refined circles of Paris, or London, or New York, I know not. But I do know that she inculcated and exemplified that fundamental principle of all good Christian manners, that we should treat all men with kindness, because we feel kindly towards them in our hearts. Such manners were always acted out, as her numerous friends can testify, in her truly hospitable home in this place. But if any parents felt dissatisfied with this Christian education and Christian politeness, and preferred a fashionable education for their daughters, Miss Lyon did not aspire to be their teacher, nor felt emulous of the laurels that might be won in such a field. It was enough for her if she could send forth pupils with minds well disciplined and stored with knowledge, with physical constitutions invigorated by exercise, temperance, and the practice of all other important hygienic laws, and with hearts glowing with a desire to do good. And when we recollect that nearly three thousand such, scattered over the whole face of the globe, still survive, what an impression do we get of the mighty work which this single woman has accomplished, and of the vast influence she is at this moment exerting upon the human family! *

* I am indebted to Mrs. Banister (Miss Z. O. Grant) for the following statement of the fundamental principles on which, in her opinion, Miss Lyon's superior skill in teaching was founded. It is interesting to observe the thoroughly Christian character of these principles.

"Some of Miss Lyon's excellences as an educator consisted, —

"In her knowledge and love of the character and government of God.

"In her knowledge of the human mind — its capacities; its destiny; of the effects of habits, and the way to form them aright; of the relation of the human mind to its Creator and to its fellow-creatures, and of the obligations growing out of those relations.

"In her entire and cordial reception of the Bible as a revelation of God to man; in her knowledge and love of this blessed book.

"In having the first and second table of the moral law written on her heart; in her peculiar facility in leading others to an intellectual understanding of this law.

"In her deep appreciation of the gospel as opening a way for the salvation of the lost; her living faith in all its truths — especially in Him who is *the* truth.

But there was another work, still more difficult to execute, and probably more important in its effects, which she accomplished; and that was, to found, or rather create, the Mount Holyoke Seminary. A minute history of that undertaking, from its inception to its completion, would show how wonderfully Miss Lyon and all concerned in it were prepared and led along by an overruling Providence. But justice to my subject and to the principal agents will not allow me to pass it entirely over.

The prominent features of the Mount Holyoke Female Seminary, as it was ultimately established, and by which it differed from any other in New England, were the following. I do not mean that in no other institution have they been introduced partially; but here alone have they been fully carried out and brought into harmonious action.

1. This seminary is permanently endowed.

2. From its foundation to its topstone, it was carried forward by an appeal to Christian benevolence; and the donors were not encouraged to expect any other reward than that which springs from doing good. Many judicious friends did not believe it possible to procure the means on such exclusively benevolent principles. But it was done triumphantly.

3. Hence, thirdly, no one connected with the seminary as

"In her glowing benevolence to all for whom Christ died.

"In her burning zeal to do all in her power towards extending the knowledge of the Redeemer to every creature.

"In her understanding and heartfelt sense of the necessity of bringing great and unalterable truths in contact with the human mind in a way suited to produce their legitimate effects.

"In a practical belief that what ought to be done can be done.

"In a deep sense that, without God's blessing, all will be in vain.

"In an abiding reliance on God, and a cheerful expectation of his blessing."

trustee, teacher, steward, or benefactor has any pecuniary interest in it, except that some receive a small fixed salary.

4. Hence, fourthly, the charges to the pupils could be put at a very low rate — not more than one third of the expense usually incurred at our best female seminaries where a similar course of study is gone through.

5. Hence, fifthly, instruction in doctrinal and practical evangelical religion could be made, as it ever has been, the most prominent feature of the institution, without any influence from that worldly policy which, under the name of excluding sectarianism, shuts out all religion of any practical value.

6. All connected with the school constitute but a single family.

7. The domestic affairs are all managed by the members.

The germ of this seminary may probably be found in a remark made by Rev. Joseph Emerson to Miss Grant (now Mrs. Banister) in 1823, when advising her to take charge of the Adams Female Academy in Derry, New Hampshire: "If you can put into operation," said he, "a permanent school on right principles, you may well afford to give up your life whenever you have done it." It was the hope of realizing this thought that induced that lady to take charge of the Adams school, where for five years she labored, with Miss Lyon, to accomplish this object, and another five years in the same school removed to Ipswich. It was not, however, till they had been two years at Ipswich — that is, in 1830 — that Miss Lyon could believe it possible, however desirable, to obtain means for a permanent institution. At length, however, she saw its importance; and the two ladies labored together for a year or two to find a permanent residence for their school, which they intended should be adapted for bringing the higher and middle classes together. But at this time the health of Miss Grant failed, and she went away. Before she was again able to resume her place, all hopes of bringing about this specific object were abandoned, and all associations, whether called committees or trustees, were dissolved; though Miss Grant still clung, as with a death grasp, to her favorite idea of permanency.

But though Miss Lyon thus yielded to this providential blasting of her hopes, yet as she mused and prayed over the subject, her interest deepened; and this probably was the object of Providence in the disappointment; for success demanded a spirit ready for any labor and any sacrifice. Several new projects occupied her attention, and she became more and more impressed with the desire of laboring for the middle and more indigent classes of society. This led her to devise every possible mode of lessening the expenses of the new seminary; and among the rest, to the plan of having the domestic affairs managed by the inmates of the school. She at last made up her mind to leave her present place as teacher at Ipswich, and go forth and see whether Providence would open any way for accomplishing her favorite object; although for a time it was doubtful whether she or Miss Grant, whom she still consulted, should take this course. Indeed, she seemed as yet to be very much in the dark as to the way in which she was to go, and did not expect such results as she lived to witness. In a letter to Miss Grant, dated March 1, 1833, she thus remarks: —

"For myself, if I should separate from you, I have no definite plan; but my thoughts, feelings, and judgment are turned towards the middle classes of society. For this class I want to labor, and for this class I consider myself rather peculiarly fitted to labor. To this class in society would I devote directly all the remainder of my strength, (God permitting;) not to the higher classes, not to the poorer classes. The middle class contains the main springs and main wheels which are to move the world. Whatever field I should occupy, it must be a humble, *laborious* work. How I could get a footing sufficiently firm for my feet to rest upon the remainder of my days, where my hands could work, I know not. But by wandering about a year or two, perhaps Providence might open the door. I should seek for nothing permanent after my decease as to the location of my labors; but I should consider it desirable that I should occupy but one more field, that I should make but one more remove, till I remove into my grave."

What a beautiful development of Christian character does this extract present! What a waiting upon God, and confidence in his providence! How and where she could get a foothold to labor she knew not; "but by wandering about a year or two, perhaps Providence might open the door." How does such faith remind us of that other servant of God, who, *when he was called to go out into a place which he should after receive for an inheritance, obeyed; and he went out, not knowing whither he went.* What humility and readiness to labor is here shown! "Whatever field I should occupy, it must be a humble and *laborious* work." Yet what holy sagacity is exhibited in strongly desiring to labor for the middle classes, because "they are the main springs and main wheels to move the world"! That is, she wished to labor where her efforts would do the most good. And finally, what perfect freedom from the ambition of having her name attached to some great institution, by which many have supposed she was actuated in her severe labors! "I should seek for nothing permanent after my decease as to the location of my labors." How evident that such a state of mind was just the one that was needed for the herculean task of founding this institution! and how obviously it was the natural result of that long and severe discipline through which she had passed!

Could we have looked forward to the results which are before us to-day, it would indeed have been a scene of high moral sublimity to have seen this female going forth on this great enterprise almost single-handed. I well remember the first meeting, in this part of Massachusetts, of some eight or ten friends of education, which was held at my house to hear her statements. We saw the object, indeed, to be a noble one, and therefore we could not but wish it God speed; and the address to the public, which that meeting called forth, signed by John Todd, Joseph Penney, and Roswell Hawks, did, indeed, express confidence in its ultimate success; but I fear, that had there not been faith somewhere else stronger than ours, the walls of this seminary would not yet have risen. Nevertheless, she who was willing to wait one or two years to see if some door would not open, could discover a bow of promise where others saw only a black cloud. Steadily did she move onward in the work, cheered by the slightest indication of success, and undiscouraged by ridicule, hostility, and discomfiture. And it was not mere indifference which she had to meet; but respectable periodicals appeared, charged with sarcasm and enmity to her plans. So ungenerous did some of these attacks seem, that I volunteered a defence, and consulted her as to its publication. I found her entirely unruffled by these attacks, and without any personal feeling in respect to a vindication. She did not object to the spirit or style of my defence, and I left it in her hands, to be published, if she thought it best. But that is the last I ever heard or saw of it.

I need not further detail the progress of this work to its completion, because it is too familiar to most of those who hear me. It was, indeed, a long, and sometimes apparently a doubtful struggle; and faith less firm than that of the presiding genius of this enterprise would often have given out. But remarkable wisdom seemed to have been given her in the formation of her plans, and in the selection of agents and guardians. She lived to see not less than sixty thousand dollars contributed by the Christian public; yonder noble edifice erected, with its accommodations for two hundred pupils; the debts of the institution all liquidated; and the whole plan in successful operation for twelve years; during which sixteen hundred young ladies enjoyed its privileges, and eleven revivals of religion stamped the seal of God's approbation upon the enterprise and the institution. How much larger these results than the anticipations of its founder when she said, "I should seek for nothing permanent after my decease"! and what a lesson of encouragement to all those who are waiting in patient faith and hope to know what God will have them do!

Such was Miss Lyon; such the discipline through which she was made to pass to fit her for her work; and such the magnificent results. We are amazed when we look back at the amount and magnitude of her labors. Very few females have done so much for the world while they lived, or have left so rich a legacy when they died. Nor is the fair picture marred by dark stains, save those of microscopic littleness. From the days of her childhood to the time of her death, all her physical, intellectual, and moral powers were concentrated upon some useful and noble object, while selfishness and self-gratification seem never to have stood at all in the way, or to have retarded the fervid wheels of benevolence. I cannot, therefore, believe that it is the partiality of personal friendship which leads me to place Miss Lyon among the most remarkable women of her generation. Her history, too, shows the guiding hand of special Providence almost as strikingly as the miraculous history of Abraham, of Moses, of Elijah, or of Paul. O, it tells us all how blessed it is to trust Providence implicitly when we are trying to do good, though the darkness be so thick around us that we cannot see forward one hand's breadth, and bids us advance with as confident a step as if all were light before us.

This picture, too, is a complete one. Her life was neither too long nor too short. She died at the right time, with her armor on and yet bright. But her friends saw that, strong as her constitution naturally was, it was giving way under such severe and protracted labor, and the infirmities of declining years beginning to show themselves even at the age of fifty-two. But with her Saviour she could say, "*I have finished the work which Thou* (God) *gavest me to do.*" All her important plans had been carried into successful operation, and tested by long experiment; and the institution was in the right condition to be committed to other hands. She had also of late been rapidly ripening for another sphere of labor. One of her friends, who had been more intimately connected with her for several years past than any other, when at a distance she heard of her sickness, felt confident that it would be unto death; for she had known how, for some months previous, her friend had been feeding daily on manna, and pluming her wings for her upward flight. Severe, therefore, as her removal seemed, when first announced, it happened just at the right time, and I cannot wish to call her back. But I do feel, and many who hear me, I doubt not, feel it too, — I do feel a strong desire to be borne upward, on an angel's wing, to the Mount Zion where she now dwells, and to hear her describe, in the glowing language of heaven, the wonders of Providence, as manifested in her own earthly course, as they now appear in the bright transparencies of heaven. Yet further, I long to hear her describe the still wider plans she is now devising and executing for the good of the universe and the glory of God; and how admirably her earthly discipline fitted her for a nobler field of labor above; so that those providences which appear to us to have been consummated on earth, were in fact only a necessary means of adapting her to a work which shall fill and delight all her powers throughout eternal ages. Gladly, too, would I listen to her intensely earnest inquiries respecting her beloved seminary and friends on earth, and learn whether, in some way unknown to us, she may not be still able to administer to their welfare. O, how sweet, too, would it be, could we listen to that rapturous song of praise, which ever and anon she would pour forth to her Redeemer, as his glories strike her eye, or his past kindness touches a chord of gratitude in her heart.

But alas! how vain are all such aspirations! And yet, my Christian friends, if we are faithful to God and duty as she was, in a very few days all this intercourse and communion will be a reality. Some of us may not, indeed, be able to sound so lofty a note of praise as our glorified friend, but our song and our communion shall nevertheless be the music and the intercourse of heaven; and that will be enough.

WASTE OF MIND.

WHAT more, or better, on the subject of female education, can be said, than has been presented by the distinguished gentlemen who have occupied this place on former anniversary occasions? This was my involuntary inquiry, when invited to address this audience to-day; and it would have decided me to decline the honor, had not another inquiry been started: Why is it necessary that these addresses should be confined to the subject of female education? Why should not the speaker be allowed the same wide field in which to choose his subject, as is given to those who address young men in our colleges, at their annual commencements? I adopt the opinion that such ought to be the case, and shall act accordingly on the present occasion, leaving it to my successors to follow my example or not, as they shall prefer.

The subject which I propose to bring before you is, in its nature, of melancholy interest. Nevertheless, it is not easy to excite human sympathy deeply in respect to it, although it unfolds a wider and darker history of human wrongs than that accursed traffic in flesh and blood which has justly aroused the Christian world for its extermination. Slavery and the slave trade are, indeed, a part of my subject; yet only a small part. For I shall speak of the slavery of the immortal mind — of its subjection, whether voluntary or involuntary, to any of the thousand petty tyrants that, from the beginning, have lorded it over the human soul, and made merchandise of its lofty powers, and crushed its expanding energies. The wrongs which the human family have endured from slavery, technically so called, terrible as they have been, sink into comparative insignificance when we take this wider view of the subject, and behold, as I shall endeavor to show, not a few millions merely, but earth's almost entire and vast population, deprived of rights infinitely more precious than personal liberty — the right and the power of cultivating the faculties by which alone they are distinguished from the brutes that perish. Here is a chapter on oppression and slavery which has never yet been written. Indeed, what arithmetic can tell us the value of the rights which have thus been wrested from man, or the amount of the losses and sufferings he has endured! And yet, as I said above, unless we bring physical sufferings into the account, there is little sensibility among men to the subject. It will not need an armed police here to-day to defend me from violence while I discuss it. But on the other hand, I have reason to fear that the strong array of urbanity, and attention, and benevolence, and patience, which I know form a strong body guard around this audience, will hardly be able to defend them against drowsiness, or nervousness, as I proceed.

But I am dealing too much in enigmas. I denominate my subject THE WASTE OF MIND. It is not necessary, before this audience, to enter into an argument to show that, unless the intellectual powers are cultivated, man scarcely rises above the brutes; nay, in many respects, is their inferior. Nor will it be any more doubted that the Creator endowed us with these powers, with the precise design of having them cultivated; and of course, that he surrounded us with circumstances favorable to their cultivation. If, then, individuals, or communities, or nations do not cultivate their minds, either through their own neglect or the fault of others, there is so much dead loss to the world, so much waste of what God placed within its reach, and whose value can be estimated neither by gold nor by numbers. This is one variety of what I call *the waste of mind.*

Again, let us suppose an individual or a community to subject their powers to some sort of discipline, but to devote them to things useless or hurtful. It is surely the mildest language we can use, to call such perversion of the noblest gifts and acquisitions a waste of mind. And this is, in fact, the most common mode in which men incur the charge of squandering away their noble powers and attainments. If their newly-developed faculties promote neither their own happiness nor that of others, nor advance the cause of sound learning, nor the cause of religion, — if employed only to aid in pampering gross bodily appetites, or in accomplishing the destruction of their fellow-men, the pearl of Cleopatra, dissolved to grace the feast to Mark Antony, is but a faint emblem of this infinitely greater sacrifice.

In these two ways, then, I maintain that the waste of mind always has been, and still is, immense. And to establish and illustrate this position, I propose to present the subject in three aspects: —

1. *Historically.*
2. *Geographically.*
3. *Individually.*

1. *Historically.* — To enable you justly to appreciate this first part of my argument, it is not necessary to go into a detailed history of nations, but only to seize upon some of its leading features. As a preliminary, I assert that there is no

important difference between the members of the human family, when placed in the same circumstances, in the facility with which they acquire useful knowledge, and adopt the arts and rules of civilized life. There is, indeed, a great diversity in these respects between individuals; but I am here comparing nations, or tribes, with one another. And if their susceptibilities of improvement are nearly equal, then, since Providence furnished them in the earlier stages of society with nearly equal means of improvement, it is fair to take those who are the most advanced as a standard by which to estimate the deficiencies of the others. Let us take for an example our progenitors of Great Britain. They were not, indeed, quite as low on the scale of intellect as some other heathen nations. But the horrid system of Druidism, which there prevailed, which could be satisfied with nothing but human victims for sacrifice, must have been like the blast of death to every thing pure, and lovely, and noble. They who could submit century after century to such a system of gloomy superstition, must have been about as much degraded as human nature can be. Nor did the Saxon conquest, which brought in little more than swarms of pirates, with a religion almost as debasing as Druidism, afford much alleviation to the gloomy picture. Nevertheless, in the amalgamated character which resulted, there were certain elements, which have, in the course of centuries, brought out the noblest development of human nature which the world has ever witnessed. What a vast storehouse of cultivated intellect has the Anglo-Saxon race been, all over the world, for the last three hundred years! What brilliant discoveries, what immense acquisitions, what mighty conquests, have they made in art, science, and literature! And as a consequence, what vast accessions have they made to the means of human usefulness and happiness!

what streams of knowledge and of salvation are at this moment flowing out from the little island of Britain, over more than half the globe! and what almost countless millions feel the giant strength of her arm!

But is there any thing peculiar in Anglo-Saxon blood, which enables that race to rise higher in intellect and art than any other? Surely not; for even now other races compete with them. The present state of that race, then, is only a fair index of what the whole world is capable of becoming — nay, of what it might have been, almost from the beginning, if it had not perverted the gifts of Providence. Indeed, even among the Anglo-Saxon race, there is, at this moment, an immense waste of mind, as I shall attempt to show in the sequel; so that even their brilliant career of knowledge and civilization is far inferior to what the whole world might have exhibited in past ages, if man had not been recreant to his powers and privileges.

But from a picture so bright and fascinating, turn back your eye, and see what the world has actually been during the six thousand years of her history. Read that history; and what is the prominent idea which remains upon your mind? It will be war — merciless, heart-withering war! Read again; and retain the next strongest impression, and I know you will say the second time — nay, the third time — that the clangor of war drowns every thing else. But consult the history once more, to ascertain what have been the employments of man during the intervals when they have paused amid their conflicts, and you will find the crafty and ambitious few engaged in intrigues with one another, and in riveting more firmly the yoke of oppression upon the necks of the ignorant and abused multitude. These are the items, I say, that constitute ninety-nine hundredths of the history of man.

Small, indeed, has been the space occupied by the deeds of the noble few who have tried to stem the general current, and to cultivate the arts of peace — to promote the progress of science and civilization, of pure liberty, and the elevation of the mass of mankind, by education and religion. Though their history deserves folios, and will live when that of political intrigues and of wars shall be forgotten, yet if given only in a proportionate space, it will be scarcely visible. For the business of man, thus far, has been to persecute and destroy his fellows, instead of blessing them; to waste and pervert his powers on unworthy or wicked objects, instead of using them for the good of the world. That, I say, has been his business; while benevolent effort has been only the infrequent exception.

I shall doubtless be referred to Greece and Rome, as sufficient examples to redeem the ancient world from the heavy charge of an almost universal waste of mind. These republics are, indeed, the brightest spots on the picture. But seen through the optics of Christianity, their light is mostly a lurid glare. With all their boasted wisdom, the inhabitants were idolaters; they were slaveholders; they were engaged in almost perpetual wars; and Rome, especially, in those most unjustifiable of all wars, — wars of conquest. They had more light than other nations; but they employed it all for the subjugation and destruction of their fellow-men, instead of their salvation. A few among them did, indeed, cultivate the arts of peace, and would gladly have blessed mankind. But those who controlled the public affairs suffered the people to grow up in ignorance, and made use of the discoveries and reputation of their philosophers and sages to aggrandize the nation, or a favored few, while the great mass, with much seeming liberty, were in fact under the worst kind of bondage.

Strike from the annals of these republics the history of their wars, foreign and domestic, scarce one of which can bear the light of Christianity, — strike from them the history of their domestic oppressions, and add to them what never has been written, the history of female degradation there, and of the insufferable despotism which those exercised over their slaves at home, who made the forum ring with their vaunts of liberty, — reduce and correct Grecian and Roman history thus, and you will find little in it which the benevolence of Christianity would not denominate *waste of mind.*

I shall probably be thought most sadly, if not criminally, deficient in reverence for the classic ground of antiquity, by this strong condemnation of the general course of conduct pursued by these ancient republics. Where shall we find oratory more overwhelming, rhetoric more correct, poetry more beautiful, or philosophy more sublime, than in the writings transmitted from the sages of antiquity, and still made the basis of instruction in our higher schools of learning? Instead of undervaluing these productions, I would appeal to them as a ground of encouragement to all literary men; for the whole history of the world scarcely furnishes such an example of success, and such extensive influence exerted by a few literary men. But, on the other hand, it should not be forgotten, that these writings are held in such high estimation not because they contain a correct philosophy, correct moral or religious principles, or even correct rules of oratory. Excepting as models of fine writing, and some rhetorical and mathematical principles, and some true common sense maxims, we are obliged to unlearn all which they contain; and were not the languages in which they were written eminently classic, — that is, chosen as the medium of thought among the learned, — there can be no doubt but these ancient authors would long since have been forgotten, or, rather, replaced by authors better adapted to modern literature, modern science, and modern religion. Nor should it be forgotten, that while a meritorious few, in ancient times, did not waste their powers and acquisitions, but devoted them to the good of mankind, scarcely any opportunity was afforded to the common people to discipline and enlarge their minds ; and thus an immense amount of talent was smothered in embryo. But what I complain of most of all is, that nearly all the talent which was elicited, and most of the discipline which was enjoyed, were turned into the war channel ; and what should have been consecrated to the good of mankind was devoted to their destruction.

Here again I shall probably come into collision with the views of some who entertain a high regard for the distinguished warriors of Greece and Rome, and who would recommend them as examples to be followed by Christian youth, and who look with a favorable eye upon wars in which such men gathered their brightest laurels. I will not, indeed, take the ground that all wars are forbidden by the spirit and letter of the gospel ; but I shall utter the almost unanimous opinion of the Protestant world, when I say that offensive wars are the very antipodes of the Bible. Now, how very few of the wars of Greece and Rome were not of this description! Some of the earlier contests — as that when Greece was invaded by Xerxes — were merely defensive. But as soon as these nations, especially Rome, became sufficiently powerful, the aggrandizement of the empire was unblushingly offered as a sufficient reason for carrying fire and sword through unsubjugated regions, however remote. A petty insult, offered by a neighboring state, was deemed cause enough for a bloody Peloponnesian war. Now, with the Bible in my hand, I boldly declare, that the talents and energies employed in such wars as these are worse than wasted, and that the leaders in them deserve execration instead of imitation. I speak not of the blood and pecuniary treasure expended in such wars. These may be, and have been, calculated; and they form a frightful aggregate. But to sacrifice upon the altar of hate and unhallowed ambition a vast and incalculable amount of immortal mind — to offer up there the intellectual hopes and glory of a nation — should receive the name of sacrilege rather than waste. And yet, what myriads of her noblest minds did Greece and Rome cast into the insatiable maw of the Moloch of war! If we can forgive it in a heathen nation, how ought it to be execrated in a land professing Christianity!

It will indeed be said that we ought not to regard all the intellect which is sacrificed, even in wars of ambition and conquest, as lost or wasted. For such wars wake up the public mind to effort; and we accordingly find that seasons of great exigency are periods when remarkable developments are made of individual talent.

There is certainly truth in this statement. But who are the men thus awakened by war to extraordinary efforts? Only that small number who are leaders in the struggle. And what effect is produced upon the community? Their means of improvement are exhausted, and they are obliged to struggle for a long time with the poverty brought on them by the expenses of the war. It requires a quarter of a century of prosperous peace to recover from the withering influence of a single protracted war. Hence the aggregate of loss to the community at large far outstrips the aggregate of gain to individuals, even if we look only to mental improvement; and hence the energies expended in such wars are worse than wasted. And the same is true of all wars. Though they may promote the interests of a favored few, and even bring out a development of individual talent, they effectually extinguish the intellectual vitality of the great majority, whose elevation is of far more importance to the world than that of an aristocratic few. But it may be stated as a general fact, that wars tend to degrade the many and exalt the few. Thus the leaders soon learn to regard the life of a common man with as much indifference as they would that of a beast of burden. In France, during the reign of Bonaparte, conscripts were styled by the leaders *raw materials, and food for powder;* and the question was discussed, how long a conscript would last. Some said thirty-three, and others thirty-six months; and Napoleon once remarked, that he had *a revenue of three hundred thousand men.* How different the spirit of Christianity, which almost forgets the trifling distinctions of worldly ambition, in looking at that infinitely more important distinction which every man may claim — the possession of an immortal mind! Hence it is, that while Christianity does not overlook the few, it aims chiefly to instruct and elevate the many.

I am led by this remark to say in this connection, that the introduction of Christianity into the world affords us the most remarkable example of success in the cultivation of the human faculties which history can furnish. The gospel had a higher object in view than to promote intellectual cultivation, and the few obscure men by whom it was first promulgated were mostly uneducated. And yet that *College of Fishermen* has done more to advance the cause of public education than all other colleges and universities combined. And this has been done by the principle just alluded to, viz., by extending its instructions and regards to the whole human family. All other systems for doing good to mankind have been exclusive in their regards; and while they have benefited a few, they have left the multitude to grovel in ignorance and wretchedness. And so long have the latter been treated as if they were but one step removed from the brutes, that, by a curious principle of human nature, they have come to believe it, and to hug the chains by which they are bound down to the dust. But when the Bible has convinced the most degraded human being that he is immortal, and capable of boundless progress in knowledge and happiness, it has taken the greatest bar out of the way of his advancement in human literature and science. Accordingly we find, that in those countries where the Bible has been most widely circulated, and its influence felt, popular education has achieved its greatest triumphs — as in Greenland, Prussia, Great Britain, and North America. But so soon as we enter those regions where the Bible is unknown, or restricted in its circulation, we have entered also the domains of popular ignorance and degradation; even though it may be a land of colleges and universities, and boasting not a few prodigies of genius and learning. He therefore who means that his name shall stand high among the pioneers and promoters of public education, must connect it with the Bible. That is the only Archimedean lever by which he can raise the world.

2. *Geographically.* — In entering upon the second division of the subject, where I am to treat it geographically, it would greatly aid our conceptions could I call in an experienced missionary as a witness. Many such, however, have given us their testimony, and to that I shall appeal. Let us suppose such a one, of Anglo-Saxon origin, to go forth on a tour of exploration, to form an estimate, not only of the moral, but the intellectual condition of the world. As he quits our

shores, probably forever, he almost forgets our many defects and crying sins, when he recollects how many salutary influences are here at work; how the Bible finds a place in almost every family; how the school house is seen at almost every corner; how thickly the select school, the academy, and the college are scattered over our soil; and how, by these and other means, knowledge is carried to the meanest hovel, and elevates and dignifies its poorest inmate. He crosses the Atlantic, and in exploring the fatherland, is no less — nay, in some respects, is more gratified, and thanks God that he belongs to the Anglo-Saxon race. He visits the continent, and as he wanders through Prussia, Sweden, and some of the German states, and some of the countries of Switzerland, he begins to fancy that wherever he meets with a Caucasian physiognomy, he shall find intelligence and freedom. He enters France, and while he surveys the splendid monuments of the Louvre, the Garden of Plants, and a thousand other repositories of art and science in the capital of that empire, he seems to have reached the emporium of knowledge, and can hardly imagine that he is to meet with deep degradation and ignorance in such a nation. But as he wanders over the streets and lanes of that city, and especially through the Departments, he is amazed to find, beneath such a splendid exterior, so much that is dark and disgusting, so much of ignorance and infidelity among the mass of the population. But when he learns that the Bible is in a great measure withheld from circulation, he sees an adequate cause for all the ignorance, corruption, and infidelity. And when he traverses Spain, Portugal, and Italy, and sees how much deeper is the cloud of ignorance and wickedness which broods over those nations, and how much more sedulously the Bible is excluded, he finds full confirmation of his conclusion that it is this book, rather than a Caucasian physiognomy, which brings light and liberty, as well as salvation. Among the teeming millions on the banks of the Danube, he finds the same truth illustrated; and the degraded serfs of Russia's vast plains confirm his impressions. In short, he finds that where the Bible is a prohibited or scarcely known book, there the common man is left unenlightened and undisciplined, and an incalculable amount of wasted and perverted mind is the result.

But though we find so much to deplore in the mental condition of Catholic Europe, and much also in many parts of Protestant Europe, still, in all those countries there does exist a great amount of mental activity. Amid much that is saddening to the missionary's spirit, there is much to cheer and inspire with hope for the future. It is not till he enters the Oriental dominions of Mohammedanism, that he has any just conceptions of what is meant by an utter waste and perversion of mind. The noble features of the Caucasian race do indeed meet him under the turban of the Turk, the cap of the Persian, in the sun-burned complexion of the Arab, even in the savage aspect of the Koord and the Tartar, and especially in the elegant countenance of the Circassian and the Georgian. But he is amazed to witness what a dreadful stagnation of mind pervades all these nations. It is not utter barbarism and destitution of all intelligence, but that strange state of the human soul, when there is just light enough to make it feel its own importance, and excite the idea that it has reached the acme of knowledge, and that others, especially those of another religion, can furnish no additional light. In short, it is just such a state of mind as the Koran is calculated to produce, and which its author meant it to produce. Its spirit is well illustrated in the syllogism by which the Caliph Omar consigned the famous Alexandrian library, where was gathered most of the literature of antiquity, to the use of the common soldiers for cooking their food. "If these books," said he, "are opposed to the Koran, they ought to be destroyed; if they agree with the Koran, they are unnecessary, and may therefore be burned." That is the spirit which chimes in admirably with the demands of despotism, and which in fact keeps at this moment one hundred millions of Asia and Africa in deep and almost hopeless political and intellectual bondage.

But the missionary on his tour of observation has yet to meet with examples of human ignorance, prejudice, and degradation still more revolting to the benevolent heart. He enters the self-styled "Celestial Empire" of South-eastern Asia, and encounters the self-sufficiency and dogmatism of the Mongolian race, still more insufferable than that of the Caucasian followers of the false prophet. In China, almost every thing is perfect; in view of the native, it is perfect wisdom, perfect intelligence, perfect freedom, and perfect happiness; in the eye of the missionary, perfect folly, perfect ignorance and self-conceit, perfect bondage to prejudice and custom, and perfect wretchedness to the soul of Christian benevolence. At any rate, the intellect of those almost countless millions, which, if properly cultivated, might send a blaze of light all over the globe, is now shut up in a nutshell; and woe be to the individual who ventures to look upon the outside. Strange, that no one of the vast population, which from generation to generation has swarmed in that empire, should ever have ventured a step beyond his predecessors, and that the highest ambition of those who might have filled the world with their literary and scientific glory has been to fill it with bohea and young hyson.

The Chinese mind, however, is by no means in as degraded

a state as that of some other nations. The wide and populous region of Hindostan and Japan, Farther India, and especially of Australasia and Polynesia, as well as the almost entire continent of Africa, exhibits an utter and almost unalleviated waste of mind. Of all the animals inhabiting those regions, man is doubtless the farthest below what his Creator intended him to be ; and, I had almost said, probably he is the lowest on the scale of intellect. There is no part of the world which the civilized man cannot penetrate, in spite of the fiercest and strongest wild beasts. But there are many regions which he has never been able to explore, because the untamed savage is more dangerous than beasts of prey. This fact is a fine comment upon those Utopian theories which represent the savage state as more desirable than the civilized. Those same beings whose cultivation might make not only the region which they inhabit a paradise, but shed blessings on other lands, are now the most degraded and disgusting objects which the earth contains, and the terror of civilized man, and even of one another. Yet this is the condition of almost the whole of the two wide continents of Africa and Australasia, and of vast regions in Asia. What a terrific waste of mind the picture exhibits !

In all the regions we have now examined beyond the limits of Christianity, there is one feature which I ought not to pass unnoticed on this occasion. In all Christian countries, we find woman brought into free companionship, if not equality, with man. Unrestrained by any thing but propriety and religion, she goes abroad to enjoy the beauties of nature, and to mingle freely in society, of which, indeed, she constitutes the chief life and ornament. But as soon as we enter the dominions of the false prophet, she is shut out from all society save that of her own sex and of her tyrannical husband, or rather master; or if we meet her, it is only as a walking mummy. Not even in her own house can she be seen, though in the presence of her lord; and to inquire of him concerning her welfare, or that of her children, is an unpardonable breach of etiquette. And the reason of this contemptuous and barbarous exclusion and neglect, the traveller is gravely informed, is, that woman has no soul. Well might the traveller retort upon the ignorant Mussulman that such an opinion could be entertained only by the man who has no soul. It is, indeed, one of the strongest marks of the grovelling and dastardly spirit of Mohammedanism and paganism that they degrade and abuse woman because she is feeble and defenceless. There is no meanness so great as his who takes advantage of the power which Providence gave him to protect the weak and confiding in order to enslave them. Yet, aside from the influence of Christianity, this has been a characteristic of human nature; and woman has been the uncomplaining victim in all ages. The oppression has been the more severe in proportion as man has been farther removed from a civilized state. It is less in Turkey and Persia than in China, where females are sometimes seen yoked to the plough and the harrow. Still deeper is the degradation in Hindostan, where the widow must either be burned on the funeral pile or by a public opinion more terrible than literal flames. And yet more intolerable do we find the female condition in Australasia and Polynesia, in some of whose islands the first addresses woman receives from her future husband consist in being levelled to the ground by a club; next she is beaten till sense and life are almost gone, and then dragged over the rough ground to his bark hut. And, as we might expect, it is said that such a beginning of the matrimonial connection is a fair sample of its character through life.

Excepting the southern portion of our own continent, where are no bright lines to relieve the gloomy picture, we have now accompanied the missionary over the entire globe; and though, to his mind, the spiritual condition of our race may seem the most degraded and hopeless, yet their intellectual state is hardly less distressing. Few, and narrow, and far between are the oases that smile on the wide mental waste. Out of Europe and the northern part of our own continent, the eye searches almost in vain for a green spot to rest upon. And when we come to take a nearer view even of the brightest spots, we shall find that the light falls on these only in fitful and scattered rays, illuminating but a small portion of the surface. To take this nearer view will constitute the third part of the subject, where I propose to examine it *individually.* Under this head, I wish to point out some of the employments and habits of individuals and classes of men which either tend to check the progress of intellect, or exert no influence, or a bad influence, upon society — for in all these ways waste of mental power is the result. And it ought never to be forgotten that Providence intended that all the energies of the human soul, in their most cultivated state, should be devoted to useful and worthy objects, and that they cannot, without guilt, be expended upon those injurious to society or to individuals, or which are of doubtful utility.

In entering upon the catalogue of pursuits injurious to society, one of the first on the list, which will immediately occur to every person, is the manufacture and sale of intoxicating drinks. A few years since, I should have been compelled to enter into a formal argument to convince even a respectable audience that such employments are injurious. But thanks to divine mercy, which has wrought so wondrous a revolution of public opinion, this is no longer necessary.

In theory, at least, most men now entertain correct views on this subject. Yet it should not be forgotten that, as Hudibras expresses it, —

> "A man convinced against his will
> Is of the same opinion still."

For it cannot be doubted that there are many such conversions among those who join the general cry against alcohol. And the future historian of temperance will probably be compelled to say of many such as Monsieur Paradin has said of the ladies in the fourteenth century, when the monk Thomas Connecte preached with great zeal and power against their lofty head dresses. "The women," says he, "that, like snails in a fright, had drawn in their horns, thrust them out again as soon as the danger was over." It ought, also, to be remembered that, even now, no less than twelve thousand persons are directly engaged all the time in the manufacture of intoxicating drinks in the United States, — or, at least, such was the case two years ago, — and ten times as many a part of their time. It cannot be doubted that at least as great a proportion of the inhabitants of Europe, and in wine countries a much larger one, is devoted to this business; so that, in this country and Europe, millions are worse than wasting their energies in this execrable employment.

I cannot, in conscience, avoid placing in the same category the cultivation and manufacture of a poisonous plant, whose narcotic and exhilarating qualities make it a general favorite, in spite of the Counterblast of King James, the decrees of popes and emperors, and the yet more powerful attacks of physicians, clergymen, and scientific men in our own day. Rarely will you find the individual addicted to its use who will not confess the habit to be a useless and filthy one; and yet appetite triumphs over his convictions, and he is made a slave for life. The consequence is, that the demand for this weed all over the world is immense — no less than twenty millions of dollars being annually expended for it in this country. And to its preparation thousands, and even millions, of immortal minds devote all their powers, instead of consecrating them to the advancement of knowledge and the happiness of man. But I am sorry to say that, so extensive is the habit of using this intoxicating drug, that I fear I shall have but little sympathy in its condemnation, and that I shall be regarded as too ascetic for this narcotic-loving age.

Shall I now proceed a step farther, and reckon among the hurtful, or at least useless, articles of cultivation and manufacture, two other plants ranked by physicians among the narcotics and stimulants, yet reckoned almost indispensable by half the inhabitants of the globe as beverages to brace up the nerves in the morning, and to chase away fatigue and the headache in the evening? If they are useless, — if Providence has provided a better beverage to our hands, — the waste of mind is truly incalculable involved in their preparation; for how many millions does it occupy! But I forbear; for I tread here upon delicate ground, and come into collision with customs and prejudices too formidable for me to grapple with on an occasion like the present, when I would give pleasure rather than pain. I do not fear, indeed, that even a strong condemnation of these articles would give pain to the members of this institution; for so well satisfied are they with the pure nectar of nature, that they lay no tax upon China or the West Indies for their morning and evening beverage.* But I trust that both they and myself, contented

* I ought to say that the young ladies are not required to refrain from tea and coffee; but the fact is that very little is used.

with the personal benefits we derive from our aqueous sympathies, will exercise a very liberal charity towards those who in this respect cannot come up to our standard. If we cannot agree that there is a waste of mind in employing millions of men to prepare these fascinating decoctions, all reasonable Christian men can agree as to a multitude of other employments, which consume unnecessarily and wickedly the time and the talents of the human family.

We shall all agree that this is done on a wide scale by luxurious living — by pampering an artificial and fastidious appetite. I think I may safely pronounce that system of living luxurious which indulges the appetite beyond what will give the most perfect development and enjoyment to the mind and the body. No man who is not strongly Epicurean in his habits can object to this principle. And yet who does not know how grossly and widely it is violated the world over? The wants of nature are few and simple; and, until we acquire a morbid appetite, that simplicity affords even more gustatory enjoyment than the costliest viands of pampered luxury. But how early are we learned to crave factitious and stimulating compounds! and how soon do we come to regard them as indispensable! Hence human ingenuity is taxed to the utmost to meet the demands of a vitiated and fastidious appetite; and the culinary art becomes so complicated as to need an encyclopædia to explain it, and a seven years' apprenticeship to learn it. In short, the whole time and physical and intellectual energies of three fourths of the human race are devoted, at this moment, to cultivating, preparing, and compounding food for the body. Is it possible that such was the intention of Providence, in endowing man with so many noble faculties? Was it meant that the great business of life should be to gratify the palate? Why, then, was man made superior to the brutes, if, with his exalted powers, he can accomplish no more than the brutes? O, no — those powers were given us to be employed upon noble objects. We have departed from nature, and given to our animal and inferior constitution so exalted a regard that the intellect, the immortal part, has become its servant. Man can be healthier and happier, if he will substitute simplicity for compound cookery, and a natural appetite for a vitiated palate.

And, on this occasion, I ought not to forget that the evils of this artificial state of things fall most heavily upon woman. Among the great mass of the community, she is expected to take the responsibility of culinary manipulations; and, indeed, eminent skill in this department is generally thought to be the perfection of her education. Almost the whole of her time must be devoted to the preparation of delicacies for the table; and it is only the shreds and patches of life that she can devote to the cultivation of her mind. Gladly would she introduce more simplicity and temperance at her domestic board — not that she might escape responsibility and care, but that she might store her mind with a richer fund of knowledge, and thus furnish her guests with something to feast the intellect and the heart, as well as the palate. But tyrannical custom and tyrannical man bind her down in hopeless servitude to morbid appetite. Her husband frowns upon any diminution of the usual variety and delicacy at the table; and then, to reward her for her compliance with his wishes, he gravely pronounces her the weaker vessel, and becomes convinced of her inferiority to himself in intellect. Verily I believe that, if ever there comes a millennium of learning, along with a millennium of religion, woman will obtain some relief from her culinary thraldom. Then, and not till then, can the question be fairly discussed and decided which forms a standing topic in the college, the academy, and the lyceum — whether she be inferior to man in intellectual power.

I have already alluded to war as eminently hostile to mental improvement. Probably no custom of society has been more so; and consequently it is chargeable with a vast waste of intellect. It exerts this pernicious influence in part by destroying the lives of many who might be the intellectual ornaments of their country; for the highest and most enterprising minds are most apt to be drawn into the vortex of vice, because they love its powerful excitement. The wars of Julius Cæsar destroyed not less than two millions; those of Alexander of Macedon, as many; those of Napoleon, twice as many. Nor can it be doubted that all the wars which have blasted the globe have swept from its surface as many human beings as now inhabit it. Again, war inevitably produces a state of things most unfavorable to the advancement of knowledge. Literature and science can flourish only amid the calm and security of peace. The war spirit awakens too much excitement, and brings into too powerful action the ferocious passions, to allow of the cultivation of the intellect. The public mind becomes a stormy sea, ingulfing every thing which cannot live in a tempest. Finally, the great pecuniary expenses of war, which fall most heavily upon the middling and poorer classes, deprive them in a great measure, and for a long time, of the leisure and money necessary for extending the blessings of education through the community. The agricultural and manufacturing interests of a country are left by war in a deranged state, and a heavy public debt is usually entailed upon the nation; and to pay this debt, and restore the business of the country to a healthy condition, demand the time and strenuous labors of the citizens. A few facts may more strikingly illustrate this point.

There is, perhaps, no part of the world where a more efficient system of general education is in operation than in the State of New York. In 1830, with a population of one million nine hundred and eighteen thousand six hundred and eighteen, she expended one million one hundred and twenty thousand dollars for common schools and academies, where nearly all of her half million of children and youth were in a course of education. To provide the same means of instruction for the seventeen millions of the United States, in 1840, would cost ten millions of dollars ; and to provide the same for the twenty-five millions of Great Britain would need fifteen millions; and for the eight hundred millions of the entire globe it would require four hundred and seventy millions of dollars. Now, let us compare these sums with the expenses of war.

The revolutionary war of this country with Great Britain cost our government six hundred millions, while the individual losses by the citizens of both countries must have been many times as great. Suppose it the same, and here we have expended on the American side, in seven years, money enough to provide the present population of the whole country with instruction like that enjoyed in New York for one hundred years, and the population of Great Britain for eighty years. The last war with Great Britain cost our government fifty millions ; and, on the same principle as above stated, enough money was spent to afford similar instruction to both countries for ten years, although the war lasted but two and a half years. A single war with Bonaparte cost Great Britain five thousand two hundred and fifteen millions of dollars — sufficient to afford the means of instruction to all her population for three hundred and fifty years, and to give the same means to all the world for eleven years. In 1835, the national debt of Great Britain, incurred for war purposes, amounted to three thousand eight hundred and ninety millions of dollars. The interest on this is one hundred and forty-two millions, and would furnish her inhabitants with the means of education for ten years; that is, she pays a yearly interest that would do this. The daily expenses of a man-of-war, when in service, are about fifteen hundred dollars, or more than half a million for a year. Nineteen such ships would of course cost as much as to educate all the children and youth in the United States. Ten such ships, to say nothing of the sum requisite for their construction, would require a pecuniary outlay as great as the income of all the benevolent societies in Great Britain and the United States, which in 1840 was five million one hundred and thirteen thousand four hundred and twenty-two dollars.

The average expense of the Florida war, carried on with only a few hundred Indians in the swamps of that country, has been from two to five millions, from 1836 to 1840 — a sum nearly equal to that collected, with vast labor, as the fruit of Christian benevolence, among the forty millions of Great Britain and the United States.

But the expenses of war are not confined to the period during which the war lasts; for it is the common maxim of rulers, in time of peace to prepare for war. The sum paid for this purpose by the United States from 1791 to 1832, a period of forty-one years, was seven hundred and seventy-seven millions, or nineteen millions annually. This was twelve times more than all the other expenses of the government during the same period, and would give instruction to all the children of the United States for twice that number of years. In 1837 and 1838, we paid twenty-six millions annually for the same purpose. The expenses of the English government, from the same cause, from 1816 to 1837, a period of twenty-one years of peace, was two thousand and ninety-one millions of dollars, or one hundred millions per year — sufficient to educate her entire population for nearly seven years. If we suppose the expenses of the United States and the other governments of Europe to be only half as great as those of Great Britain for war purposes during peace, we should still have the startling aggregate of five hundred millions annually — a sum sufficient for the education of all Europe and the United States for more than three years, and of all the world for more than one year. If the whole world expend as much in proportion to their numbers for war purposes during peace, it would form the frightful sum of one thousand six hundred millions of dollars — sufficient to educate all its population three and a half years. Truly this is a peace establishment with a vengeance.

These statements seem more like the dreams of disordered fancy than like sober fact. But they are most painfully true; nay, they fall far short of the reality. But, instead of looking on the dark side of the picture, as I expected to do when I began these statistics, they have thrown a bright beam of promise upon the future condition of the world. They show us how immense are the pecuniary capabilities of the human family. They show us what an incalculable amount of funds the world will have at its disposal, for the promotion of science, literature, and religion, when they shall be brought to act according to the principles of reason and religion; for all that now goes into the war channel will then be consecrated to the service of knowledge and benevolence. In spite of all the oppressions and disadvantages under which the human family have hitherto labored, they have been able to sustain this immense war tax which I have described. Nay, I have mentioned only the direct expenses of war. But the losses always sustained by withdrawing men from their regular pursuits, by blocking up the outlets of trade, by idleness and discouragement, and in a multitude of other ways, are far greater. In addition to all this, in most countries men have been compelled to sustain the extortions of tyrannical rulers. Yet has the world borne all these immense taxes; and a few years of peace are generally sufficient to enable a nation to recover its pecuniary independence. How vast, then, will be its surplus pecuniary resources when war and oppression shall cease, and all its energies can be devoted unobstructed to the various pursuits of business! Instead of the stinted sums which men are now persuaded, with great difficulty, to bestow upon objects of education and benevolence, and which leave those devoted to such pursuits to discouragement and heart sickness, because their hands are so tied and their energies so cramped, there will then be ready for every noble object more than is wanted. Millions will then be substituted for thousands. This is indeed a bright page of human history, on which we are permitted to gaze in anticipation; and it affords a cheering resting place for the eye, when placed in contrast with the terrific waste of mind which has been the consequence of war.

Do I seem to any to be indulging in dreams when I say that most assuredly such a bright period will come? But do they doubt that the Bible predicts unequivocally a period of universal peace, and the prevalence of general, if not universal, benevolence? In such a state, why will not the vast treasures that have been wasted upon the destruction of men be consecrated to the diffusion of knowledge and religion through all the earth? — objects that claim the first regard of every benevolent heart. Assuredly this vision is not imagination; and it looms up in the future, — and I would fondly hope not in the distant future, — a bright star of hope for this abused and down-trodden world. The little which has hitherto been contributed to raise man out of the slough of ignorance and sin has accomplished a great deal. What splendid results, then, will be witnessed when ample means shall be placed within the reach of every human being for the highest attainments in knowledge and holiness!

Although war has been thus preëminently instrumental in the perversion and waste of human intellect, there is a kindred evil scarcely less hurtful to man's highest interests, though more unnoticed in its operation. I refer to the various oppressions from tyrannical rulers and masters, under which the human family have been sighing and groaning for thousands of years. If I were to draw out in detail the physical sufferings which result from such oppression, I could reach a tender chord of sympathy in your bosoms. But when I merely calculate the intellectual loss which the world has thereby sustained, I feel that I can draw forth no responsive sigh. And yet this is in reality a darker part of the picture than the physical suffering presents; for in this way have unnumbered millions of minds been shut up in the hopeless dungeon of ignorance and sin. But the world is incapable of estimating its loss, because it has never enjoyed the blessing, and therefore it cannot feel that loss. Nor can I describe it. I will only refer you to one dark feature in that domestic oppression which reigns in our own country, and for which, therefore, we as a nation are responsible. In most of the states of this Union where slavery exists, the law forbids that the slave should be taught to read by severe penalties; and in one state, at least, that penalty, upon a repetition of the offence, is death. Now, if we admit all the reports that have ever been circulated as to the physical cruelties practised upon the slave to be true, they are hardly worth naming in comparison with this effort to stifle and crush the undying souls of two and a half millions of our inhabitants. Nor does the injury stop here; for when we find that the poor black man, whose intellect has been thus crushed into the dust from generation to generation, shows less of mental acumen than the free Caucasian, we proudly and presumptuously infer his intellectual inferiority, and hence justify his enslaved condition. We have, however, the testimony of missionaries from almost every tribe under heaven, which demonstrates that the minds of young children every where exhibit almost equal mental strength and aptness to learn. Hence the slaves of our own land might have risen as high on the scale of knowledge and civilization as the free white man; and the immense disparity in this respect which now exists may all be imputed to their degraded condition; and hence, too, the world must hold us responsible for all this mental waste, who keep the chains of slavery riveted upon these millions. O, this is a fearful responsibility! I leave out of the account the bodily sufferings of the slave. He who maltreats my body injures only what was once brute matter, and will soon be brute matter again. But he who mars and manacles my soul lays a ruthless hand upon that immortal principle which is an emanation of the Deity, which allies me to the Deity, and which a righteous God will not see abused with impunity.

In a free country like ours, there is a prodigious waste of mind in the excitement and discussions of party politics. The mental efforts devoted often to a gubernatorial, and especially a presidential, election would be sufficient, if turned into the channels of literature and science, to raise our country at once to the highest rank on the scale of knowledge. Did these periodical excitements prepare the mind to engage with greater ardor in literary pursuits, they ought not to be viewed as a waste of intellect; but their tendency is decidedly the reverse. No men are so little likely to become eminent in science or literature as strong political partisans. The organs of combativeness and self-esteem soon become so excessively developed as to stifle the reflective faculties. In a few cases, indeed, these electioneering battles must be fought to save the liberties of the country; but, in general, an impartial and uncommitted man will see that there is scarcely any thing to choose between the rival candidates as to general character. And when he perceives how sharp and furious the contest becomes between the partisans, he will be reminded of Dean Swift's couplet respecting disputes about music: —

> "Strange that such high disputes should be
> 'Twixt tweedle dum and tweedle dee."

Notwithstanding the awful predictions by the defeated party of the loss of liberty and every thing else valuable, the government and the affairs of the country generally move on as usual, leaving the philosopher and the Christian, while they rejoice in the calm that has succeeded, to lament that such powerful interests and giant efforts should not be devoted to worthier objects.

In the strong passion for accumulating property which exists among men, and which is said to be eminently characteristic of Americans, we find another source of a waste of mind. In this country, students, like others, are usually obliged to build up their pecuniary, as well as literary, fortunes. The consequence is, that the love of money in too many cases supplants the love of knowledge; and it is a painful fact that a vast proportion of our publicly educated youth close their literary labors with the day that gives them a professional license. They seem to have submitted to the drudgery of an eight or ten years' course of study chiefly for the purpose of learning how to accumulate property. Professors and tutors have taken them to the Castalian fountain, and tried to make them drink deeply of the pure waters. They have been led abroad into the wide fields of nature, and shown every thing there "sublimely great and elegantly little." They have been taught to take those enlarged views of men and things, and of their own responsibilities and capabilities, which will lead them to sacrifice selfish and petty worldly interests to the cause of science, and to consider themselves devoted through all their days to the advancement of human knowledge and happiness. And now behold the magnificent result. They have attained the sublime art of acquiring money a little faster than the farmer or mechanic; and most heroically do they consecrate the remainder of life to this most noble enterprise. They have been so long so near the sun of science that their Dædalian wings are melted off; and from their lofty flights through the wide universe, they quietly settle down into the nutshell of a lynx-eyed money catcher. To apply the remark of the poet, with a slight variation, —

> "They narrow their mind,
> And to money give up what was meant for mankind."

These remarks may seem unreasonably severe. But can the fact be doubted that a large majority of educated men do give up almost entirely the further prosecution of science and literature after they are established in one of the learned professions? And how few ever accomplish more than to accumulate a moderate fortune by a diligent attention to their profession! And ought a man who has enjoyed so many advantages, and held converse with so many of the master minds of former times, — ought he to catch none of their spirit, and to be willing to abandon the noble pursuits of knowledge, and to be satisfied with the mere ordinary routine of a profession, useful, indeed, but requiring scarcely any of the acquisitions which he has made during his education — especially when the continued pursuit of some branch of literature or science would make him more eminent and successful in that profession? But the difficulty seems to be that this continued devotion to literary pursuits would make his profession less profitable in a pecuniary point of view. Money, indeed, is not to be despised by any man; and, after all, very few of our professional men are burdened with it. If it comes into a man's hands as the fruit of his intellectual labors and his economy, he ought to be thankful, and to make a wise improvement of it. But I complain that so many should consider its acquisition as the chief object of an education, and abandon the prosecution of science and literature, because the two objects are thought to be incompatible. And the fact is that, so well understood is this incongruity, a large proportion of the youth in our colleges, even though not compelled to it by poverty, are in the habit, after going through them, of selling off the standard works which they study there, and which they are taught to regard as next to the Bible in value, just as if they should have no further use for them. This appears to me to be the same almost as if the mechanic should dispose of his tools after he had learned the use of them by a seven years' apprenticeship. How many men, also, who have become attached to some branch of literature or science in early life, soon abandon it, on entering upon their profession! — not, surely, because it would make them less learned or respected, but because they find that the charlatans with whom they have to compete, having no learning to impede them, are able to bear away the pecuniary palm. In this case, the fault lies chiefly with the community, who prefer the prompt, pliable, and voluble empiric to the more modest and cautious, yet learned, lawyer or physician.

In the early relish which is acquired, in the present state of society, for things artificial, I find another prolific cause of a waste of mind. God has filled the world with a vast variety of objects, animal, vegetable, and mineral, far more attractive and beautiful than any result of man's invention. He has scattered them in immense profusion all around us, and brought them into contact with all our senses. He has also implanted in the human soul a strong love for these objects. I never saw a young child who did not exhibit a decided relish for natural objects. How eagerly will children pluck the opening flower, or gather up the sparkling mineral, or chase the gay insect, and gaze upon the brilliant bird! Indeed, they are constitutionally naturalists, and it is easy to excite in them so much enthusiasm, that they will forget their ordinary food, if you will lead them forth into the fields, and point out to them the wonders of creation. But in the present condition of society, this natural taste is not cultivated. They are sent to the primary school, and there their attention is turned to subjects that have little connection with nature. I do not complain that they are taught grammar, and geography, and history, and arithmetic; but I do complain that there is not mingled with these studies, so dull to them, some instruction in zoölogy, botany, and mineralogy. The first lines of these branches might be taught to children as early at least as they learn the alphabet, and it would be a very easy matter to make four fifths of them no mean adepts in these branches in very early life, and that, too, without interfering at all with other studies. Once call into action their enthusiasm for natural history, and you will find it a most powerful means of preserving them from idleness and wicked companionship.

But instead of this course, evidently pointed out by the providence of God, the attention of children is directed almost wholly to things artificial. The boy soon learns that money is the most important thing in this world, because it will procure for him toys, and delicacies for the palate ; and as he grows older, he looks forward for happiness to the possession of a fashionable equipage, and other means of sensual enjoyment. The girl finds very early that dress and personal appearance are the grand objects for which she should live; and as she grows up to womanhood, this is too apt to become the ruling passion of her life. Every freak and every change in fashion are watched with more carefulness than her health, her mental improvement, or any thing else. Thus does she unconsciously waste enough of mental power to make her very wise and very learned. Indeed, were all the anxiety, and study, and ingenuity, and expense, which woman now devotes, throughout the world, to these objects, to be given to the cultivation of her mind, permanently endowed female seminaries would be as common as colleges and universities, and the world would have its admired galaxy of female authors, encircling the whole heavens — not, as now, a few scattered stars, scarcely noticed.

Let me not be thought, however, by these remarks, so utilitarian in my views as to suppose that attention to personal appearance, and to objects generally whose principal use is to gratify the love of the harmonious and the beautiful, is a mere waste of money and of mind. The elegant symmetry of Nature's works, and the lavish manner in which she has adorned her infinitely varied productions, often for no assignable cause but to gratify the beholder, teach me a very different lesson, and show me that it is not only right, but a duty, to imitate nature, by expending time and money to give an attractive and elegant appearance to our persons, our dwellings, our streets, and indeed to all the products of our labors, so far as it can be done consistently with higher duties. If a man gives that time and attention to these objects which are indispensable to the acquisition of knowledge, or if he devote to them that wealth which should have been bestowed upon the poor and the distressed, or any other object of benevolence, who would not say that he was doing wrong, morally wrong? If he can satisfy the just claims of learning and benevolence, no matter how much of his surplus time and surplus money he gives to objects whose chief use is to gratify the taste; and I doubt not, that when men shall spend their time and property more as God would have them than they now do, a much greater portion will be devoted to works of taste and ornament. But as the world now is, with so much ignorance to be enlightened, and misery to be relieved, when the calls of learning and benevolence are so loud upon us, it is a most difficult point to determine how much we may consecrate to purposes of mere ornament. And I complain, that the noble powers of woman, so eminently adapted, if turned into the right channel, to bless mankind, should so extensively be suffered to waste themselves upon an affair comparatively so unimportant as dress; especially when I recollect, that

35

"Loveliness
Needs not the foreign aid of ornament,
But is when unadorned adorned the most."

And confident am I that such would not be the case, were the constitutional bias of the young for natural objects more faithfully cultivated, and artificial objects made to assume in their estimation a proper, that is, a subordinate place.

Another most pernicious effect resulting from this artificial state of things in society, is that strong love of romance, which now almost constitutes a universal passion. At least one fifth part of all the works published in this country are works of fiction; and probably one half of the works actually read are of this description. And they are devoured with epicurean greediness by almost all classes, especially by the young. Need I stop to convince this audience, that the time and mental effort devoted to the preparation and perusal of such works are much worse than wasted? that they engender views and feelings decidedly hostile to thorough mental discipline, and to temporal and eternal happiness? Now, if a love of nature were early and thoroughly cultivated in the youthful bosom, I am confident that usually it would forestall the love of fiction. For does the youth resort to works of romance because he wishes to gratify a natural taste for the new and the beautiful? Where can he find such novelty and such beauty as nature unfolds? Is it a love of variety that makes romance so fascinating? Here, too, nature is as superior to human invention as the Author of nature is to man. Or is it a love of the marvellous and the magnificent that constitutes the chief attraction of the dreams of imagination? O, where are the wonders and sublimities that can be compared to those which open before the student of nature at every step? — wonders of fact, and not of fiction; on which, therefore, the mind may feast continually without fear, and find all its powers invigorated and refreshed. In short, to him who has cultivated that love for the works of creation which is originally implanted in all our hearts,

> "God makes all nature beauty to his eye,
> And music to his ear."

And yet what multitudes there are, even of refined and cultivated minds, to whom nature is but a synonyme for vulgarity; who can recite fluently every tale in the Waverleys and the Bozziana, but whose knowledge of nature is limited to an acquaintance with a few roses, dahlias, and other exotics, whose stamens have been changed to petals by cultivation, so as to have lost the delicate beauty of their natural state!

Gladly would I linger on this part of my subject, and present other arguments to win the young to the study and love of nature. As they advance in life, they will find that a love of artificial objects and pleasures will pall upon the mind, and ere long be succeeded by disgust. But a genuine love of nature clings to the heart in all the vicissitudes of life; in adversity as well as in prosperity; in sickness as well as in health; even to extreme old age, when almost every other worldly source of pleasure is dried up. Hear the testimony of Hannah More, at the age of eighty-two. "The only one of my youthful fond attachments," says she, "which exists still in its full force, is a passion for scenery, raising flowers, and landscape gardening." Well, indeed, will it be for the young, if they will follow the example of this venerable woman, and early acquire a passion for scenery and flowers. For as they pass through life, they will find the world often frowning upon them; but the flowers will always smile. And it is sweet, in the day of adversity, to be met with a smile.

The last prolific cause of mental waste, which I shall mention, is indolence and irresolution. Among the vast numbers of men capable of rising to eminence in art, science, or literature, and of making a deep impression on the world, how few confer any lasting benefit upon their generation, by their works, inventions, or discoveries! And it seems to me that the want of perseverance — in other words, indolence and irresolution — is the principal cause of their failure. Go to the primary school, and, among a hundred boys you will usually find fifty exhibiting nearly equal natural abilities, and making equal progress in learning. In the academy and the college you will find as large a proportion, between whose talents and scholarship you will see scarcely any difference. Year after year, they will move forward shoulder to shoulder, and come to the end of their literary course so nearly abreast, that it requires a nice application of the merit gauge to give them a difference of rank on the scale of honorary appointments; and the most sagacious application of the doctrine of probabilities will not enable any one to predict with confidence which of them will be distinguished above his fellows in future life. But let the history of those boys and young men, whether from the primary school, the academy, or the college, be consulted at the end of their lives, and you will scarcely find a dozen, out of a hundred, who have risen to high distinction in their business or profession, or made valuable discoveries, or left a deep impression upon the world. The others may have done much good; but why have they not done as much as their dozen comrades, who, during the years of their elementary education, were not able to outstrip them? We must allow something for feeble health, and other unforeseen difficulties, hedging up the path of a few. But in respect to the great body of these men, difference in application and perseverance will alone explain their difference of success. The twelve had acquired, during their early days, an ardent love of knowledge, and a deep sense of their responsibilities to God and the world, and the result was, a strong determination to make use of the vantage ground which they had attained, for pushing their conquests still farther into the dominions of art and science. Having prepared themselves by an elementary acquaintance with the circle of knowledge, they selected some particular department, to which taste or duty invited, and concentrated their energies upon its thorough examination; being convinced that he who attempts to master all subjects, though he may become respectable in all, can be accurate and successful in none. Having chosen their field, they went about its exploration as a business for life. The morning's dawn and the evening's darkness found them still at their work. Those seasons which most men devote to relaxation witnessed in them little more than a change of objects, whereby their exhausted energies were recruited. Time they regarded as a treasure too rich to have any of it wasted; and therefore all its shreds and patches were carefully used. The difficulties which they encountered in their researches served only to awaken new effort, and every new conquest gave them an earnest of future victories. Feeble health may have retarded their progress; poverty's skeleton hand may often have been laid with a crushing weight upon their heads; the world may have passed them by in cold neglect, or cast upon them a contemptuous frown, while the discerning and liberal few may not have found them out. But the unconquerable spirit within them stood erect in spite of all these obstructions. The delight which every step of their progress afforded by opening new wonders before them; the increased power which each acquisition gave them to advance to other victories; the desire of leaving their names permanently inscribed upon the history of man; and perhaps also those higher motives to diligence derived from a sense of responsibility to Heaven; all these motives were continually sounding in their ears the onward cry. And onward they went, triumphing over one difficulty after another, until the world at last confessed their superiority, sought from them the lessons of wisdom, and lavished upon them its honors. But their former companions lingered in the race. They were wanting in the untiring industry and indomitable spirit of perseverance which these twelve men exhibited, and therefore they have not stood forth as the master spirits of their times, nor secured the homage of the world; and the wave of oblivion has rolled over their memories. But having equal talents in the commencement of their course with their more energetic companions, their failure and the world's loss must be imputed to their indolence and irresolution.

But I will not further weary your patience by pointing out other causes of that waste of mind of which the world exhibits so many melancholy examples. Melancholy indeed is the dark catalogue which I have already presented; incalculable the amount of that loss which the world has always sustained, and still sustains, from perverted and neglected intellect. Now, I maintain that God has given to the human family, as a whole, an inalienable right to all the intellectual labor of which the individuals of that family are capable. Whatever deficiency, or perversion, or waste, there is in those labors, it is just so much downright robbery, for which somebody is accountable. So long, however, has this robbery been practised, that the world has become insensible to its rights, and knows not how to estimate its loss; and individuals have forgotten their responsibility. How great that responsibility is, the views which I have presented may assist us in determining. Who of us does not shudder when he thinks of that deep stain of guilt which rests on his soul who tears the wretched African from his home, and shuts him up in hopeless servitude for life on the cotton, rice, and sugar plantations of the tropics? Why are we so insensible to that far darker crime by which a whole world have been kept in ignorance and wretchedness for so many thousands of years? Probably the reason is that, in this sense, we are all of us slave dealers and slave holders; nay, we enslave our own souls.

Such views as I have presented cannot but exalt our estimation of literary and scientific pursuits, and of all efforts which are made to promote the cause of education. The heart sickens when it sees how many and how powerful are the causes in operation to pervert, and crush, and waste man's intellect, and to keep those powers grovelling in the dust which should be rising and soaring among the stars. But it is cheering to know that there are some, and in this country many, who are striving to rescue the noblest thing on earth, the human soul, from its thraldom and degradation. They stand, indeed, in the world's Thermopylæ, and struggle against a fearful odds. But they shall not fall there, like the band of Leonidas. Nay, they shall see the deluge of ignorance and sin which has so long been dashing over the fairest portion of the globe beaten back; and the dry land of knowledge and virtue shall appear, and the flowers of hope and happiness shall spring up, and the rich fruits of science and religion shall fill the garners of every land.

A beautiful bow of promise already spans the horizon; for, when Christianity prevails in all lands and fully controls all hearts, then those powerful causes of intellectual waste and perversion which I have pointed out shall pass away. Intemperance in every form, and cruel war, and fierce party collisions, and inordinate selfishness, and factitious and unnatural desires shall all be sacrificed upon the altar of benevolence; and man shall shake off his indolence, and ample means and motives shall be placed before the whole human family for intellectual and moral culture. Then shall such progress be made in science, literature, and art as will throw into the shade all former bright spots in human history; then will the world learn for the first time how deep has been her degradation, how incalculably valuable are the rights of which for thousands of years she has been deprived, and how truly frightful has been the waste of mind since the beginning. O, how cheering to the lover of science to look forward to those halcyon days which Christianity tells us shall assuredly come! Imagination need not fear that her most vivid colors can outdo the original; for if the little benevolence and the little knowledge which have been in the world hitherto have accomplished so much, what imagination can sketch the picture when the hearts of earth's vast population shall all be swayed by benevolence, and their minds all disciplined and expanded by science?

The institution whose anniversary we celebrate to-day is to me an earnest that such a bright period is coming on. A brief sketch of its history is, therefore, an appropriate close to my remarks.

There is a place in Essex county, called Agawam by the natives, which was visited by our pilgrim fathers nine years before the settlement of Plymouth, and of which Captain John Smith, of Virginia, gave the following account six years before the Mayflower entered Massachusetts Bay. "Here," says he, "are many rising hills, and on their tops and descents are many cornefields and delightful groues. On the east is an isle of two or three leagues in length — the one half plain marsh ground, fit for pasture or salt ponds, with many fine high groues of mulberry trees. There are also okes, pines, walnuts, and other wood, to make this place an excellent habitation." Nineteen years afterwards, the pilgrims located themselves in this spot; and, more than one hundred years after, two young ladies had made the pleasant village which had sprung up there the seat of a flourishing female seminary. God had greatly smiled upon their efforts; for while they placed their standard of literary attainments high, religion, not nominally only, but practically, was made paramount to every thing else. The consequence was, that Ipswich female seminary soon attracted the attention, not only of the wise and the good in our own land, but even of visitors from Europe; for it sent a benign influence to the remotest portions of this country, and even to far distant heathen lands. Its moulding power gave to the female character that happy shape which, while it fitted woman for great energy of action, did not hide those milder virtues and that grace of manners which make her influence almost irresistible over the human heart.

The ladies who had charge of this seminary were not insensible to the blessings with which God had crowned their labors. They had the joy of witnessing, from month to month and from year to year, a silent yet transforming divine influence, whereby a large proportion of all who came there unconverted returned to their paternal roof with the new song of redeeming love upon their lips. They went back, also, with a new and deeper sense of their responsibilities to their fellow-beings, and with a strong determination henceforth to devote the energies of their minds to the cause of human improvement and happiness. But as these teachers mused on the subject, often would the inquiry arise, How shall the blessings of our institution be perpetuated? Often, when the labors of the day were ended, and the silence of evening was broken only by the whip-poor-will's song or the distant surf breaking on the shore, would they muse upon this question until the fire burned within them, and an irrepressible desire arose to do something more than they had done for placing the means of education permanently within the reach of the daughters of America — especially those whose pecuniary means are small, but to whom Providence has made up in mind what is wanting in money. As they cast their eyes over the land, though colleges and universities met them at almost every step, not a single permanent female seminary could be found. In many places, such schools had risen up and become distinguished while some able teacher was at their head; but as soon as she was gone, the glory of the institution departed. Their own would probably share the same fate. Already did the occasional sinking of nature, under their arduous labors, remind them that those labors must soon forever cease. But could an institution like theirs be moderately endowed by a benevolent public, so that rooms, and apparatus, and books should be gratuitously furnished, the same system of instruction might pass from teacher to teacher through successive generations. After long deliberation and much prayer, one of these teachers resolved to consecrate herself for the remainder of life, if necessary, to carry this plan into effect. The other has not, indeed, been permitted to build the temple; but it was not because, like David, she was unfit, but because an enfeebled constitution has compelled her to retire from the arduous duties of public instruction; though I am happy to say that she is able to fill a private station with great dignity, usefulness, and happiness.

The plan was thus laid, and the agent ready for the work; but what an herculean task to carry it into execution! Who could be made to believe that permanence in a female seminary was desirable? Who, especially, could be persuaded to give money for an enterprise of so doubtful utility and uncertain success? I believe the effort must have been a failure, if, in the first place, the prime mover had not been a woman; if, in the second place, she had not in the outset appealed to woman; and if, in the third place, she had not acquired so firm a conviction of the excellence of her cause as to feel assured that God would ultimately make it triumph — so that coldness, ridicule, and enmity would produce no effect but to stimulate her to greater efforts and more fervent prayer. Yes, she did first appeal to women; and, to the everlasting honor of the ladies of Ipswich, be it known that they raised a purse of five hundred dollars to give the first impulse to the cause; and, what is still more to their credit, they did this when they knew that the proposed seminary would be located in some other part of the country. This was soon increased to one thousand dollars by other ladies; and if that sum had not been raised, probably the walls of this seminary would never have gone up. Thus the prompt impulse of woman's generous heart has secured that object which man's cold wisdom would have deemed quixotic, but which he is now willing to acknowledge to be most noble in character and rich in promise.

It cannot be expected that, on this occasion, I should go into minute details respecting the means used to advance this enterprise, and the many difficulties which have been overcome to bring it into its present condition. There is but one individual who could write such a history; nor could even she give us an adequate idea of the toils and sacrifices which this great work has cost — how hard it was at first to gain the ear of the Christian public long enough to unfold the plan; how much harder still to make even a few believe in its feasibility; how the way seemed often so hedged up that prayer was the only resort; and, what was worse to bear with a Christian spirit, how even influential fellow-Christians endeavored to put down the enterprise by scorn and ridicule. Even most of us, who have viewed it with deep interest from the beginning, will recollect how the pleadings of its eloquent advocate produced in us only faith enough to say to her, We admire the plan, and wish it might succeed, and any influence we possess shall be cheerfully given to it; but you must expect a hard struggle to accomplish it. And, in fact, while we could not but speak encouraging words, there was within us a fainting of the heart in anticipation of defeat. We forgot the sentiment of Elliot, that "prayers and pains through Jesus Christ can do any thing." And as we look around us to-day, we stand rebuked for our misgivings and unbelief. Little did I ever imagine that my eyes would be allowed to behold one of the finest edifices in New England so soon completed, and with its two hundred inmates already exerting a strong influence in arresting the waste of female mind in our country. I had thought of it as one of the visions which the early Christian friends of this institution might be permitted to enjoy, long after they had gone to their final rest, as they came down hither on some errand of mercy. But to most of them the vision is granted this side the grave; and to-day are they permitted to mingle their congratulations at the completion of this noble enterprise, and to unite in thanksgiving to that infinite Being whose blessing has crowned every effort to advance it with success.

The blessing of God, my friends, is indeed to be specially acknowledged, on this occasion, as having been experienced from the first conception of this institution to its completion. Those who have borne the heat and burden of the enterprise have found his providence their cloud by day and their pillar of fire by night, and therefore their courage has not fainted. The success of the seminary thus far has been only a fulfilment of the promise of Jehovah, *Them that honor me I will honor;* for holiness to the Lord was engraved upon its foundations, and stands out in bold relief upon the top stone. From the first it has been distinctly understood that, while an elevated and thorough system of instruction should be here pursued, religion should receive a still higher attention, and take the precedence of every thing else. This I conceive to be the grand fundamental principle on which the institution rests, and the secret of all its success hitherto, and the only ground of hope for the future. God has set his seal to this principle by the almost constant presence of that divine energy by which the soul is converted. And while that principle is practically regarded, it will continue to be blessed. Its teachers, its present mode of instruction, its peculiarities of domestic arrangement, may all be changed without essentially affecting its prosperity, so long as this principle is made the pole star of action. Nay, its influence shall become wider and wider, deeper and deeper. By means of its example and its well-educated pupils, it shall operate all over the land to raise the standard of female education, and to rescue woman from the perversion and waste of her powers. Man, too, shall come under its humanizing influence, and be awakened to new efforts in the cause of learning and benevolence. Nor shall that influence be limited to the civilized portions of our continent. Its daughters shall go forth, as some have already gone, with minds well disciplined and hearts burning with a desire to bless mankind, to the persecuted red man of our western wilds, and to the degraded heathen and Mohammedan of far distant continents and islands; and in every quarter of the globe shall the ignorant, the oppressed, and the miserable, especially abused and suffering woman, call down a blessing upon its founders and its pupils. It shall add new power to that lever which benevolence has placed beneath the regions of ignorance and sin, and which is fast heaving them up into the daylight of Christianity and science. It shall form one of those radiant points from which the blended rays of knowledge and religion will go forth, to aid in forming that halo of light which shall at length encircle the whole earth, and make it noonday among all the nations.

HISTORY.

Prescott.

HISTORY OF THE REIGN OF PHILIP II.

By William H. Prescott. With Portraits, Maps, Plates, &c. Two volumes, 8vo. Price, in muslin, $2 per volume.

The reign of *Philip the Second*, embracing the last half of the sixteenth century, is one of the most important as well as interesting portions of modern history. It is necessary to glance only at some of the principal events. The War of the Netherlands — the model, so to say, of our own glorious War of the Revolution — the Siege of Malta, and its memorable defence by the Knights of St. John; the brilliant career of Don John of Austria, the hero of Lepanto; the Quixotic adventures of Don Sebastian of Portugal; the conquest of that kingdom by the Duke of Alba; Philip's union with Mary of England, and his wars with Elizabeth, with the story of the Invincible Armada; the Inquisition, with its train of woes; the rebellion of the Moriscos, and the cruel manner in which it was avenged — these form some of the prominent topics in the foreground of the picture, which presents a crowd of subordinate details of great interest in regard to the character and court of Philip, and to the institutions of Spain, then in the palmy days of her prosperity. The materials for this vast theme were to be gathered from every part of Europe, and the author has for many years been collecting them from the archives of different capitals. The archives of Simancas, in particular, until very lately closed against even the native historian, have been opened to his researches; and his collection has been further enriched by MSS. from some of the principal houses in Spain, the descendants of the great men of the sixteenth century. Such a collection of original documents has never before been made for the illustration of this period.

The two volumes now published bring down the story to the execution of Counts Egmont and Hoorn in 1568, and to the imprisonment and death of Don Carlos, whose mysterious fate, so long the subject of speculation, is now first explored by the light of the authentic records of Simancas.

HISTORY OF THE REIGN OF FERDINAND AND ISABELLA, The Catholic.

By W. H. Prescott. With Portraits. Three volumes, 8vo. Price, in muslin, $2 per volume.

"Mr. Prescott's merit chiefly consists in the skilful arrangement of his materials, in the spirit of philosophy which animates the work, and in a clear and elegant style that charms and interests the reader. His book is one of the most successful historical productions of our time. The inhabitant of another world, he seems to have shaken off the prejudices of ours. In a word, he has, in every respect, made a most valuable addition to our historical literature." — *Edinburgh Review.*

HISTORY OF THE CONQUEST OF MEXICO,

With the Life of the Conqueror, Fernando Cortez, and a View of the Ancient Mexican Civilization. By W. H. Prescott. With Portrait and Maps. Three volumes, 8vo. Price, in muslin, $2 per volume.

"The more closely we examine Mr. Prescott's work the more do we find cause to commend his diligent research. His vivacity of manner and discursive observations scattered through notes as well as text, furnish countless proofs of his matchless industry. In point of style, too, he ranks with the ablest English historians; and paragraphs may be found in his volumes in which the grace and eloquence of Addison are combined with Robertson's majestic cadence and Gibbon's brilliancy." — *Athenæum.*

HISTORY OF THE CONQUEST OF PERU;

With a Preliminary View of the Civilization of the Incas. By W. H. Prescott. With Portraits, Maps, &c. Two vols., 8vo. Price, in muslin, $2 per volume.

"The world's history contains no chapter more striking and attractive than that comprising the narrative of Spanish conquest in the Americas. Teeming with interest to the historian and philosopher, to the lover of daring enterprise and marvellous adventure, it is full of fascination. A clear head and a sound judgment, great industry and a skilful pen, are needed to do justice to the subject. These necessary qualities have been found united in the person of an accomplished American author. Already favorably known by his histories of the eventful and chivalrous reign of Ferdinand and Isabella, and of the exploits of the Great Marquis and his iron followers, Mr. Prescott has added to his well-merited reputation by his narrative of the Conquest of Peru." — *Blackwood.*

Mr. Prescott's works are also bound in more elaborate styles, — half calf, half turkey, full calf, and turkey antique.

Barry.

THE HISTORY OF MASSACHUSETTS,

By Rev. John Stetson Barry. To be comprised in three volumes, octavo. Volume I. embracing the Colonial Period, down to 1692, now ready. Volumes II. and III. in active preparation. Price, in muslin, $2 per volume.

Extracts from a Letter from Mr. Prescott, the Historian.

BOSTON, June 8, 1855.

Messrs. Phillips, Sampson, & Co.

Gentlemen. — The History is based on solid foundations, as a glance at the authorities will show.

The author has well exhibited the elements of the Puritan character, which he has evidently studied with much care. His style is perspicuous and manly, free from affectation; and he merits the praise of a conscientious endeavor to be impartial.

The volume must be found to make a valuable addition to our stores of colonial history.

Truly yours,

WILLIAM H. PRESCOTT.

Hume.

THE HISTORY OF ENGLAND,

From the Invasion of Julius Cæsar to the Abdication of James II., 1688. By David Hume, Esq. A new edition, with the author's last corrections and improvements; to which is prefixed a short account of his life, written by himself. Six volumes, with Portrait. Black muslin, 40 cents per volume; in red muslin, 50 cents; half binding, or library style, 50 cents per volume; half calf, extra, $1.25 per volume.

The merits of this history are too well known to need comment. Despite the author's predilections in favor of the House of Stuart, he is the historian most respected, and most generally read. Even the brilliant *Macaulay*, though seeking to establish an antagonistic theory with respect to the royal prerogative, did not choose to enter the lists with *Hume*, but after a few chapters by way of cursory review, began his history where his great predecessor had left off.

No work in the language can take the place of this, at least for the present century. And nowhere can it be found accessible to the general reader for any thing like the price at which this handsome issue is furnished.

These standard histories, Hume, Gibbon, Macaulay, and Lingard, are known as the *Boston Library Edition*. For uniformity of style and durability of binding, quality of paper and printing, they are the cheapest books ever offered to the American public, and the best and most convenient editions published in this country.

Macaulay.

THE HISTORY OF ENGLAND,

From the Accession of James II. By Thomas Babington Macaulay. Four volumes, 12mo., with Portrait. Black muslin, 40 cents per volume; red muslin, 50 cents; library style and half binding, 50 cents; calf, extra, $1.25.

"The all-accomplished Mr. Macaulay, the most brilliant and captivating of English writers of our own day, seems to have been born for the sole purpose of making English history as fascinating as one of Scott's romances." — *North American Review.*

"The great work of the age. While every page affords evidence of great research and unwearied labor, giving a most impressive view of the period, it has all the interest of an historical romance." — *Baltimore Patriot.*

Gibbon.

THE HISTORY OF THE DECLINE AND FALL OF THE ROMAN EMPIRE,

By Edward Gibbon, Esq. With Notes by Rev. H. H. Milman. A new Edition. To which is added a complete Index of the whole work. Six volumes, with Portrait. 12mo., muslin, 40 cents per volume; red muslin, 50 cents; half binding, or library style, 50 cents per volume; half calf, extra, $1.25.

"We commend it as the best library edition extant." — *Boston Transcript.*

"The publishers are now doing an essential service to the rising generation in placing within their reach a work of such acknowledged merit, and so absolutely indispensable." — *Baltimore American.*

"Such an edition of this English classic has long been wanted; it is at once convenient, economical, and elegant." — *Home Journal.*

Lingard.

A HISTORY OF ENGLAND,

From the first Invasion by the Romans to the Accession of William and Mary in 1688. By John Lingard, D. D. From the last revised London edition. In thirteen volumes; illustrated title pages, and portrait of the author. 12mo., muslin. Price, 75 cents per volume.

"This history has taken its place among the classics of the English language." — *Lowell Courier.*

"It is infinitely superior to Hume, and there is no comparison between it and Macaulay's romance. Whoever has not access to the original monuments will find Dr. Lingard's work the best one he can consult." — *Brownson's Review.*

"Lingard's history has been long known as the best history of England ever written; but hitherto the price has been such as deprived all but the most wealthy readers of any chance of possessing it. Now, however, its publication has been commenced in a beautiful style, and at such a price that no student of history need fail of its acquisition." — *Albany Transcript.*

Lamartine.

HISTORY OF THE FRENCH REVOLUTION OF 1848,

By Alphonse de Lamartine. Translated by F. A. Durivage and William S. Chase. In one volume, octavo, with illustrations. Price, in muslin, $2.25.

Same work, in a 12mo. edition, muslin, 75 cents; sheep, 90 cents.

A most graphic history of great events, by one of the principal actors therein.

"The day will come when *Lamartine*, standing by the gate-post of the Hotel de Ville, and subduing by his eloquence the furious passions of the thousands upon thousands of delirious revolutionists, who sought they knew not what at the hands of the self-constituted Provisional Government of 1848, will be commemorated in stone, on canvas, and in song, as the very impersonation of moral sublimity." — *Meth. Quarterly Review.*

"No fitting mete-wand hath To-day
For measuring spirits of thy stature, —
Only the Future can reach up to lay
The laurel on that lofty nature. —
Bard, who with some diviner art
Hast touched the bard's true lyre, a nation's heart."

James Russell Lowell, "To Lamartine."

Hale.

HISTORY OF KANZAS AND NEBRASKA,

With a Map. Compiled with the assistance of the New England Emigrant Aid Society, by Rev. E. E. Hale. Price, in muslin, 75 cents.

This work is the result of labor and research, and will be found invaluable to those who contemplate removing to Kanzas, as well as to those who for other reasons would acquire a knowledge of the geography and capabilities of the territories. The extraordinary scenes which have transpired during their recent rapid settlement are sufficient to attract the public attention strongly to whatever may give authentic information.

Ballou.

THE HISTORY OF CUBA,

Or Notes of a Traveller in the Tropics. By M. M. Ballou. In one volume, 12mo., with illustrations. Price, 75 cents.

In this volume Mr. Ballou has given a well-written, but concise history of Cuba from its discovery to the present time. Following this the author endeavors to place the character and manners of the people and the scenery of the beautiful island directly before the reader's mental vision. Authentic and valuable in matter, attractive in manner, the book combines greater merits than any other similar work.

Craig, D'Aubigne.

HISTORY OF THE PROTESTANT CHURCH IN HUNGARY

From the Beginning of the Reformation to 1850. With reference also to Transylvania. Translated by the Rev. J. Craig, D. D., Hamburg. With an Introduction by J. H. Merle D'Aubigné, D. D., President of the Theological School of Geneva. 550 pages. Price, $1.25.

"This is a translation of a German work, of great reliability and value. The matter it contains has been collated from a large mass of public and private documents, and every pains has apparently been taken to render it what it professes to be, a complete History of Protestantism in Hungary. The hearty indorsement of the work contained in the introductory chapter, by Dr. Merle D'Aubigné, the distinguished author of the 'History of the Great Reformation,' will not fail to secure for the book the confidence of the Christian public, while its attractive style and instructive character entitle it to a place in the library of the clergyman, the Sabbath school, and the private Christian."—*National Era.*

ESSAYS, REVIEWS, AND LECTURES.

Emerson.

ESSAYS, BY RALPH WALDO EMERSON,

First Series, in one volume, 12mo. Price, $1. Second Series, in one volume, 12mo. Price, $1.

It is too late to present any labored analysis of the writings of Emerson, — too late to set down any eulogy. Whoever loves to deal with first principles, and is not deterred from grappling with abstract truths, will find in these essays a rare pleasure in the exercise of his powers. The popular ridicule which was heaped upon the so-called transcendental literature, at least so far as Emerson is concerned, has passed away; and these volumes are universally admitted to be among the most valuable contributions to the world's stock of ideas which our age has furnished. Every page bears the impress of thought, but it is thought subtilized, and redolent of poetry. Obscurity there is none, save to the incapable or the prejudiced, or to those averse to metaphysical speculations.

NATURE; ADDRESSES AND LECTURES,

By R. W. Emerson. In one volume, 12mo. Price, $1.

REPRESENTATIVE MEN,

Seven Lectures, by R. W. Emerson. In one volume, 12mo Price, $1.

"It is certainly one of the most fascinating books ever written, whether we consider its subtile verbal felicities, its deep and shrewd observation, its keen criticism, its wit or learning, its wisdom or beauty. For fineness of wit, imagination, observation, satire, and sentiment, the book hardly has its equal in American literature." — *E. P. Whipple.*

"It is a thoughtful book, and better adapted to please the majority of readers than any previous attempt of the writer." — *H. T. Tuckerman.*

"This is not an ordinary book." — *London Athenæum.*

Carlyle.

CRITICAL AND MISCELLANEOUS ESSAYS,

By Thomas Carlyle. In one volume, octavo, with Portrait Price, in muslin, $1.75.

This vigorous and profound writer has been chiefly known to the public at large from the caricatures of his style published by those to whom drapery and ornament are of more consequence than vital force. The faults of Carlyle are sufficiently obvious; they lie upon the very surface; but for nicety of analysis, power, and closeness of logic, manliness of utterance, and genuine enthusiasm for what he deems the good and true, no critic is more justly entitled to admiration

THE LATER ESSAYS OF THOMAS CARLYLE,

(Latter Day Pamphlets.) In one volume, 12mo. **Price, in** muslin, 60 cents.

Macaulay.

ESSAYS, CRITICAL AND MISCELLANEOUS,

By Thomas Babington Macaulay, author of a History of England. In one volume, octavo, with Portrait. Price, in muslin, $2.

Whoever wishes to gain the most extensive acquaintance with English history and English literature in the briefest space of time, will read the Essays of Macaulay. It is emphatically the book to direct the student in his researches; and at the same time the brilliancy of the author's style, his learning and vast fund of information, and the pertinency of his illustrations, render his writings as fascinating to every thinking mind as the most splendid work of fiction. More scholars and critics of the present day owe their first impulse to self-culture to Macaulay than to any other writer.

"Undoubtedly the prince of the English essayists."

Sydney Smith.

THE WORKS OF REV. SYDNEY SMITH,

(Consisting principally of articles contributed to the Edinburgh Review.) In one volume, octavo, with Portrait. Price, in muslin, $1.25.

The Edinburgh Review, so long known as the leading Quarterly of Great Britain, perhaps owed its existence and its reputation more to Sydney Smith than to either of his illustrious compeers — Brougham, Macaulay, and Jeffrey. The good sense and simplicity of his style, no less than his vigorous logic and bristling wit, have rendered his name known wherever the English language is spoken. The interest in his writings will outlive the occasions which called them forth, and they may now be placed among the British classics.

Jeffrey.

CONTRIBUTIONS TO THE EDINBURGH REVIEW,

By Francis Lord Jeffrey. In one volume, octavo, with Portrait. Price, in muslin, $2.

In these articles of Jeffrey, the curious reader may see a history of English literature for the last fifty years. Now that Scott, Campbell, Wordsworth, Byron, and a few others are immortal beyond cavil or peradventure, with what interest do we look for the first impressions which their works made upon the mind of their contemporary and reviewer! Aside from his learning, vigor, acuteness, and general impartiality, Jeffrey will be read for many years to come for his association with the eminent names which have made the early part of this century so illustrious.

Wilson.

THE RECREATIONS OF CHRISTOPHER NORTH,

(Contributed to Blackwood's Magazine.) By John Wilson. In one volume, octavo, with Portrait of "Christopher in his Shooting Jacket." Price, in muslin, $1.25.

The fame of Wilson, under his chosen pseudonyme, Christopher North, is universal. The wonderful vigor, the wit, satire, fun, poetry, and criticism, all steeped through in his Tory prejudices, with which his contributions to Blackwood overflowed, commanded the attention of all parties, and have left a deep if not a permanent impression in the literature of the age. These articles are full of the author's peculiar traits. Humor and pathos succeed each other like clouds and sunshine in an April day. The character of the Scottish peasantry in some of the Recreations, is depicted with as much power as in the author's famous "Lights and Shadows of Scottish Life."

Mackintosh.

THE MISCELLANEOUS WORKS OF THE RIGHT HON. SIR JAMES MACKINTOSH,

In one volume, octavo, with Portrait. Price, in muslin, $2.

This edition contains all the miscellanies of the author, reprinted from the London edition of his works. The topics are various, from literature to politics. The Revolution of 1688. it is well known, had engaged much of the author's attention, and his articles upon that subject are among the most important and valuable in the language.

Alison.

MISCELLANEOUS ESSAYS,

By Archibald Alison, F. R. S., author of a History of Europe during the French Revolution. In one volume, octavo, with Portrait. Price, in muslin, $1.25.

The distinguished author of the History of Europe, in a series of critical articles, mostly upon modern historical, subjects, has apparently given to the world many of the studies upon which his great work is based. These Essays will be read with profit by every student of European history.

Talfourd, Stephen.

THE CRITICAL AND MISCELLANEOUS WRITINGS OF THOMAS NOON TALFOURD.

Author of "Ion," a Tragedy, &c., with a Portrait, and

THE CRITICAL AND MISCELLANEOUS ESSAYS OF JAMES STEPHEN,

In one volume, octavo. Price, in muslin, $1.25.

The author of "Ion" may surely claim a place among the classic writers of Britain. The essays here collected, though lacking the force and splendor of style that belongs to Macaulay, are among the most elegant and attractive in the language. They refer generally to lighter literary topics, instead of the severe subjects with which Mackintosh, Alison, or Carlyle choose to grapple.

Mr. Stephen, also, has long been known as among the ablest of the great modern essayists.

THE MODERN BRITISH ESSAYISTS,

Comprising the eight volumes octavo preceding. Price, in muslin, $12; in sheep, $16; half calf, or half morocco, $18.

Prescott.

BIOGRAPHICAL AND CRITICAL MISCELLANIES.

By W. H. Prescott. With a finely engraved Portrait. One volume, 8vo. Price, in cloth, $2; in sheep, $2.50; half calf, or half antique, $3; full calf, or antique, $4.

"Mr. Prescott is an elegant writer, and there is nothing that comes from his pen that does not strongly bear the marks of originality. The present volume contains a series of papers on different subjects; biography, belles-lettres, criticism, &c., in which Mr. Prescott has put forward some beautiful ideas on the attributes of mind, the formation of character, and the present condition of various sections of society. It will be read with avidity by the scholar and general inquirer." — *New Orleans Bulletin.*

Ware.

LECTURES ON THE GENIUS OF WASHINGTON ALLSTON,

By Rev. William Ware. Author of "Zenobia," "Aurelian," &c., &c. In one volume, 12mo. Price, 75 cents.

"The illustrious painter has found a splendid exponent of his genius in Mr. Ware. No one can read these Lectures without being impressed with the congeniality and perfect knowledge of the art upon which, in connection with his subject, he expatiates. They are clear as crystal, showing in the transparency of words the gemmed and brilliant ideas. The pictures of the great artist are described in language whose coloring rivals the brightness of the objects themselves, setting them before the mind of the reader with such vividness as to make them almost visible to sight. * * * * The whole book is full of feeling, and radiant with beauty." — *Albany Knickerbocker.*

PRACTICAL AND SCIENTIFIC.

THE MECHANIC'S TEXT BOOK,

And Engineer's Practical Guide. Containing a concise Treatise on the Nature and Application of Mechanical Forces, the Action of Gravity, the Elements of Machinery, the Strength, Pressure, and Resistance of Materials, &c., &c. Compiled and arranged by Thomas Kelt. To which is added, Valuable Hints to Mechanics on various Subjects, by John Frost, LL. D. In one volume, 12mo. Price, $1.

THE ENGINEER'S POCKET GUIDE,

By Thomas Kelt. 18mo., muslin. Price, 75 cents; with tucks, $1.

The most valuable information for the mechanic, in a small compass, and in clear and intelligible language.

MANUAL OF MAGNETISM,

By Daniel Davis, Jr., with 180 original illustrations. In one volume, 12mo. Price, $1.

Extracts from the Preface.

"The present work is principally occupied with magnetism in its connection with electricity. But the general phenomena of both these sciences are described as fully as the thorough comprehension of the relations existing between them appeared to require. It has been the aim to give the book a practical rather than a theoretical character, and to introduce hypotheses no further than was essential to a clear explanation of the phenomena described."

"In the preparation of this (2d) edition, alterations and additions have been made to adapt it better to the purposes of a text book for colleges and high schools, and also as a companion to the apparatus."

www.ingramcontent.com/pod-product-compliance
Lightning Source LLC
LaVergne TN
LVHW021144110826
845150LV00005B/1125